Theatre and Anti-Theatre

Theatre and Anti-Theatre

New Movements Since Beckett

Ronald Hayman

New York
Oxford University Press
1979

ISBN 0–19–520089–6

Library of Congress Catalog Card Number 78–73778

Acknowledgments are recorded on p. viii.

Printed in Great Britain

For Catharine
with love and gratitude

Contents

Acknowledgments

The author and his publishers make grateful acknowledgment for permission to quote material:

Edward Albee, *Zoo Story*, by permission of Jonathan Cape Ltd, London, and Coward McCann & Geoghegan, Inc, New York; *Who's Afraid of Virginia Woolf?* and *A Delicate Balance*, by permission of Jonathan Cape Ltd, London, and Atheneum Publishers, New York; *The American Dream* by permission of Samuel French Ltd, London. Samuel Beckett, *Proust, Watt* and *Murphy*, by permission of John Calder Ltd, London; *Waiting for Godot* and *Endgame*, by permission of Faber and Faber Ltd, London, and Grove Press, Inc, New York; 'Dante, Bruno. Vico . . . Joyce' from *Our Exagmination Round the Factification for Incamination of Work in Progress*, by permission of Faber and Faber Ltd, London. Claude Bonnefoy, *Conversations with Eugène Ionesco*, translated by Jan Dawson, by permission of Faber and Faber Ltd, London. Interview with Peter Brook, by permission of *Transatlantic Review*. Judith Cook, *Directors' Theatre*, by permission of George G. Harrap & Co. Ltd, London. Gilles Deleuze, *Proust and Signs*, by permission of Allen Lane Penguin Books Ltd, London, and George Braziller, Inc, New York. Article by Jerzy Grotowski in Vol III, No. 10, by permission of *Theatre Quarterly*. Jerzy Grotowski, *Towards a Poor Theatre*, by permission of H. M. Bergs Forlag ApS, Copenhagen. Ronald Hayman, *Playback*, by permission of Davis-Poynter Ltd, London. John Heilpern, *Conference of the Birds*, published by Faber and Faber, London, by permission of A. D. Peters & Co Ltd, London. Eugène Ionesco, *Notes and Counter-Notes*, by permission of John Calder Ltd, London. John Lahr, quoting Joseph Chaikin in *Acting Out America*, by permission of Penguin Books Ltd, London, and John Cushman Associates Inc, New York. Charles Marowitz, *Confessions of A Counterfeit Critic*, by permission of Eyre Methuen Ltd, London. Harold Pinter, *The Dwarfs*, copyright © 1961 by Harold Pinter; *The Birthday Party*, copyright © 1959, 1960 and 1965 by Harold Pinter; *The Caretaker*, copyright © 1960 by Theatre Promotions Limited; *The Homecoming*, copyright © 1965 by H. Pinter Ltd, by permission of Eyre Methuen Ltd, London, and Grove Press, Inc, New York. Sam Shepard, *The Unseen Hand, The Tooth of Crime*, and *Angel City*, by permission of Faber and Faber Ltd, London, and The Bobbs-Merrill Co, Inc, Indianapolis; interview in the *Guardian* with Sam Shepard, by permission of the author and Lois Berman, New York. A. C. H. Smith, *Orghast At Persepolis*, by permission of Eyre Methuen Ltd, London. Susan Sontag, excerpts from *Styles of Radical Will*, by permission of Martin Secker & Warburg Ltd, London, and Farrar, Straus & Giroux Inc, New York. Copyright © 1966, 1967, 1968, 1969 by Susan Sontag. Tom Stoppard, *Jumpers, Travesties*, by permission of Faber and Faber Ltd, London, and Grove Press, Inc, New York; *Another Moon Called Earth* and preface to *Dogg's Our Pet* by permission of Fraser & Dunlop Ltd, London.

And now I am going to say something which people
may find quite stupefying.
I am the enemy of theatre.
I always have been.
I love the theatre so much
I am, for that reason, hostile to it.

Antonin Artaud

Introduction

Negative currents in contemporary art are unprecedentedly strong. Would a playwright have designated any of his work as an 'anti-play' before Ionesco dubbed *La Cantatrice chauve* 'anti-pièce'? Could the term anti-theatre have been used before 1968, when Rainer Werner Fassbinder and nine actors called their theatre in Munich *Anti-Teater*? There was a nineteenth-century magazine called *Anti-Theatre*, but the term had no anti-art connotation before Alfred Jarry.

One premiss for this book is that the development of theatre since Beckett has been more anti-literary and more influenced by anti-art attitudes than has generally been recognised. An aversion to current practices in literature, art and theatre has inspired an alternative method of procedure. To use the term 'anti-theatre' is to emphasise the negative, destructive, revolutionary, reductionist and abstractionist tendencies in the new theatrical art. The anti-play is less mimetic than satirical, not so much a story about life in a particular place at a particular time as an object in its own right, non-referential, implicitly denying the feasibility of referential art.

Without attempting an encyclopaedic survey of world theatre since the première of *En attendant Godot* in Paris on 5 January 1953, I have tried to give a critical account of what I consider to be the most important innovations made by playwrights and directors. That it is necessary to consider production alongside text is itself an index of the way theatre has changed. Literature has not been squeezed out, but there has been a drastic shift in the balance of power between writer, director and actors. Peter Brook and Jerzy Grotowski, for instance, have not been as dependent on playwrights as Stanislavski was on Chekhov or even as Meyerhold and Vakhtangov were on playwrights. But Grotowski's reductionism parallels Beckett's: both have enriched theatre by using a minimum of the resources available to it.

I have devoted about half the book to Beckett, Ionesco, Genet and Handke, the four playwrights who will turn out, I believe, to have been the most important innovators. I hope these chapters will show that the term 'anti-theatre' can be useful.

I would not apply it to Pinter, Stoppard, Albee or Sam Shepard, but just as yesterday's anti-art is today's art, anti-theatre influences are absorbed into the theatrical mainstream, and the two chapters divided between these four playwrights give me a chance to analyse how this is happening. Apart from Brook and Grotowski the only director I have discussed at length is Joseph Chaikin of the Open Theatre in New York. With directors, therefore, as with playwrights, I am laying myself open to the charge of choosing the ones whose work I most admire. 'What about Arrabal?' it may be objected, or 'What about the Living Theatre?' While the work of both is vitiated, in my opinion by self-indulgence and indiscipline, I cannot deny that this book ignores a great many playwrights, directors and ensembles that have produced important work. But books which cover too much ground are always bad books, and, rather than over-extend my survey of the present, I have made two excursions into the past, one *à propos* writing, one *à propos* staging. Beckett's theatrical achievement, I contend, cannot be appreciated fully without understanding how much he has learnt from his Symbolist, Expressionist and Dadaist precursors. The chapter on 'Beckett and Before' deals mainly with Dadaism, Duchamp, Mallarmé, Proust and with Beckett's early work, critical, fictional and dramatic. *En attendant Godot* was his first successful play and his first published play, but not his first play or even his first play to be performed. Similarly, the achievements of Brook, Grotowski and Chaikin cannot be appreciated fully without an understanding of Artaud, whose achievements as a director amounted to very little, but whose influence has been enormous.

Except where another translator has been credited, all the translations from French and German are my own.

1 Godot and After

'Nothing to be done' are the first words spoken in *Waiting for Godot*, and the phrase is repeated twice within the first three pages of dialogue. Virtually every previous play had started from the opposite premiss, that there was something to be done, a mystery to be solved, an injustice to be righted, a crime to be punished, an obstacle to be removed, a pair of lovers to be united. Usually, within minutes of curtain-rise, we were presented with an unsatisfactory situation which could not be allowed to continue; in *Waiting for Godot* we are presented with an unsatisfactory situation which cannot be altered. When Estragon says 'Nothing to be done', he is on the point of giving up the struggle to pull his boot off, but Vladimir's answer comically widens the focus:

> I'm beginning to come round to that opinion. All my life I've tried to put it from me, saying, Vladimir, be reasonable, you haven't yet tried everything. And I resumed the struggle.

So the premiss for the dramatic action is that action is useless.

But what constitutes dramatic action? The play provides a new answer to this question. As Tom Stoppard has said, *Waiting for Godot* 'redefined the minima of theatrical validity'.[1] And when William Saroyan saw the play, he said: 'It will make it easier for me and everyone else to write clearly in the theatre.'[2] Beckett made it easier by showing how to erect inaction into valid theatrical action. The act of waiting is itself a contradictory combination of doing something and doing nothing, and if you put a pair of characters on stage, with no apparent objective except to wait for someone, the contradiction can come playfully into play. If the characters are aware that there is nothing they can usefully do, this gives them the basis for a theatrical action. The medium abhors a vacuum, and even if they sit on stage trying not to move and not to talk, the effort to make no effort becomes a game, and the game fills the space.

Though it is often said that nothing happens in *Waiting for Godot* – Vivian Mercier's summary of the two acts is 'Nothing happens, twice' – inaction does not entail inactivity. The four characters who wear bowler hats all have a lot of vaudeville-type business with them, and there is some farcical comedy with stinking boots and stinking breath. Vladimir's diseased bladder compels him to rush offstage and pee in the wings when he laughs. The entrance of Pozzo and Lucky introduces a great many new props – rope, stool, picnic basket, whip, pipe, baggage – which are all used in preventing the conversation from becoming static, and Lucky's monologue (the only long monologue in a script consisting mainly of very short lines) is violently counterpointed by protests from Vladimir and Estragon and groans from Pozzo, who starts pulling on the rope tied around Lucky's waist until all four of them are in a struggling heap on the ground. Lucky still goes on shouting his text until they silence him by putting his hat on. A small act of violence, such as the kick Lucky delivers to Estragon's shin, is comically inflated, and generally there is no shortage of stage movement, as there is, progressively, in Beckett's later plays.

Side by side with this activity, there is a great deal of game-playing that does not involve much movement. 'What shall we do now?' is, in effect, what Vladimir and Estragon are always asking each other, and some of their improvisations are like children's ways of passing time. They play a game of being Pozzo and Lucky, they play at being very polite to each other, at abusing each other, at making it up, and they stagger about on one leg trying to look like trees. The audience is involved most directly when they look out in horror at the auditorium, but it is involved in the game all through, because Beckett is playing with the fact of having actors on a stage playing roles. Instead of working to keep the audience guessing about what's going to happen next, he gives the impression of having written the play without himself knowing how he was going to go on.

Vladimir and Estragon are not *characters* in the conventional sense of the word. There is more contrast between their personalities than there is between Rosencrantz's and Guildenstern's in Tom Stoppard's comparable play about waiting: Vladimir is more tormented, more idealistic and more nostalgic than Estragon, who is more physically involved with the needs of the moment. But there is no firm outline around either character, and only the scantiest biographical data. They are defined not in relation to time, place, or social circumstance, but in relation to eternity and to human longings for a sense of purpose. From Shakespeare to Brecht, dramatists had operated character causally: for Mutter Courage and Galileo, as for Hamlet and Lear, what happens is partly a result of what they are. With different personality traits, we are made to feel, they would have reacted in such a different way to the same circumstances that they would not have had the same problems. The problem of Vladimir and Estragon is that they are alive. Like everyone and like Everyman, they are trapped between birth and death. What is happening to them does not seem to be consequent either on a specific set of circumstances (situation) or on their behaviour patterns (character). Nor do they remind us of anyone we have ever met.

The audience, then, is deprived of nearly all its normal sources of theatrical pleasure. In a realistic play much depends on recognising something familiar in people, in places and circumstances. Heroic action encourages us to identify with the heroes. We picture ourselves wielding Orestes's sword or Hamlet's rapier.

Beckett gives us nothing we can envy or admire: no courage, no gallantry, no glamorous lovers, beautiful costumes, handsome settings or desirable furniture. There is no possibility of tragedy, even when Vladimir and Estragon consider suicide. There is not much theatrical illusion, and very little suspense. It is even difficult to admire the acting. To the average member of the average audience, the actor playing Estragon is less obviously giving a performance than the actor playing Romeo or Jimmy Porter. Admittedly, all these points could be made about two comedians doing a music-hall act. There is no heroism, nothing to admire and not much illusion. So is it by introducing vaudeville comedy into existential drama that Beckett manages to take away so many of our toys without reducing us to tears? Is this the secret of the alternative distraction that *Waiting for Godot* offers?

In the theatre it is easy to make an impact by doing something that has never been done before. In 1896 when Alfred Jarry's *Ubu Roi* was premièred, the opening word 'Merdre' was – despite the extra *r* – enough to provoke fifteen minutes of pandemonium among the audience. Many of the Dadaist performances at the Cabaret Voltaire and many Expressionist dramas were equally defiant of convention, but a play stands no chance of staying in the repertoire unless its negative gestures are accompanied by positive achievement. Beckett has taken a great deal away but also given a great deal. The sheer quantity of argument and critical writing his work has provoked is itself evidence of its power to intrigue, to engage the imagination. *Waiting for Godot*'s resonance depends partly on the impression that the central argument is going on inside a single consciousness.

> VLADIMIR: What are you insinuating? That we've come to the wrong place?
> ESTRAGON: He should be here.
> VLADIMIR: He didn't say for sure he'd come.
> ESTRAGON: And if he doesn't come?
> VLADIMIR: We'll come back tomorrow.
> ESTRAGON: And then the day after tomorrow.
> VLADIMIR: Possibly.
> ESTRAGON: And so on.

VLADIMIR: The point is –
ESTRAGON: Until he comes.
VLADIMIR: You're merciless.
ESTRAGON: We came here yesterday.
VLADIMIR: Ah no, there you're mistaken.
ESTRAGON: What did we do yesterday?
VLADIMIR: What did we do yesterday?
ESTRAGON: Yes.
VLADIMIR: Why . . . (*angrily*) Nothing is certain when you're about.

But if everything seems uncertain, it is partly because the form and rhythm of the dialogue disconcertingly resemble the form and rhythm of internal monologue. The components which normally give opacity to drama have been so attenuated that we can see a consciousness arguing with itself. With setting, plot and character almost at the point of vanishing, the reality of the play is defined entirely by its dialogue, and since we are conditioned into the expectation that drama mirrors reality, the appearance of a dramatic argument in a vacuum carries the implication that there is no reality except the reality created by reasoning. Defining scepticism, Hegel wrote: 'The mind becomes perfect thought, annihilating the world in the multiple variety of its determinations, and the negativity of self-consciousness becomes real negativity.' *Waiting for Godot* is, in this sense, the most sceptical play ever written.

In some of Beckett's novels and stories the analytical commentary acts like acid to dissolve the actuality of the events described. In a play there is no space for commentary: the writer's corrosive irony must be absorbed into the self-deflation and self-parody of the characters. One of Beckett's most astonishing successes in *Waiting for Godot* is in making the lightweight banter of Vladimir and Estragon into a powerful solvent. In their suicide attempt, for instance, reality disintegrates:

ESTRAGON: Let's hang ourselves immediately.
VLADIMIR: From a bough? (*They go towards the tree.*) I wouldn't trust it.
ESTRAGON: We can always try.

VLADIMIR: Go ahead.

ESTRAGON: After you.

VLADIMIR: No no, you first.

ESTRAGON: Why me?

VLADIMIR: You're lighter than me.

ESTRAGON: Just so!

VLADIMIR: I don't understand.

ESTRAGON: Use your intelligence, can't you?

VLADIMIR: *uses his intelligence.*

VLADIMIR (*finally*) I remain in the dark.

ESTRAGON: This is how it is. (*He reflects.*) The bough . . . the bough . . . (*angrily*). Use your head, can't you?

VLADIMIR: You're my only hope.

ESTRAGON: (*with effort*) Gogo light – bough not break – Gogo dead. Didi heavy – bough break – Didi alone. Whereas –

VLADIMIR: I hadn't thought of that.

ESTRAGON: If it hangs you it'll hang me.

VLADIMIR: But am I heavier than you?

ESTRAGON: So you tell me. I don't know. There's an even chance. Or nearly.

VLADIMIR: Well? What do we do?

ESTRAGON: Don't let's do anything. It's safer.

VLADIMIR: Let's wait and see what he says.

ESTRAGON: Who?

VLADIMIR: Godot.

The style of the writing prevents us from taking the possibility of suicide seriously. The experience that the characters might have seemed to be having is de-realised in the process of enactment, as it might be in a music-hall sketch or a Laurel and Hardy film. But this sequence is not merely farcical. Beckett is making a new mixture of slapstick and theatrical poetry. The poetry depends as much on atmosphere as on words, and as much on its references to the human situation in general as on its development of events involving particular people in a particular place. Jacques Vaché, an eccentric who influenced the Surrealists, defined humour as 'a sense of the theatrical and joyless uselessness of everything, once you know'. If *Waiting for Godot* is sad and funny at the same time,

part of the reason is that the functioning of the human consciousness is made to seem not only intrinsically theatrical but
intrinsically comic.

In what sense, though, does the play imply an annihilation of the
world? Is it even possible to imagine an annihilation of the world?
Writing a chapter on 'The Idea of Nothing' in his *Evolution créa-
trice*, Henri Bergson argued that if you close your eyes, block your
ears, and suppress all the impressions that have been flooding in,
you remain with an impression of yourself and the present state of
your body. If you try to imagine the extinction of your consciousness, another consciousness apparently comes into play, 'because
the first could disappear only for the second and in the presence of
the second'. You can imagine annihilation only by erecting a viewpoint from which to look at it. Vladimir can watch Estragon
asleep, and he can ask himself whether he is dreaming, but he
cannot watch himself sleeping, which is one reason for needing
Estragon, or, better still, Godot, a witness outside space and time.
'At me too someone is looking, of me too someone is saying, he is
sleeping, he knows nothing, let him sleep on.' But the conversation Vladimir has with himself or with Estragon proceeds like
Hegelian dialectic. For the movement from thesis through antithesis to synthesis Hegel used the word *Aufhebung*, which means
both cancellation and preservation. But for him the significance of
the ambiguity was determined by a view of history as guided by
spirit. Beckett's ambiguity is different, slung between religious
images and agnostic assumptions. References to the crucifixion
are recurrent in the dialogue of *Waiting for Godot*, and Estragon
says that throughout his life he has compared himself to Christ.
In *The Imitation of Christ* Thomas à Kempis quotes *Romans* VI 8:
'Learn now to die to the world that thou mayst begin to live with
Christ.' The religious imagery in *Waiting for Godot* has the effect of
tantalising the men who have no option but to die, gradually, to
the world, tormented by the notion of transcendence but without
any means of achieving it.

At the same time, the play is jokily a play about the theatrical
situation. As in music hall, but as in few previous modern plays,
the performers do not pretend that the audience is not there. The
faces in the stalls inspire them with comic horror, but the overall

effect is to make the spectator an uncomfortable accomplice in the act of waiting. Why are we sitting there? What are we waiting for? The play to be over? It is partly a play about habit, and we are in the habit of going to the theatre. It is hard to imagine that drama could ever be wholly non-representational or non-referential, but Beckett was taking an important step towards making the play an object in its own right, pointing insistently and amusingly inwards at the fact of its being a play. The possibility of Godot's coming is no more real than the possibility that Vladimir and Estragon will hang themselves. The self-consciously literary cadences and the recurrent dissolution of character into comedian not only undermine our willingness to suspend disbelief but mock us for having started out with it. Beckett is simultaneously demonstrating the hollowness of the theatrical situation and the humiliating similarity between the procedures of consciousness and a dialogue between two clowns.

At the same time as pointing forwards, the allusions to the audience's presence point backwards: Shakespeare produced something of the same effect when, as so often, he resorted to the device of the play-within-the-play. Symmetry and circularity are also important in giving *Waiting for Godot* its resonance and its theatrical poetry. 'Do not despair, one of the thieves was saved; do not presume, one of the thieves was damned.' Without quoting his favourite sentence from St Augustine, Beckett writes several variations on it, and he is fruitfully influenced by both form and attitude. The short lines of dialogue balance each other; thrust is succeeded by counter-thrust, inflation by deflation.

> VLADIMIR: We are not saints, but we have kept our appoint-
> ment. How many people can boast as much?
> ESTRAGON: Billions.

There is strong patterning in the exchanges and in the overall structure: in each act there is a major interruption to the duologue with the entrance of Pozzo and Lucky, a minor interruption with the entrance of the Boy. Each act ends with the same words

> Well? Shall we go?
> Yes, let's go.

But in the first act Vladimir is agreeing to Estragon's proposal, in the second Estragon to Vladimir's. In neither case do they actually make a move.

In *Waiting for Godot*, all five characters had unrestricted use of their limbs – a luxury Beckett would never again allow. In *Endgame* (written 1954–6; produced 1957) only Clov can move freely. The blind Hamm is confined to his armchair, which can be pushed about on castors. Nagg and Nell are visible only when their heads pop up out of their dustbins. In *Krapp's Last Tape* (written 1958; produced 1959) the drab interior setting is populated only by an old man who moves about with difficulty. In *Happy Days* (produced 1961), Winnie is half submerged – more than half after the interval – in a low mound, while the only other character, Willie, who can move only by crawling, does not emerge fully into view until just before the end. In *Play* (produced 1963) all three characters are imprisoned up to their necks in urns. In *Not I* (produced 1973) most of the stage space is in darkness. We see only a human mouth with about two inches of surrounding flesh, and, lit more dimly, a listening figure, its head wrapped in the loose garment that covers its body. In *That Time* (produced 1976) nothing is visible except a man's head. Even his voice has been disembodied: it comes to us over loudspeakers from three different angles. In *Footfalls* (produced 1976) only a strip of the stage is lit and the old woman shambles in and out of view, but we see her face and her hands. Not that Beckett is wasting the stage space that remains unused: in each case it contributes in much the same way that an area of blankness can contribute to a painting. But the progression is towards an increasing concentration on the conditions of consciousness. Beckett's use of the medium has been determined by the same overwhelming need that is evident in his novels, the need to investigate the non-stop flow that goes on inside our heads, mixing words (heard, spoken and remembered) with images (observed, remembered and evoked).

In contrast to his stage plays, Beckett's first radio play, *All That Fall* (1957), is full of movement and rich in scenic detail, suggested by words and sound effects. Mr Rooney seems to be enunciating a principle basic to Beckett's drama when he says: 'Once and for all do not ask me to speak and move at the same time.' Beckett, we feel, is allowing characters to move from place to place only because we can see neither the movement nor the places. Proust had said 'The need to speak obstructs not only hearing but seeing'; the assumption behind Beckett's theatre is that the need to listen is obstructed by the need to watch movement or change. Like the radio audience, spectators in the theatre must be made to work with their ears. At the same time, his ascetic disposition has combined with his determination to avoid repetition of what other playwrights have done, inducing a progressive rejection of the amenities that the medium offers. The presupposition may be that the negative approach leads, if not to positive results, at least to an avoidance of distortion. In the same way that a man whose body seems to be wasting away can cure himself by fasting, a medium's potentialities can effectively be enhanced by refusing to exploit them. In leaving stage space empty and dark, Beckett is giving an unfamiliar perspective to whatever happens in the area he uses. By showing us nothing of an actress except her mouth, he makes us oddly aware of the apparently absent body; as in listening to a radio play, we use our imagination more in visualising than we would in seeing. It is both stimulating and disconcerting to have our attention riveted by the movements of lips, teeth and tongue, as words pour out rapidly, desperately, almost incomprehensibly. It is like watching both sound and pain, while the movement strikes us, simultaneously or alternately, as inhuman and ultra-human. In the television production (1977) we could see the anguished lips and flailing tongue more clearly, but this did not compensate for the absence of the empty space. The reality of close-up was less compelling than the illusion of close-up, partly because close-up on television is so familiar. In all good anti-art, the shock waves of unfamiliarity are integral to the emotional pressure on the audience. If the surprise is a pebble dropped into a pool, the statement is a paper boat which is not seen at its best once the ripples have subsided.

In *Endgame* the central image is derived from chess, and we are made to watch the game from the players' point of view, understanding why neither of them can merely walk away from the chessboard, though both wish the stalemate could be checkmate. The allusions to *Oedipus* and *Lear* suggest that art is part of the game which is ending, but the text is full of self-deflating devices to discourage us from reacting to it as to art.

HAMM: We're not beginning to . . . to . . . mean something?
CLOV: Mean something! You and I, mean something! (*Brief laugh.*) Ah that's a good one!

The action is less circular than it was in *Waiting for Godot*. Both plays drift (or at least aspire) towards an indeterminate viewpoint outside space and time, but the set of *Endgame* presents an outsize visual pun which (without committing itself any more than a verbal pun) admits the possibility of equating the action with life inside the brain. The two windows can be taken to represent eyes, and Clov's business of opening the curtains and removing the dust-sheet from Hamm to represent the process of waking up in the morning. The dustbins would then be a very disenchanted reference to Proust's vases – containing useless memories of the past.

Undeterred by the built-in warning about 'meaning', critics go on proposing one-to-one correlations between intrinsic and extrinsic; but anticipating this, Beckett has booby-trapped the play with contradictory indications. The evidence to support the equation between Hamm and God is contradicted by evidence to suggest that the man is an incarnation of the void.

HAMM: I was never there.
CLOV: Lucky for you. (*He looks out of window.*)
HAMM: Absent, always. It all happened without me. I don't know what's happened.

Underneath the dark glasses, his eyes have gone all white, and seeing nothing, he can see Nothingness.

The play progresses by cancelling itself out: there are sequences which can have been introduced only to discredit the vision already presented. Hamm talks about a madman who thought the end of the world had come:

I'd take him by the hand and drag him to the window. Look! There! All that rising corn! And there! Look! The sails of the

herring fleet! All that loveliness! (*Pause*.) He'd snatch away his
hand and go back into his corner. Appalled. All he had seen was
ashes.

When Clov looks out of the window, he reports 'nothing' and
'zero', but if Hamm is mad to think the end of the world has come,
Clov may be a function of his madness. At the end of the play, the
appearance of the small boy contradicts all the indications we
have had that nothing outside has survived. Not that we have to
choose between these mutually exclusive versions of the central
situation. Beckett deliberately maroons us between the two. The
play is working acidly on our habit of assuming that information
contained in dialogue and action must be self-consistent, that a
situation must be coherent, that a character must seem to exist as a
whole, that the total work of art represents 'reality'. Occasionally
it is the words that contradict themselves, as when Hamm says
'The bigger a man is the fuller he is . . . And the emptier.' More
often it is the indications about situation that cancel each other
out, and this has the effect of making the words more like objects
in their own right than component elements in a theatrical illusion
of reality. In a 1945 article about painting, Beckett had written,
'each time that one wishes to make words do a true work of trans-
ference, each time one wishes to make them express something
other than words, they align themselves in such a way as to cancel
each other out.'[3] Peter Handke was later to occupy the same
position.

One of the sentences Beckett quotes in his *Proust* from *A la
recherche du temps perdu* is 'A being scattered in space and time is no
longer a woman but a series of events on which we can throw no
light, a series of problems that cannot be solved, a sea that, like
Xerxes, we thrash with rods in an absurd desire to punish it for
having engulfed our treasure.' *Krapp's Last Tape* brilliantly illus-
trates the disintegration of the self into a series of events scattered through time. Having kept a sort of diary on tape for more
than forty years, the old man is in imperfect sympathy with the
younger men who made the recordings. Thirty years ago he was
already liable to laugh at what he had been twelve years before
that. And now he starts a new tape with the comment:

Just been listening to that stupid bastard I took myself for thirty years ago, hard to believe I was ever as bad as that.

For Krapp, who is a writer, the only reality is words. His own past selves are real for him only in the form of words on a tape, and the pleasure he enjoys most in the present is the pleasure of words. Within the first minute of the action, we see him relishing the word 'spool'. 'Spoooool,' he croons. But he can no longer regard himself as creative, and, as John Pilling points out, 'it is no accident that Krapp should switch off the tape when he hears the words "When I *look*", and fortify himself with drink and a song celebrating the delights of darkness'.[4] The idea is Proustian, but Krapp's *recherche du temps perdu* is not going to bring him any understanding or fulfilment.

Happy Days is the third and last of Beckett's full-length plays. To be presented in female guise, the Beckettian consciousness has to be characterised. The mixture of intellectuality and vulgarity in Winnie is not altogether convincing, and performance depends more on personality than in any other Beckett play; but the main mistake is in prolonging the theatrical statement beyond its natural length. The paper boat is not very interesting to watch when it is not in motion, and the ripples have subsided long before the end of the first act. It soon becomes clear that Winnie's optimism will survive the incessant deterioration in her circumstances: it is a habit which screens her from the suffering of being. She is not totally unaware of what is happening, so there is some courage in her apparent mindlessness, but the polarity in her consciousness does not produce much tension. At the beginning of the second act, a theatrical impact is made by showing that she is now embedded in the mound up to her neck, and, just before the end, we get something of a climax when Willie, dressed like a bridegroom, tries to crawl up the mound, but most of the theatrical points have been made already, while the monotony is not sufficiently extreme to constitute a point in its own right.

The subsequent plays are all, by contrast, extremely economical, and, though much depends on the performers' expertise, little depends on their personality. All we see of the actor and the two actresses in *Play* is their heads. 'They face undeviatingly front throughout the play. Faces so lost to age and aspect as to seem almost part of urns.' Beckett also demands 'faces impassive throughout. Voices toneless except where an expression is indicated.' And the only expressions that are indicated are 'faint, wild laugh' once for the second woman (W2), 'vehement' once for W1, 'hopefully' once for W2 and two peals of wild, low laughter for her. The man is required to hiccup several times but to talk tonelessly throughout.

A great deal depends on the use of a spotlight, which cues the speeches by shining on the character who is to talk. He has to go on talking, it seems, until the light switches to the next.*

Beckett's *Not I* is even shorter than *Play*, running only about twelve minutes, but, though the theatrical image is one of the most striking in modern drama, it would not have been wise to base a full-length play on it, and, having once made the mistake of over-extending his material, Beckett has scrupulously avoided it.

In his unpublished novel *The Dream of Fair to Middling Women* (1932) he had written: 'The experience of my reader shall be between the phrases, in the silence, communicated by the intervals, not the terms.' *Not I* comes as close to realising this ambition as any of the fictions. It is not merely that the syntax is broken

---

* This is a development of an Expressionist device, though the Expressionists may, as Walter Sokel suggests, have learnt it from Rembrandt's technique of using light to put a character 'on the spot'.[5] In Reinhard Sorge's *Der Bettler* (*The Beggar*, 1912; 1917) the script gives detailed instructions for lighting changes. In key monologues, the stage is darkened except for the beam of light on the speaker. The shifting of light from one group of characters to another mimics the shifting of the dreaming mind. And in Richard Weichert's 1918 production of *Der Sohn*, the spotlight was used 'for the first time as a kind of persecutor, throwing the characters into vivid relief against the surrounding blackness of the minimal set . . . free-standing door and window frames set in black drapes'. The theatrical ideas central to Expressionism had been pioneered by Adolf Appia and Gordon Craig, who, at the turn of the century, had introduced abstract geometry into set design, and lighting that could depersonalise the actor, either magnifying him by making him cast a huge shadow, or dwarfing him in relation to the stage picture's non-human components.

and the disjunction between the phrases is expressive, the main statement about the speaking self is made through its attempts to fend off its own identity. The experience that Mouth has to retail is so painful that even now, about seventy years since it began, she can only talk about herself in the third person. All four movements of the listening figure are movements of 'helpless compassion', and all four are made at moments when she seems to be about to say 'I' but baulks at it: '... what? ... who? ... no! ... she!' is her refrain. In the same way that Proust's painter, Elstir, uses land and sea to define each other by making their unlikeness into a resemblance, Beckett characterises only the distance between this consciousness and its image of itself.

The originality of Beckett's theatre is rooted in a vision that could hardly have seemed more unlikely to be expressible in words and actions that the medium allows. Beckett has lost faith in words as corresponding to anything but themselves, and in some of his later plays, the importance of words dwindles. In both *Play* and *Not I*, the syntax is so complex, so fragmentary and so breathless that the dialogue would be partially incomprehensible to an audience, even if the actors delivered it much more slowly than he wants them to. He has moved beyond aspiring to the condition of radio drama. The emotional impact, which is considerable, depends as much on tone, inflection, audible pain, as on construable statements. Through speech, an emotional pressure can be put on an audience even without its assimilating all the words.

At the same time, the later plays contain not only less action but less activity. Beckett's Schopenhauerian attitude tends towards a cult of inaction. If unsatisfied desire is the cause of all misery, the closest we can come to satisfaction is through the abandonment of desire. In the novel *Watt* (written 1942-5; published 1953) Mr Knott's house represents an area in which there is no suffering because there are no unfulfilled needs; the characters in Beckett's plays are all suffering from being shut out of some such negative paradise. Even the word *characters* is misleading. They are precipitates from a consciousness which never stops – never can stop – meditating on the conditions of its own existence, and they exist in what is almost a vacuum of non-action, which almost succeeds in sucking the audience into awareness of those conditions. His art corresponds to his description of the van Velde brothers: 'An endless unveiling, veil behind veil, level upon level of imperfect transparencies, an unveiling towards what cannot be unveiled, the nothing, the new thing.'[7]

2 Beckett
and
Before

What Beckett has given to playwrights depends on what he has taken away from audiences: the gift of freedom is the result of asking: 'how little does one need to offer?' One of my reasons for thinking the term 'anti-theatre' may be useful is that I believe we can arrive at a better understanding of how he wrote *Waiting for Godot* if we look at his earlier development in the context of minimalism, reductionism and the other negative tendencies of anti-art.

Does the anti-artist want to destroy the medium? If he could and if he did, he would be condemning himself to silence. The *via negativa* chosen by several of the greatest modernist innovators has led to either silence or suicide. Cesare Pavese, who killed himself in 1950, said that literature was one form of defence against the attacks of life, and silence was the other. Rimbaud was no older than twenty-five and possibly as young as twenty when he gave up writing; Marcel Duchamp turned from art to chess, but according to Octavio Paz, his inactivity has been as fruitful for the twentieth century as Picasso's prolific vitality: 'Our time is one which affirms itself only by negating itself and which negates itself only to invent and transcend itself.'[1]

Duchamp's method was not only theatrical but farcical. Using the exhibition hall as Jarry used the stage, he introduced a caustic, iconoclastic comedy that questioned the conventions and assumptions of all previous painters.

Most anti-artists have been more ambivalent, inspired by an uncomfortable mixture of love and hatred for other practitioners in the medium. Destruction is intended only as a preliminary to creation. 'The man who wants to be a creator,' said Nietzsche, 'must first be a destroyer and disrupt values'; Beckett has approvingly quoted a parallel pronouncement by the nineteenth-century Italian critic Francesco de Sanctis: 'He who lacks the strength to kill reality lacks the strength to create it.'[2]

The history of art is a history of movements and countermovements; a history of parody would have to go back at least to the eighth or ninth century BC. Cratinus, who lived in the fifth century BC, was probably one of the first playwrights to parody Homer. Aristophanes compared him to an impetuous torrent that sweeps everything in front of it, but he could hardly be called an anti-artist. Nor could the word be applied to Pope, though, like Greek and Roman satirists, he applied the Epic style mockingly to trivial events. Eighteenth-century Augustanism could envisage no higher objective than to imitate the achievements of classical poets, rather in the way that the believer may imitate the achievements of the saints, without any ambition to outstrip them. But the modern secularisation of culture has intensified the savagery artists have shown in rejecting the work of their predecessors, and since the Romantic revolution, destructiveness has been integral to originality, as originality has to self-definition.

Walter Benjamin has said that 'The history of each form of art contains critical periods in which art aspires towards results that can be achieved only after a drastic modification of the technical *status quo*; that is to say by a new form of art. This is why the seeming absurdities and extravagances that emerge in times of so-called decadence, far from being mere symptoms of decay, stem from what is most vital in the artistic forces of the period.' When the anti-artist behaves outrageously, it may be partly because he himself is outraged by the comfort that has seeped into the relationship between the public and works of art that should disturb it. Edges have been blunted. Masterpieces are being used as subjects for dinner-party chatter, financial speculation, superficial aesthetic frissons and facile moral reassurance.

But what is anti-art? We cannot define it simply in terms of hostility to the audience, though this is an important factor, sometimes producing outbursts of direct provocation, sometimes an attempt to break off all relations with the public. The preparatory activity can become all-important. Mallarmé went on throughout his life making notes for a *magnum opus* which he probably never started; Duchamp began working on his 'Large glass', 'La Mariée mise à nue par ses célibataires, même', in 1915 and finished it in 1923, having brought it to 'a state of incompletion'.

At the same time, anti-art is always anti-realistic, because it always rejects the assumption that art's function is to mirror reality. Duchamp repudiated 'the possibility of recognising any two things as being like each other'. The tradition of landscape painting rests on the assumption that the painting resembles the landscape. Even a Cubist still life is assumed to be like the objects that are depicted – an assumption Magritte amusingly challenged when he painted a pipe and captioned it 'This is not a pipe.' The statement is true: an image of a pipe is not a pipe.

If anti-art has been important during the last hundred years, as never before in the history of art, it is partly because this is a period of decadence with a vast amount of mediocre artistic activity. Decadence has been defined by the Russian Symbolist poet Vyacheslav Ivanov as 'the feeling, at once oppressive and exalting, of being the last of a series'. This is implicitly to give decadence a special relationship to *avant-garde* art, which Massimo Bontempelli characterises as 'an exclusively modern discovery, born only when art began to contemplate itself from a historical viewpoint'.[3] But the second-rate *avant-garde* artist may not recognise that the history of art has already made his work redundant. Duchamp's ready-mades were meaningful at the time of the first world war; since the end of the fifties Pop Art has gone on *ad nauseam* giving us meaningless repetitions of them. If there were no decisive silences, no strongly negative gestures, mediocre artists would make all art meaningless by their endless, uncritical repetition of themselves and each other.

Waiting for Godot is a good example of the anti-art in which game-playing bulks large, partly because negative principles have asserted themselves so strongly. Since no serious activity can have worthwhile consequences, the artist is in the same position as the characters, who have nothing to do but while away the time with games. Game-playing also introduces the element of chance, and it is sometimes a premiss of anti-art that accident should supersede intention. Tristan Tzara would create a poem by cutting up a newspaper article into single words, shaking them up in a bag and letting them flutter down on to a table-top. Chance would arrange the words better than he could.

André Gide called Dadaism 'a negating operation', and the Dada manifesto of 1918 ridiculed Art as 'a parrot word – replaced by Dada . . . Art is a pretension, warmed by the diffidence of the urinary tract, hysteria born in a studio.' But while Tzara enjoyed carrying on like the leader of an artistic demolition squad, other pressures were at work within the movement. In 1916, when Hugo Ball founded the Cabaret Voltaire in Zurich, the war, observed from a neutral country, formed a mad perspective that made the excesses of Dadaism seem non-violent, therapeutic and perhaps even spiritual. 'We were seeking an art based on fundamentals,' wrote Hans Arp in *Dadaland*, 'to cure the madness of the age'; and Ball believed that art could help towards the regeneration of the European mind. When he had been laying plans for the new theatre, he had been influenced by Kandinsky, who had argued the case for breaking down the barriers between the arts in *Über das Geistige in der Kunst* (*On the Spiritual in Art*, 1912), a book which had a strong tidal pull on Expressionism. The first post-Freudian generation of playwrights followed the example of the painters, introducing anti-realistic scenery, costumes and lighting as a means of articulating the inner life, the spirit. The eye of the artist, wrote Kandinsky, 'should be focused on his inner life and

his ear should constantly be open to the murmur of inner necessity.' Interested, like Rimbaud, in making the senses work together'
he believed in radical experiment with form and in an interpenetration between the arts. His ultimate objective was what
the Expressionists called *Durchgeistigung* – a permeation of spirit
into artistic expression.

Art becomes anti-art when the spirit becomes hostile to artistic
expression. As Susan Sontag has put it,

> Art becomes the enemy of the artist, for it denies him the
> realization – the transcendence – he desires. Therefore, art
> comes to be considered something to be overthrown. A new
> element enters the individual artwork and becomes constitutive
> of it: the appeal (tacit or overt) for its own abolition – and,
> ultimately, for the abolition of art itself . . . Committed to the
> idea that the power of art is located in its power to *negate*, the
> ultimate weapon in the artist's inconsistent war with his audi-
> ence is to verge closer and closer to silence.[4]

The aggressiveness of the Dadaists was directed partly against
artistic tradition, partly against the public. At the Cabaret Voltaire,
poets and painters presented themselves provocatively as performers. There were songs, recitations, dancing, exhibitions of
abstract art, simultaneous poems in three languages, and
'Bruitist' music, consisting of noises taken from machinery,
engines, traffic. Both these last ideas were borrowed from the
Italian Futurists.

The idea of the *Gesamtkunstwerk* was a background influence
on performances at the Cabaret Voltaire and, later, in the larger
space at the Dada Gallery, where the arts were drawn into new
combinations. The aggressive confrontation with the audience
was itself theatrical, while Tzara's method of composing poems
was more theatrical than literary. As in television cooking pro-
grammes, the spectacle mattered more than the result. The
Dadaists also produced plays; in 1917 Oscar Kokoschka's
Expressionistic *Sphinx und Strohmann* was staged. Tzara appeared
in the role of a parrot, while Ball played a man doubly deceived by
an evil scientist, who kills him by implanting the idea that fear of
cuckoldry can be lethal. As the victim dies, horns sprouting from

his forehead, the scientist pokes his head through the backcloth to
declaim nonsensical aphorisms.

A still more anti-theatrical event had been staged in July 1916
at the Dada evening in the Zunfthaus zur Waag, when Hugo Ball
gave a solo performance. He wore a costume made of cardboard –
a witch-doctor's cylindrical hat with blue and white stripes, and a
huge collar, gold outside and scarlet inside. This was fastened at
his neck so that he could flap it like wings by moving his elbows.
Around his legs was a shiny cylinder of blue cardboard, designed
to make him look like an obelisk. He was carried to the platform
in a blackout. When the lights came up, he began slowly and
impressively:

> gadji beri bimba glandridi laula lonni cadori
> gadjama gramma berida bimbala glandri galassassa laulitalomini
> gadji beri bin blassa glassala laula lonni dadorsu sassala bim . . .

Long before he got to the end, he was playing to loud laughter.
The best stratagem was to remain serious, but the only movement
at his disposal was flapping his wings. Without taking any decision
about what to do, he found his voice was imitating the cadences
of a parish priest celebrating High Mass. By chanting, he stopped
himself from laughing, and brought his performance successfully
to its close.

In nearly all anti-art there is an implicit rejection of the conditions in which previous artistic statements have been made, and
the criteria by which they have been judged; in Ball's performance, there was also an undertone of insult to the audience. As in
Peter Handke's more overtly insulting *Publikumsbeschimpfung*
(*Offending the Audience*, written 1965; produced 1966) the public
was implicitly being challenged not to submit to the entertainment which was being substituted for the usual fare. Invariably
the audience does submit – not always without heckling – but the
tension is intrinsically theatrical, and therefore enjoyable. Wanting
to cause embarrassment, the performers are themselves not
immune to it. Ball's success came from improvising an escape
route from his embarrassment. The impact of the shock had worn
off; by modulating he launched a second shock-wave.

It could be said that all anti-art depends on shock, on presenting the audience with a package of surprises, but this could also be said of all art. Marcel Duchamp argued that 'A painting which does not shock is not worth painting.' He maintained that the life of a painting was limited to forty or fifty years: 'I think a picture dies after a few years like the man who painted it. Afterward it's called the history of art. There's a huge difference between a Monet today, which is black as anything, and a Monet sixty or eighty years ago, when it was brilliant, when it was made.'[5]

Duchamp's 'Nude Descending a Staircase' cannot have the impact today that it would have had in 1912, if it had been shown, as he intended, at the Salon des Indépendants in Paris. The shock would have come more from the title than the painting, which would not have been recognised as a nude descending a staircase, since the lady has no skin and her limbs are approximately cylindrical. There was no impropriety in painting a nude, but it seemed offensive to catch her on her way downstairs, and the implications seemed so anti-religious that the Indépendants, then the most *avant-garde* group in Paris, asked him to withdraw it. It was after this, at the age of twenty-five, that he gave up painting on canvas. Four years later, at the New York Salon des Indépendants, which he had himself helped to found, he tried to exhibit a urinal with the title 'Fountain'. It could not be rejected, but it was concealed behind a partition for the duration of the exhibition.

Duchamp's 'readymades' are classics of anti-art. The first, a bicycle wheel mounted on a kitchen stool, was put together in 1913, two years before he arrived at the name 'readymades'. He denied wanting to be provocative. 'I didn't have any special reason to do it,' he told Pierre Cabanne, 'or any intention of showing it, or describing anything.' The following year he bought a cheap reproduction of a landscape, added two dots, red and green, and called it 'Pharmacy' because of the red and green jars of coloured water in the windows of French chemists' shops. In 1915 he bought a bottle-rack in a bazaar and gave it an inscription. In 1919 he added a beard and a moustache to a reproduction of the Mona Lisa. Any schoolboy could have done the same; no doubt many schoolboys have.

He understood the importance of limiting himself to a small number of 'readymades'. 'It's very difficult to choose an object, because, at the end of fifteen days, you begin to like it or to hate it . . . The choice of readymades is always based on visual indifference and, at the same time, on the total absence of good or bad taste.' Taste he defined as 'A habit. The repetition of something already accepted. If you start something over several times, it becomes taste. Good or bad, it's the same thing, it's still taste.' This revulsion against 'taste' drove him towards dependence on the mechanical, which 'upholds no taste, since it is outside all pictorial convention', and on chance. 'Pure chance interested me as a way of going against logical reality: to put something on a canvas, on a bit of paper, to associate the idea of a perpendicular thread a meter long falling from the height of one meter on to a horizontal plane, making its own deformation. This amused me. It's always the idea of "amusement" which causes me to do things . . .' After his eight years of work on 'La Mariée mise à nue par ses célibataires, même', which he painted on glass, he claimed to like it better after it had been smashed as the result of careless packing in Brooklyn. 'It's a lot better with the breaks, a hundred times better. It's the destiny of things.' He admired the painter Francis Picabia as 'a negator . . . Whatever you said, he contradicted. It was his game.'

According to Richter, Picabia also had a strong catalytic influence on Tzara, who 'seemed to switch suddenly from a position of balance between art and anti-art into the stratospheric regions of pure and joyful nothingness'.[6] Picabia's canvases incorporated words and collages of hairpins, feathers and string. He used the paintbrush very little but produced a great deal of work. He ran an aggressive periodical called *391*, writing in it with wry acumen about the meaninglessness of all artistic creation, anticipating Beckett's 1949 summary of Tal Coat's painting as 'The expression that there is nothing to express, nothing with which to express, nothing from which to express, no power to express, no desire to express, together with the obligation to express.'[7] Nihilistically denying that life could have any meaning, and wanting to reject art in so far as it could not help being an affirmation of life, Picabia was kept helplessly afloat by inexhaustible energy and compulsive inventiveness. Temperamentally, he lived at the opposite pole from the other 'negator' who influenced Duchamp – Raymond Roussel. In 1911, the year he met Picabia, Duchamp went to see the play Roussel had based on his novel *Impressions d' Afrique*. 'On the stage there was a model and a snake that moved slightly – it was absolutely the madness of the unexpected. I don't remember much of the text. One didn't really listen . . . that man had done something which really had Rimbaud's revolutionary aspect to it, a secession.'

Roussel spent his time either living in a caravan with the curtains drawn or travelling around the world, trying not to see it, living in cabins and hotel rooms. His life conforms with attitudes expressed in Villiers de l'Isle Adam's *Axel* ('Living? Our servants can do that for us.') and in Huysmans's *A Rebours*. ('Travel he considered a waste of time, for he believed that the imagination could provide a more than adequate alternative to the vulgar reality of actual experience.'). Huysmans's hero, des Esseintes, was partly modelled on Comte Robert de Montesquiou-Fezensac, a friend of Proust, who based his Baron de Charlus on him.

Extreme revulsion against reality can grow into a fascination with the idea of Non-being. Stéphane Mallarmé, whom Octavio Paz shrewdly identifies as Duchamp's direct antecedent, came to equate truth with nothingness. In March 1866 he wrote to Henri Cazalis: 'Unfortunately, burrowing into the verse down to this point, I have encountered two abysses, which dismay me. One is Nothingness. I have reached it without any knowledge of Buddhism and I am still too overwhelmed to be able to believe in my poetry and go back to the work this shattering thought made me abandon.'

All through the rest of his life, he was on the verge of madness. Suicide seemed like a possibility of positive action. His identity appeared to flow away from him into his thinking, and his thinking into the literature he produced. Fourteen months later, writing to Cazalis again, with a mirror on the table, he had to keep looking at it, for fear of 'reverting' to the Nothingness into which he had made 'rather a long descent'.

This is to let you know that I am impersonal now, no longer the Stéphane Mallarmé you knew – but a capacity the Spiritual Universe has for seeing itself and developing itself through what used to be me.

He had let literature float him to a transcendentalist belief in ideal forms. The ordinary functioning of language swerves constantly towards abstraction; Mallarmé was intensely aware of the bias. To write 'flower' is to substitute a generalising name for the particular flower you are looking at. Its colours, contours and blemishes are obliterated, to be replaced by a pure idea. The poet can impart fragrance to the idea, but the whiff of imaginary scent that reaches the reader is quite different from the real scent, and the suggestion of the ideal depends on the suppression of the real. The word blots out the thing. The point is very close to one Hegel made when he said: 'The first act by which Adam made himself master of the animals was to impose a name on them. Which is to say that he annihilated them as existent beings.' Paul Valéry made the converse point in his essay on Degas when he wrote: 'To look is to forget the names of the things you are seeing.'

In his poetry Mallarmé could evoke not only the presence but the absence of an object:

> *Une dentelle s'abolit*
> *Dans le doute du Jeu suprême*
> *A n'entrouvrir comme un blasphème*
> *Qu'absence éternelle de lit.*
>
> *Cet unanime blanc conflit*
> *D'une guirlande avec la même,*
> *Enfui contre la vitre blême*
> *Flotte plus qu'il n'ensevelit.*
>
> *Mais chez qui du rêve se dore*
> *Tristement dort une mandore*
> *Au creux néant musicien*
>
> *Telle que vers quelque fenêtre*
> *Selon nul ventre que le sien,*
> *Filial on aurait pu naître.*

A lace curtain effaces itself
In the uncertainty of the supreme Game
To half-open like a blasphemy
Only on eternal absence of bed.

Unanimous white conflict
Of a garland with the same
Escapes against the pale pane
More floating than burying.

But with one who plumes himself on dreams
Sadly sleeps a mandola
With a hollow music-making void

Such that towards some window
According to no other belly
Filial one could have been born.

With elegant ambiguity, Mallarmé shuts himself out from the space of his own literary creation. The meaning is so elusive, the relationships so tenuous, the co-ordinates so far apart, that the statement seems hardly to exist. He once said he was like a 'holy spider, holding myself on the main threads (*fils*) which have already come out of my mind and with which I will weave, at the points of intersection, wonderful lacework, which I guess, and which already exists in the bosom of beauty'.[8] Samuel Beckett is comparably compulsive in believing the work of art pre-exists the writer's realisation of it: it is 'neither created nor chosen, but uncovered, excavated'[9].

Some of the connections Mallarmé makes are dependent on verbal relationships which already exist in the French language. Another sonnet plays on the fact that *cygne* (swan) is homophonous with *signe* (sign). Some depend on visual associations he makes voluntarily or involuntarily. The lace curtains suggest sheets. Sheets suggest both love-making and conflict in the undivided mind of the writer who confronts blank pages. The window is both transparent and a reflecting surface. But the reflecting emptiness of the mind is destructive. The poem may seem to be saying that there is more floating than burying, but the stress of the eighth line falls on burying. The lace curtains have become a shroud. Then the sestet hints at pregnancy in the womb of the instrument. Resonance comes from the inner emptiness. The birth might have been directed towards a view through the window of a world outside the room, but there is nothing there, no lace curtains, no bed, no poet.

One of the reasons this sonnet is so disturbing is that creativity and vacancy are nihilistically equated. If anything is born inside the emptiness of the womb, the instrument, the mind, how much substance can it have? Is artistic creation always a matter of fabricating names and abolishing existing animals?[10]

In Mallarmé's final poem *Un Coup de Dés* the words are scattered sparsely over the pages: it was his intention to make blank white space predominate, take the initiative. He succeeded so well that even before the poem was printed, Paul Valéry, hearing the poet read it, had the impression of 'infinity speaking, thinking, giving birth to temporal forms. Expectation, doubt and concentration were visible objects. My understanding had to cope with silences that had become incarnate.'

Like Baudelaire, Mallarmé was deeply influenced by Edgar Allan Poe, whose theories of cosmic unity derived from Coleridge's. Poe's *Eureka* equates logic with 'the science of Relation in the abstract – of absolute Relation – of Relation considered solely in itself'. Baudelaire wanted, through poetry, 'to create a suggestive magic containing simultaneously object and subject, the world exterior to the artist and the artist himself'. As he said in his essay on Poe, our instinctive sense of beauty makes us regard the world as a glimpse, a correspondence with heaven. Poe said in *Eureka* that the movement of a finger displacing a speck of dust is integral to a universal movement that involves sun, moon and stars. This assumption of a correspondence between minutiae of private life and movements in the universe can generate analogies, metaphors and pregnant juxtapositions which evoke a vivid impression of spiritual life: Baudelaire spoke of 'almost supernatural' states of soul in which 'familiar sensations are invested with universal significance'. And for Mallarmé, life would have been unbearable if he had not believed that his cobweb of relationships corresponded to the design of the universe. Literature must be 'architectural and premeditated, not just a collection of chance impressions, even marvellous ones'.

Without believing in God, he needed to believe in perfection and eternity. Like Nietzsche, he lived under a pressure that was almost insufferable and superbly fruitful. Nietzsche said that no artist could tolerate reality. 'What strikes me as beautiful, what I would like to do is a book about nothing, a book without external attachments, which would hold itself together by itself through the internal force of its style.' Mallarmé tolerated reality resentfully. There is wistful regret in his acknowledgment that 'Certainly there is nothing except what there is'. But we have a right to draw a void out of ourselves in our boredom with things 'if they established themselves, as solid and dominant'. One would like to have the power of 'extending, simplifying the world' according to one's inner state.[11]

Paul Klee wrote: 'Formerly we used to represent things visible on earth, things we either liked to look at or would have liked to see. Today . . . things appear to assume a broader and more diversified meaning, often seemingly contradicting the rational experience of yesterday. There is a striving to emphasize the essential character of the accidental.' Mallarmé's constant concern was to extract the essential from the accidental, the pure idea from the object. 'What would be the point,' he asked in *Divagations*, 'to transpose a fact of nature into its virtual disappearance in the vibration of a word, unless it is to make the pure idea emerge without the embarrassment of a specific summoning?'

The poem *Igitur* had asked whether thought is governed by chance or superior to it. The central statement of *Un Coup de Dés* is 'A throw of the dice will never abolish chance'. In the uncertainty of the supreme game, we throw the dice by making love or writing a poem, but though we should prefer to imagine it was written in the stars that we should couple with that lover, or that what we are writing already existed in the bosom of eternal beauty, we know that there is no valid comfort to be had from the idea of fatality. If necessity is not an illusion, it is visible only from our point of view. There is no extra-human viewpoint from which the shipwreck is necessary or advantageous. It may seem to us that the whirlwind which sinks the boat is both cruel and irresponsible,

but if the captain dies with the dice still in his hand, there is no
way he could have thrown it to win the game, no means for
thought to transcend eventuality. In the end, no sign of the
human catastrophe is visible on the ocean.

The *magnun opus* that Mallarmé talked about was not entirely a
fantasy. Valéry saw his notes for it. But Mallarmé left instructions
that they were to be destroyed on his death, and he died at the age
of fifty-six with the book still unwritten. Accident or design?
Killed by a strong death wish? Or by the knowledge that the great
work was unwritable? Like the final silence of Rimbaud and
Duchamp, his death was almost integral to his work.

When Samuel Beckett wrote *En attendant Godot* (October 1948–
January 1949) he had been an unbeliever for at least twenty years.
He had been living in France for more than ten, and writing in
French since 1945. His Irish childhood, his four undergraduate
years at Dublin University, and his six terms of teaching had combined with the influence of James Joyce to involve him with the
figures and forms of pedantry and theology, but the involvement
was ironically compensated by fierce blasts of anti-pedantry and
anti-theology. Medieval scholasticism now had the appeal of a
climbing frame in the gymnasium of an abandoned school. A
resentful ex-pupil, he kept coming back to exercise with virtuoso
self-awareness, mercilessly mocking the instructor who was no
longer there. He was still fixated by the notion of a relationship
between microcosm and macrocosm long after he had abandoned
all hope that it could be meaningful.

In 1937, when he settled in Paris, literature was still basking in
the freedom left by the Symbolist revolution. If Symbolism had
succeeded where Romanticism had failed – in breaking down the
rigidities of metrical regularity and Cartesian logic – one reason, as
Edmund Wilson pointed out, was that the Symbolists had built up
pressure by admitting foreign influences.[12] Baudelaire had
translated Poe into French; Verlaine had lived in England;
Mallarmé had taught English; two of the Symbolist poets, Stuart
Merrill and Francis Vielé-Griffin, were Americans who lived in
France and wrote in French. In a foreign language, words are
more like objects in their own right, opaque, musical, slightly

mysterious. Syntax is governed by rules that are less easily taken for granted. Though Joyce (who lived on the Continent from 1904 onwards) went on writing in English, English for him had become more like a foreign language, while failing eyesight tended to heighten his sensitivity to sound and rhythm, increasing his pleasure in onomatopoeia, his interest in composing a word-music that mimicked the sound of the action. As the twenty-three-year-old Beckett put it in an essay,

> His writing is not *about* something; *it is that something itself.* . . . When the sense is dancing, the words dance. Take the passage at the end of Shaun's pastoral: 'To stirr up love's young fizz I tilt with this bridle's cup champagne, dimming douce from her peepair of hideseeks tight squeezed on my snowy-breasted and while my pearlies in their sparkling wisdom are nippling her bubblets I swear (and let you swear) by the bumper round of my poor old snaggle-tooth's solidbowel I ne'er will prove I'm untrue to (there!) you liking so long as my hole looks. Down.' The language is drunk. The very words are tilted and effervescent. How can we qualify this general esthetic vigilance without which we cannot hope to snare the sense which is for ever rising to the surface of the form and becoming the form itself?[13]

This helps to explain why Beckett wrote only in French from 1945 till about 1952 (when he stopped writing until the end of 1955). But Mallarmé had been equally critical of French as abstract in this sense:

> Compared to the opacity of the word *ombre*, the word *ténèbres* does not seem very dark; and how perversely frustrating it is that *jour* has dark tones and *nuit* bright tones. We dream of a word brilliant at once in meaning and sound, or darkening in meaning and sound . . . *But* we must not forget that if our dream were fulfilled, *verse would not exist* – verse which, in its wisdom, atones for language's sins, nobly comes to their rescue.

If Joyce's prose aspires to the condition of verse, Beckett's reactions to it show how he read Renaissance literature through spectacles that had been tinted by Symbolism. His essay argues that Vico's cyclical theory of history was evolved out of Giordano Bruno's identification of opposites:

> Minimal heat equals minimal cold. Consequently transmutations are circular. The principle (minimum) of one contrary takes its movement from the principle (maximum) of another. Therefore not only do the minima coincide with the minima, the maxima with the maxima, but the minima with the maxima in the succession of transmutations. Maximal speed is a state of rest . . . And all things are ultimately identified with God, the universal monad.

In Vico's reading of history, progress is determined neither by individuals nor by fate: 'Individuality is the concretion of universality, and every individual action is at the same time super-individual.' History is the outcome of a Necessity which he equated with Divine Providence, and Beckett assumes that he made the equation with his tongue 'very much in his cheek'. 'This Providence is not transcendental but immanent, and it works by natural means . . . In a word, here is all humanity circling with fatal monotony about the Providential fulcrum – the "convoy wheeling encirculing abound the gigantig's lifetree".' If Vico's theory of history prefigures Hegel's, the scepticism of Beckett's essay prefigures the scepticism of *Waiting for Godot*.

This essay also helps to explain how Proust did so much to condition the early development of the mind that was to produce *Waiting for Godot*. Whereas Dante's Purgatory is conical, implying culmination, James Joyce's is spherical.

> In the one movement is unidirectional, and a step forward represents a net advance: in the other movement is non-directional – or multi-directional, and a step forward is, by definition, a step back. Dante's Terrestial Paradise is the carriage entrance to a Paradise that is not terrestrial: Mr Joyce's Terrestial Paradise is the tradesmen's entrance on to the sea-shore. Sin is an impediment to movement up the cone, and a condition of movement round the sphere. In what sense, then, is Mr Joyce's work purgatorial? In the absolute absence of the Absolute. Hell is the static lifelessness of unrelieved viciousness.

Paradise the static lifelessness of unrelieved immaculation. Purgatory a flood of movement and vitality released by the conjunction of these two elements.

Waiting for Godot presents a very different image of Purgatory, while the Absolute, though not unambiguously present, is not absolutely absent. But the mechanically circular movement proceeds more or less according to the principle Beckett formulated nearly twenty years before he wrote his play:

> Vice and Virtue – which you may take to mean any pair of large contrary human factors – must in turn be purged down to spirits of rebelliousness. Then the dominant crust of the Vicious or Virtuous sets, resistance is provided, the explosion duly takes place and the machine proceeds. And no more than this; neither prize nor penalty; simply a series of stimulants to enable the kitten to catch its tail. And the partially purgatorial agent? The partially purged.

Waiting for Godot would not be what it is if Beckett had not proceeded from a deep involvement in the work of Joyce to a deep involvement in the work of Proust. Proust's language was less eccentric than Joyce's, but his rejection of the realistic tradition was equally extreme; Beckett's early stories and novels recoil even further away from it. His critical book on Proust (1931) bears something of the same relation to the creative work which followed as Proust's *Contre Sainte-Beuve* (1908–10) does to his later fiction. Conceived as a critical article for *Le Figaro*, *Contre Sainte-Beuve* grew into a long book that mixes fiction with criticism, while making a direct statement of points which would be developed with more subtlety and more comedy in the later work. 'Each day,' wrote Proust,

> I attach less value to intelligence. Each day it becomes clearer to me that it is only without it that the writer can recapture something of our impressions. Which is to say that the only business of art is to penetrate to something inside oneself. What intelligence presents as the past is not the past.

Proust is consistently subjective. Gathering force in *A la recherche*, his assault on intelligence and realistic observation is partly an attack on himself. The voyeuristic side of his personality was highly unattractive, even to him, but after his withdrawal into the cork-lined bedroom, the Marcel Proust who enjoyed watching hatpins being stuck into rats survives in the Marcel who describes the flagellation he watches during a visit to the male brothel owned by the Baron de Charlus. In fact Proust made one of his rare sorties into the world outside the bedroom in order to refresh his memories of male brothels. It must be significant, as Martin Turnell suggests,[14] that in the narrative the most offensive homosexual incidents are invariably observed from a concealed position. When André Gide told him about his memoirs and gave him a copy of *Corydon*, Proust's comment was: 'You can tell everything, but on condition you never say "I".'[15]

A la recherche both affirms and negates Proust's life. His principle was 'to yield to one's demon, one's thinking, to write on anything to the point of exhaustion'. But was his writing an alternative to living? In what sense did it represent a repudiation of his previous life or the life that was still continuing? The book by Céleste Albaret,[16] who looked after him from 1913 till 1922, confirms the impression that his art was suicidal. He drank a great deal of coffee, but ate very little, wanting to keep his mind clear while bringing the book to birth. He worked at night, slept through the morning, drank his first cup of coffee in the afternoon. His windows were permanently shut. When he went out, it was usually at night. If he needed to observe the hawthorn in blossom, he would drive to the country in a carriage with closed windows. He gave Mme Albaret the impression that he had no sexual relationships and that except for the sake of the book he had no surviving interest in other people or in what was going on outside the room. He told her about his visit to the male brothel. He said that if he died before the novel was finished, his life would have been wasted. When he had nearly finished it, he died at the age of fifty-one, from what had begun as a mild influenza. He had been consulting doctors but disregarding their advice and refusing their medicine. The day before he died he was dictating corrections of *La Prisonnière*. For him, as for Mallarmé, the world existed only to be made into a book, but he did not die with the book still unmade.

He had created it by submitting himself ruthlessly to a negative principle. At the age of twenty, answering a personal questionnaire, he said that his main fault was 'to be unable to want anything'. By the time he was forty, he was able to want nothing. 'Perhaps it is nothingness that is real,' he wrote in *Du Côté de chez Swann*, 'and all our dreaming has no real existence.' Rejecting the normal functioning of memory as falsifyingly dependent on intelligence, he maintained that the writer 'should expect involuntary memory to provide nearly all the raw material of his work'. Accordingly, he created for himself a vacuum which would suck a variety of fragments from the past into co-existence. He called his solitude 'the life of a mental drawing-room', but only uninvited guests were welcome; voluntary memories were ejected. The living routine he established for himself tended to make his waking life approximate to dreaming with all the senses alerted. As Valéry said, 'In dreams, everything is automatically included. Nothing is left out.' The coffee, the habit of working in bed, the treatment of day as night, night as day, all helped to give him the sensation of being liberated, as the dreamer is, from time. Areas of past experience are folded into the present; the personality disintegrates as all one's past selves share the foreground with the present self. Previous experience appears less like a linear sequence of events than like a vortex which is sucking upwards and downwards simultaneously. But the predominant feeling is of liberation: it may not, after all, be too late to disentangle successions of mistaken decisions and disastrous events.

Though there are nearly one and a half million words in *A la recherche*, his attitude to words was ambivalent: 'I found words instructive only when interpreted either in the manner of a rush of blood to the face of someone embarrassed, or in the manner of an abrupt silence.' They can almost never be taken at their face value – this is one of the reasons Proust needs so many of them when they constitute his only means of expression. Unlike Mallarmé, he cannot use blank spaces on the page; unlike the dramatist, he cannot use gesture or silence or empty stage space. He must show exactly how Marcel graduates, by suffering, from believing in the possibility of direct communication with Albertine to the realisation that her words make more sense if turned upside down. One of the main lessons is 'that the truth can be revealed without being spoken, that without either waiting for words or even taking account of them it can be reached perhaps more securely through a thousand external signs, even in invisible phenomena – signs which function in the world of characters as atmospheric changes do in physical nature'. His attitude corresponds to what Georges Braque said about not believing in things, only in the relationships between them. In Proust's novel the painter Elstir is the representative of the new art. By making sea look like land and land look like sea, he is not so much realising either as essentialising both through the quality of the difference, which is also the quality of what they have in common. As Gilles Deleuze says, the essence revealed by art

> is a difference, the absolute and ultimate Difference. Difference is what constitutes being, what makes us conceive being. This is why art, insofar as it manifests essences, is alone capable of giving us what we sought in vain from life . . . Art is a veritable transmutation of substance. By it, substance is spiritualized, and physical surroundings dematerialized, in order to refract essence, that is, the quality of an original world. This treatment of substance is indissociable from 'style' . . . This is because style, in order to spiritualize substance and render it adequate to essence, reproduces the unstable opposition, the original complication, the struggle and exchange of the primordial elements which constitute essence itself.[17]

So art is revealed as the means of recovering lost time. As in dreaming, past sensations become inseparable from the present context, past contexts inseparable from the present sensation. Subject merges with object, macrocosm with microcosm. Marcel's apprenticeship may be purgatorial, but his purgatory is conical, culminating in the work of art. Beckett's purgatory is spherical, and the triumph of *Waiting for Godot* as a work of anti-art is that it assimilates Proust's anti-objectivism without becoming subjective. The play does not disguise its own identity as an artistic artefact, but it neither presents the sufferings of the sensitive artist as an interesting theme nor implies that the construction of artistic arte-facts is a solution to the problem of how to live.

As Beckett admitted to John Pilling,[18] *Proust* overstates Proust's pessimism. 'If there were no such thing as Habit,' says Proust, 'Life would of necessity appear delicious to all those whom Death would threaten at every moment, that is to say, to all Mankind.' But for Beckett it is 'the suffering of being' that supervenes, when Habit fails in its fundamental duty, which is to preserve 'the bore-dom of living'.

> Habit is a compromise effected between the individual and his environment, or between the individual and his own organic eccentricities, the guarantee of a dull inviolability, the lightning-conductor of his existence. Habit is the ballast that chains the dog to his vomit. Breathing is habit. Life is habit.[19]

He goes on to ridicule the idea that some habits can be better than others: 'An automatic adjustment of the human organism to the conditions of its existence has as little moral significance as the casting of a clout when May is or is not out.' Realistic fiction and drama had centred on adjustments of this sort, but Beckett embraces Proust's contempt for 'the penny-a-line vulgarity of a literature of notations' and 'for the literature that "describes", for the realists and naturalists worshipping the offal of experience, prostrate before the epidermis and the swift epilepsy, and content to transcribe the surface, the façade, behind which the Idea is prisoner . . . For Proust the object may be a living symbol, but a symbol of itself. The copiable he does not see.'

Using the critical licence of the artist, Beckett is dragging Proust towards the position he will occupy himself. Proust's description of the hawthorns was not an attempt to copy the hawthorns; but, unlike Duchamp, he did not reject the possibility of recognising any two things as being like each other. When Marcel first sees the great actress Berma as Phèdre, he is disap-pointed by her intonations, which define their meaning so clearly that they seem to exist in their own right. Other intelligent actresses could copy them. Imitation of this kind leads to inferior art, but one of her gestures can suggest the pose of an antique statuette which had nothing to do either with her intentions or with Racine's. When art and unconscious memory are at work, there is constant interpenetration of past and present, signs and behaviour. The artist is necessarily not in control of the references that art has, but art is not necessarily non-referential.

Taking his cue from Proust, Beckett insists:

> The artistic tendency is not expansive, but a contraction. And art is the apotheosis of solitude. There is no communication because there are no vehicles of communication . . . The only fertile research is excavatory, immersive, a contraction of the spirit, a descent. The artist is active, but negatively, shrinking from the nullity of extracircumferential phenomena, drawn in to the core of the eddy.

Or as Proust puts it, 'Man is the creature that cannot come forth from himself, who knows others only in himself, and who, if he asserts the contrary, lies.'

If the only possibility of truthful relationship is with oneself or, through unconscious memory, with one's earlier selves, what can the work of art express? Nothing, says Beckett, talking about Tal Coat. Discussing Bram van Velde, he went further, denying even that a painting can express the impossibility of expressing anything.

> It is obvious that for the artist obsessed with his expressive vocation, anything and everything is doomed to become occasion, including, as is apparently to some extent the case with Masson, the pursuit of occasion, and the every man his own wife experiments of the spiritual Kandinsky. No painting is more replete than Mondrian's. But if the occasion appears as an unstable term of relation, the artist, who is the other term, is hardly less so, thanks to his warren of modes and attitudes.[20]

Van Velde is praised for being 'the first to submit wholly to the incoercible absence of relation' between artist and occasion.

Nor is language any more expressive than paint. In a letter written to Axel Kaun in 1937, Beckett had proposed a 'literature of the un-word'. 'Grammar and Style! They appear to me to have become just as obsolete as a Biedermeier bathing suit or the imperturbability of a gentleman. A mask.' The best way to treat language, he maintains, is assiduously to maltreat it. (In an article on the paintings of the van Velde brothers in *Cahiers d'art* 1945–6, he had spoken of 'deliberate creative bad workmanship'.) If language cannot be obliterated, it can at least be attenuated.

> Is there any reason why that terribly arbitrary materiality of the word's surface should not be dissolved, as, for example, the tonal surface, eaten into by large black pauses, in Beethoven's Seventh Symphony, so that for pages at a time we cannot perceive it other than, let us say, as a vertiginous path of sounds connecting unfathomable abysses of silence.

This passage from the letter has been compared[21] with a passage in the unpublished 1932 novel *Dream of Fair to Middling Women* when Belacqua comments on

> the incoherent continuum as expressed by, say, Rimbaud and Beethoven . . . The terms of whose statements serve merely to delimit the reality of insane areas of silence, whose audibilities are no more than punctuation in a statement of silences. How do they get from point to point. That is what I meant by the incoherent reality . . .

In *Murphy* (1935), Beckett's 'vice-exister' is never happier than when he can lock the door of his room and tie himself naked to a rocking-chair. Like Belacqua, he is heavily involved in personal relationships when we first meet him, but we see him steadily withdrawing into isolation. His mind is described as 'a hollow sphere, hermetically closed to the universe', and its recoil from contact with the 'big blooming buzzing confusion' of external reality develops into an almost mystical pursuit of positive gratifications in negative qualities.

Murphy began to see nothing, that colourlessness which is such a

> rare postnatal treat, being the absence (to abuse a nice distinction) not of percipere but of percipi. His other senses also found themselves at peace, an unexpected pleasure. Not the numb peace of their own suspension, but the positive peace that comes when the somethings give way, or perhaps simply add up, to the

Nothing, than which in the guffaw of the Abderite naught is more real. Time did not cease, that would be asking too much, but the wheel of rounds and pauses did, as Murphy with his head among the armies continued to suck in, through all the posterns of his withered soul, the accidentless One-and-Only, conveniently called Nothing.

In anti-narrative like this, critical interpretation is built in, as if to invalidate both criticism and interpretation. In *Watt* (written 1942–4) too, Beckett fastidiously negates any claim tha might seem to be implicit in what the narrative seems to be offering.

> But what was this pursuit of meaning, in this indifference to meaning? And to what did it tend? These are delicate questions. For when Watt at last spoke of this time, it was a time long past, and of which his recollections were, in a sense, perhaps less clear than he would have wished, though too clear for his liking, in another. Add to this the notorious difficulty of recapturing, at will, modes of feeling peculiar to a certain time, and to a certain place, and perhaps also to a certain state of the health, when the time is past, and the place left, and the body struggling with quite a new situation. Add to this the obscurity of Watt's communications, the rapidity of his utterance and the eccentricities of his syntax, as elsewhere recorded. Add to this the material conditions in which these communications were made. Add to this the scant aptitude to receive of him to whom they were proposed. Add to this the scant aptitude to give of him to whom they were committed. And some idea will perhaps be obtained of the difficulties experienced in formulating, not only such matters as those here in question, but the entire body of Watt's experience, from the moment of his entering Mr Knott's establishment to the moment of his leaving it.

The presence of Proust in most of Beckett's fiction is comparable to the presence of Vico in Joyce's: it is less a question of substance or style than of the way the beats succeed each other. In *Murphy, Watt* and *Mercier et Camier* (written 1946–7) the narrative switches ironically between resonant *ex cathedra* pronouncements of nihilistic gloom and laborious reporting of quotidian triviality,

analysed so fastidiously that the accumulation of jejune detail
parodies all previous narrative. The brief rhyme in the 'Addenda'
to *Watt* is like a trailer of Beckett's future work:

> who may tell the tale
> of the old man?
> weigh absence in a scale?
> mete want with a span?
> the sum assess
> of the world's woes?
> nothingness
> in words enclose?

In the trilogy *Molloy* (written 1947), *Malone meurt* (written 1947–8)
and *L'Innommable* (written 1949–50), the comedy of quotidian
triviality will be pushed aside, as extravert action disappears, to
leave nothing but the self-consciously monotonous monologue
of a consciousness communing with itself. 'Every road,' said
Valéry, 'leads back to oneself', and these perfunctorily disguised
narrators are aware that the stories they tell can build only
rickety bridges between themselves and external reality. They
know that they have nothing to say. They know that they consist
only of words and that the words are not their own. They cannot
even say this without repeating what has already been said.
Rimbaud had written: 'It is misleading to say "I think". One
should say "I am being thought".' Artaud had said 'In my unconscious it is always other people that I hear.' But the voice of
consciousness cannot be silenced, and the trilogy is rigorous in
interposing a minimum of situation and character between the
unknown source of the verbal flow and the deposits it pours out
on paper. Like *Finnegan's Wake*, this writing is not about something; it is that something itself. In *Proust*, Beckett equated 'the
suffering of being' with 'the free play of every faculty'; in the
trilogy, as in the later plays, it is by limiting his characters' freedom
of movement that he approximates to a direct account of the
suffering of being.

Mercier et Camier, the last novel he wrote before the trilogy,
is so directly the antecedent of *Waiting for Godot* that sometimes
it reads like a rough draft. It continues the extravagantly literary

manner of *Murphy* and *Watt*, but the serio-comic commentary on
the human situation is more closely integrated into the ironically
formal dialogue:

> Seeing the state you were in, said Camier, it was imperative to
> go, and yet at the same time stay.
>
> You are cheap, said Mercier.
>
> We'll get down at the next stop, said Camier, and consider
> how to proceed. If we see fit to go on we'll go on. We'll have
> lost two hours. What are two hours?
>
> I wouldn't like to say, said Mercier.
>
> If on the other hand, said Camier, we see fitter to return to
> town –.
>
> To town! cried Mercier.
>
> To town, said Camier, to town we shall return.
>
> But we have just come from town, said Mercier, and now you
> speak of returning there.
>
> When we left town, said Camier, it was necessary to leave
> town. So we very properly left it. But we are not children and
> necessity has her whims. If having elected to drive us forth she
> now elects to drive us back shall we balk? I trust not.
>
> The only necessity I know, said Mercier, is to get away from
> that hell as fast and as far as possible.
>
> That remains to be seen, said Camier. Never trust the wind
> that swells your sails, it is always obsolete.

Their vague project for a journey has been conceived in terms of
departure, with no thought of arrival – this is one stepping-stone
towards *Godot*, and another is the discovery that the central figure
can be divided, like an amoeba, without altogether destroying its
isolation. The non-stop conversations we silently hold with ourselves are depressingly like the conversations we hold with other
people, while the dialogue of *Mercier and Camier* looks forward
both to the solipsistic soliloquies of Beckett's 'vice-existers' in the
trilogy and to the central images of *Waiting for Godot*.

> Why do we insist, said Mercier, you and I for example, did you
> ever ask yourself that question, you who ask so many? Shall
> we fritter away what little is left of us in the tedium of flight

and dreams of deliverance? Do you not inkle, like me, how you might adjust yourself to this preposterous penalty and placidly await the executioner, come to ratify you?

No, said Camier.

They held back on the brink of a great open space, a square perhaps, all tumult, fluttering gleams, writhing shadows.

Let us turn back, said Mercier. This street is charming. That brothel perfume.

They set about the street the other way. It seemed changed, even in the dark. Not they, or scarcely.

I see distant lands –, said Mercier.

Where are we going? said Camier.

Shall I never shake you off? said Mercier.

Do you not know where we are going? said Camier.

What does it matter, said Mercier, where we are going? We are going, that's enough.

Beckett had discovered how to divide the central isolation by means of multiplying it. He had already learned how not to claim heroic stature for it, and now, using the male couple, he could avoid the crudity of so many plays which set the hero on a level apart from all the other characters, making communication impossible and implying that they and the audience were equally lacking in the sensitivity and integrity he incarnated. Beckett has found subtler ways of provoking the audience. Many practitioners of anti-theatre have approximated to the automatic writing technique of the Surrealists, never editing or cutting or suppressing; Beckett has always been fastidious, leaving work unfinished or unpublished when it failed to satisfy him. What was probably his first play, *Le Kid*, a parody of Corneille's *Le Cid* in the manner of Charlie Chaplin, must have been written in 1930–1. It was performed in February 1931 with Beckett as Don Diègue.[22] He went on to start *Human Wishes*, a four-act play about Dr Johnson and Mrs Thrale, but abandoned it after ten pages. His 1947 play *Eleuthéria* (which was completed, extensively revised and then typed out, but never performed or published)[23] provokes the audience subtly but more directly than *Waiting for Godot* and *Endgame* do when Vladimir and Estragon look out at the audience

and when Clov points his telescope at it. *Eleuthéria* plants an actor
in the auditorium so that he is taken for a member of the audience
when he climbs on stage. He explains why he has not already
walked out:

> It's like watching a game of chess between two tenth rate
> players ... There they are like two half-wits gaping at the board
> and there you are, even more half-wit than they, riveted to the
> spot, nauseated, bored to extinction, worn out, flabbergasted by
> such stupidity. Finally you can't stand it any longer. You say to
> them: 'But for God's sake do this, do this, what are you
> waiting for, do this and it's finished, we can go off to bed.'
> There's no excuse for you, it's against all the rules of good
> manners, you don't even know the blokes, but you can't help
> yourself, it's either that or hysterics.

But why was it necessary for Beckett to slow the action down so
much? The hero, Victor Krap, is like Huysmans's des Esseintes
(and all the other Symbolist heroes who were modelled either on
him or on his prototype, Comte Robert de Montesquiou-
Fezensac), like Beckett's Belacqua in *More Pricks Than Kicks*, like
Murphy and like his later namesake, Krapp, in wanting to withdraw from the irritations and frustrations of relationships with
other people. As he is put under pressure to behave like everyone
else or at least to explain why he won't, the audience finds itself
identified with the advocates of conformism. Victor believes:
'It is perhaps time someone was simply nothing.' But the only
explanation he can offer is:

> I have always wanted to be free. I don't know why. I don't
> even know what that means, to be free . . . First I was the
> prisoner of others. So I left them. Then I was the prisoner of
> myself. That was worse. So I left myself.

This negative presentation of freedom differentiates *Eleuthéria*
from the many Expressionist plays that had centred on a filial
rebellion against a mindlessly conformist family. In Walter
Hasenclever's *Der Sohn* (*The Son*, written 1914; produced 1916) the
anonymous Son is imprisoned by his father. As in some of Strindberg's plays, metaphor is being translated directly into stage action.

The hero could have committed suicide, as so many students really did, but lust for life asserts itself with Nietzchean rapture: 'Only in ecstasy is it possible to live. Reality would cause embarrassment.' After being rescued by his friends, with Beethoven's Ninth Symphony as background music, he joins a revolutionary society dedicated to patricide. Many other Expressionist plays – such as Paul Kornfeld's *Die Verführung* (*The Seduction*, 1916; 1917) and Arnolt Bronnen's *Vatermord* (*Patricide*, 1915; 1922) – were similar in making violent affirmations of the need to burst through to full enjoyment of liberty.

Beckett's contrasting attitude is crystallised by the final stage direction in *Eleuthéria*: 'Then he lies down, his thin back turned on humanity.' Instead of being concerned with the individual's adaptations to other individuals and to the social environment, Beckett's drama is about the impossibility of adaptation. Artistic activity must be introverted.

Waiting for Godot applies negative principles to the art of theatre in the same way that the trilogy applies them to the art of fiction: Beckett comes close to making the stage space into a vacuum. Though the final script is one that wouldn't allow any improvisation from the actors – it calls for great precision in performance – it has an engaging resemblance to the patter of a well-read conjurer. Without any such direct provocation of the audience as Alfred Jarry or the Dadaist writers had depended on, Beckett was capitalising more on his talent, meticulously nurtured through his novels, for making Nothing happen. To Watt it sometimes seems 'that a thing that was nothing had happened, with the utmost formal distinctness'. This is the impression that *Waiting for Godot* gives the audience.

As a play it could not be satisfying without being provoking, and in the late seventies it is still satisfying. If it no longer provokes audiences as it did in the middle fifties, this is an index of how successful it has been in changing theatrical fashion. The antitheatrical ideas of Jarry, like those of the Expressionists, of Apollinaire, of Artaud and of Vitrac, had less influence on the theatre of their time than they have had since *Waiting for Godot* has made them admissible. In *Waiting for Godot* the ambiguities are still mystifying, but we no longer grow impatient, as audiences did in the fifties, when there are no unequivocal answers, and we are no longer irked at being deprived of a story that will keep us guessing about what is going to happen next.

One of Beckett's discoveries was a new theatrical means of representing discontinuity in the existence of the self. In the concentrated action of a play this cannot be suggested in the same way as it can in a novel, but *Proust* throws a good deal of light both on Beckett's refusal to characterise his characters, and on their inability to remember even the events of the previous day. The idea of dissolving the individual into a series of events scattered through space and time* is relevant to the apparent absent-mindedness of Estragon, Vladimir and Pozzo, and to their irritation when questioned about details of time and place:

> POZZO: Have you not done tormenting me with your accursed time? It's abominable. When! When! One day, is that not enough for you, one day like any other day, one day he went dumb, one day I went blind, one day we'll go deaf, one day we were born, one day we'll die, the same day, the same second, is that not enough for you?

> VLADIMIR: Do you not recognize the place?
> ESTRAGON: Recognize! What is there to recognize? All my lousy life I've crawled about in the mud! And you talk to me about scenery! (*Looking wildly about him.*) Look at this muck-heap! I've never stirred from it!

The implication is that material circumstances are irrelevant if not immaterial. One time and one place are so much like another time and another place that the differences do not matter. What is intolerable about the situation is that nothing can be explained in terms of events or intentions. So the conventional theatrical concatenation of actions and motives is irrelevant. Beckett's grievances about conventional theatre are indistinguishable from his grievances about the human condition. *Waiting for Godot* may fail to dissolve 'that terrible arbitrary materiality of the word's surface', and may fail to prove that 'it's nothingness which is real'. It acknowledges that 'there is nothing except what there is', but it

*See p. 12.

could not have been written as it was if Mallarmé, Duchamp and Proust had not made their protests against reality and their voyages into the void.

Coleridge had an explanation for the long-standing convention by which shaking of the head indicates the negative. Wanting a certain food, and offered something else, the baby averts its head to avoid the spoon. Twice, when Vladimir and Estragon are wanting Godot to come, Pozzo arrives with Lucky. The play is shaking its head. Just as consciousness is incapable of envisaging nothingness, the medium cannot offer a direct presentation of the void. *Waiting for Godot* suggests that reality will always offer food for human consciousness but that it will never be the food which is wanted.

3 Ionesco and the Anti-Play

While he was studying French at the University of Bucharest, Ionesco published a pamphlet ridiculing the three literary leaders of the Rumanian *avant-garde* – Tudor Arghezi, Ion Barbu and Camil Petrescu. A few days later, in another pamphlet, he launched into extravagant praise of all three. The two contradictory verdicts were then published together in his first book, *Nu* (*No*).

His French mother had an unhappy relationship with his Rumanian father, so, from the beginning, the conflict of two languages and two cultures was associated for him with a conflict of loyalties. The tension was exacerbated as the family alternated between the two countries. Born in Rumania, he was only eighteen months old when his parents settled in Paris. French is his first language, and he was scarcely aware of having been Eugen Ionescu when he became Eugène Ionesco. Two years later, in 1916, his father left for Bucharest to fight in the war. They lost

contact with him and assumed he had been killed. Eugène was
about ten when he started reading Flaubert and wrote a film
scenario about a disorderly children's party. Finally, after smashing crockery and throwing their parents out of the window, the
children set fire to the house. He also wrote poems and, when he
was thirteen, a 32-page play, called *Pro Patria*, based on the belief
that French soldiers were the bravest in the world. In 1925, when
his parents were divorced, his father was given custody of him
and his sister. Living in Rumania again, he translated his play into
Rumanian. The title remained the same and the same virtues were
now attributed to Rumanian soldiers.

Drawn to late French Symbolist poetry, he began writing
imitations of it in Rumanian. He was especially attracted to the
work of Francis Jammes, who was a leader of the poetic movement alternatively known as *Naturisme* or *Jammisme*. It had begun
in the nineties as a reaction against Symbolist withdrawal from
actuality. The principle of a 'return to nature' led to rather naïve
celebrations of rustic life and universal brotherhood.

Beckett had been forty-two when he wrote *En attendant Godot*;
Ionesco was thirty-six when he wrote his first play, *La Cantatrice
chauve* (*The Bald Prima Donna*), having consistently disliked both
plays and actors for twenty years. Since early childhood he had
loved Punch-and-Judy shows.

> It was the very image of the world that appeared to me, strange
> and improbable but true as true, in the profoundly simplified
> form of caricature, as though to stress the grotesque and brutal
> nature of the truth. And from then until I was fifteen any form
> of play would thrill me and make me feel that the world is very
> strange, a feeling so deeply rooted that it has never left me.[1]

But as soon as he became conscious of artifice, of stage trickery,
he stopped liking theatre. 'I think I realise now that what worried
me in the theatre was the presence of characters in flesh and blood
on the stage ... Every gesture, every attitude, every speech spoken
on the stage destroyed for me a world that these same gestures,
attitudes and speeches were specifically designed to evoke;
destroyed it even before it could be created.'

When he began to write *La Cantatrice chauve*, which he was later

to designate as an 'anti-play', it was without any thought of having
it performed. Teaching himself English by copying phrases out of
a conversation manual, he became actively interested in the clichés
he was transcribing and in the characters to whom they were
attributed. Mr and Mrs Smith and Mr and Mrs Martin in *La
Cantatrice chauve* are the same Smiths and Martins who exchanged
commonplaces in the Assimil Manual, and he wrote one section of
the play just by copying out their textbook dialogue. 'It was only
a parody of a play, a travesty of a comedy. I used to read it to
friends to make them laugh when they came to my house. Since
they laughed heartily, I recognised that there was a real comic
force in this text.' Reading Raymond Queneau's *Exercices du style*,
he noticed a certain stylistic similarity, and when a friend confirmed that what he had written was a comedy, he let her show it
to the young actor-director Nicolas Bataille, who almost immediately went into rehearsal with it. When Benjamin Peret and André
Breton saw it in 1951, they recognised it – according to Simone
Benmussa – as 'what we wanted to do thirty years ago'.[2]

In so far as Ionesco's conception had been theatrical, the object,
as he says in *Notes and Counter-Notes*, had been to hold theatre up
to ridicule. 'It was not for me to conceal the devices of the theatre,
but rather make them still more evident, deliberately obvious, go
all out for caricature and the grotesque, way beyond the pale
irony of witty drawing-room comedies . . . A theatre of violence:
violently comic, violently dramatic . . . We need to be virtually
bludgeoned into detachment from our daily lives, our habits and
mental laziness, which conceal from us the strangeness of the
world . . . the real must be in a way dislocated, before it can be re-
integrated.' The last sentence echoes De Sanctis.[3]

All Ionesco's theorising about theatre and anti-theatre has been
retrospective. His genuine affinity with the Surrealists derives
partly from his efforts to switch off conscious control, to exclude
what he calls 'discursive thinking' from creative activity:

When I'm writing plays, I don't really cross out at all . . . I
allow my mind a freedom that I don't allow it when I'm writing
an article where things need to be logically linked, where the
language has to be clear and coherent.[4]

In *Les Chaises*, he makes the old woman say: 'It is in talking that one finds ideas, words, and then ourselves in our own words, and also the town, and the garden, maybe one finds everything again and is an orphan no more.' This at least reflects Ionesco's experience with *La Cantatrice chauve*. Having been activated partly by hostility to the medium, he was amazed, during rehearsals, by the mixture of pleasure and fear he had in watching the actors lend their bodies to his words and ideas. He even discovered a feeling of human solidarity, a recognition that other people's fundamental hopes and fears were the same as his.

At the beginning of the play the anti-theatricality centres on parody of conventional dramatic dialogue in which the maid and the butler or the husband and wife establish a situation for the audience by telling each other what they both know already –

MRS SMITH: This evening for supper we had soup, fish, cold ham and mashed potatoes and a good English salad, and we had English beer to drink. The children drank English water.

The text would soon have become uninteresting if it had continued on the same level. Like Hugo Ball in his performance at the Dada Gallery, Ionesco had to modulate. Two other elements are introduced: the nonsensical and the pseudo-logical. Mrs Smith talks about a grocer who makes home-made Rumanian yoghurt in England, and about a doctor who, before operating on a patient's liver, went through the operation himself without needing it. Having started the action by making the clock strike seventeen and Mrs Smith contradict it by saying 'Goodness! Nine o'clock', Ionesco makes the clock contradict itself by striking seven, and, immediately afterwards, three. Studying the births, marriages and deaths column in his newspaper, Mr Smith wonders why the age of the babies is never mentioned. Seeing the announcement of Bobby Watson's funeral, he remembers that Bobby Watson died two years ago and that, eighteen months ago, he went to the funeral. After Bobby Watson had been dead for four years, people commented on what a good-looking corpse he was. His wife was also called Bobby Watson, so it was impossible to tell which was which. The self-contradiction reaches its climax in the description of her:

She has regular features, but you can't call her beautiful. She's too tall and too well built. Her features are rather irregular, but everyone calls her beautiful. A trifle too short and too slight perhaps.

The accumulating confusions and contradictions go on assaulting the basic convention by which the audience collects information as if it were factual, fitting it together to build a situation. Like Beckett in *Endgame*, but before any of Beckett's mature plays were produced, Ionesco is perversely issuing us with pieces of a construction kit that defies construction.

The next two characters to enter are under the impression that they have seen each other before, but it takes them four pages of dialogue to establish that they are married, live together, and have a two-year-old daughter with one red eye and one white. This conclusion is immediately discredited by the Maid, who says that the husband's daughter has a red right eye and the wife's daughter a red left eye.

We can see for ourselves what is happening on stage, even if it makes no sense; but in the efforts we cannot help making to resolve contradictions in information about what is happening offstage we are constantly frustrated. The doorbell rings twice before the Captain of the Fire Brigade is admitted, but when Mrs Smith opens the door in answer to the first two rings, no one is there. He says that he has been waiting at the door for three quarters of an hour, but that it was someone else who rang the bell the first two times. How can this be 'true'? And how can he know that he will have a fire to attend to in three-quarters of an hour and sixteen minutes exactly? The fire is as real as the Fireman, who has no reality once the actor has left the stage, and had none before he made his entrance. The bell was probably rung by an assistant stage manager. In the theatre nothing is real except the people and things we see, the words and sounds we hear.

Ionesco's language has a life of its own, and, as Richard Schechner has said, the characters are no more than an obstacle to it.[5] The language has its own logic. It can reproduce itself, generate off-stage characters, produce situations. At the climax of the play it goes berserk, taking possession of the action. The characters are all shouting at each other, raising their fists, ready to hurl themselves at each other's throats. The sound of the words becomes as important as the meaning, and there is a great deal of nonsensical punning:

MRS SMITH: Khrishnamourti, Khrishnamourti, Khrishna-mourti!

MR SMITH: Le pape dérape! Le pape n'a pas de soupape. La soupape a un pape.

MRS MARTIN: Bazar, Balzac, Bazaine!

MR MARTIN: Bizarre, beaux-arts, baisers!

MR SMITH: A, e, i, o, u, a, e, i, o, u, a, e, i, o, u, i!

MRS MARTIN: B, c, d, f, g, l, m, n, p, r, s, t, v, w, x, z!

MRS MARTIN: De l'ail à l'eau, du lait à l'ail!

MRS SMITH: (imitating a train) Teuff, teuff, teuff, teuff, teuff, teuff, teuff, teuff, teuff!

MR SMITH: C'est!

MRS MARTIN: Pas!

MR MARTIN: Par!

MRS SMITH: La!

MR SMITH: C'est!

MRS MARTIN: Par!

MR MARTIN: I!

MRS SMITH: Ci!

Already, describing Mrs Bobby Martin in a way that defied visualisation, Ionesco had come close to using words non-referentially. Here they have almost become objects in their own right.

Both of Ionesco's original ideas for the ending are reminiscent of Dadaist events. One idea was that the argument between the Smiths and the Martins would be interrupted by the author, who would shake his fist and shout abuse at the audience. The other idea was more violent:

The maid would reappear to announce that dinner is served. All movement would stop; the two couples would leave the stage. Two or three actors planted in the audience would then start whistling, booing, heckling, invading the stage. This

would cue the arrival of the theatre manager followed by a
Superintendent of Police and policemen. They would open fire
at the refractory audience to make an example of it and while the
manager and the inspector congratulate each other on teaching
the public a lesson, the policemen, threatening the audience with
their revolvers, drive everyone out of the auditorium.[6]

Ionesco is one of the best critics of his own work. His diary entry
for 10 April 1951 summed up *La Cantatrice chauve* as an attempt

> to make the mechanics of drama function in a vacuum. An
> experiment in abstract or non-representational drama . . . The
> aim is to release dramatic tension without the help of any
> proper plot or any special subject. But it still leads, in the end,
> to the revelation of something monstrous: this is essential,
> moreover, for in the last resort drama is a revelation of mon-
> strosity or of some monstrous formless state of being or of
> monstrous forms that we carry within ourselves. Abstract
> theatre. Pure drama. Anti-thematic, anti-ideological, anti-
> social-realist, anti-philosophical, anti-boulevard-psychology,
> anti-bourgeois, the re-discovery of a new 'free' theatre . . .
> characters without character. Puppets. Faceless creatures.

Yes, but to what extent was this theatre new, and to what extent
was he rediscovering the ideas of earlier playwrights?
In 1885 Mallarmé had predicted and prescribed a drama that
would break free from French rationality with action that would
'cut loose from place, time and recognisable characters'.[7] *Ubu Roi*,
staged in 1896 at the Théâtre de l'Oeuvre when Alfred Jarry was
twenty-three, fulfilled the demands of Mallarmé, who was in the
first-night audience and hailed Jarry's anti-hero as 'a prodigious
personage' who 'enters the repertoire of high taste and haunts
me'. Eight years earlier, when Jarry started at the *lycée* in Rennes,
he had made friends with a boy called Henri Morin who, together
with his elder brother, had written a sketch which depicted the
unpopular physics teacher, M. Hébert, as King of Poland. The
schoolboy Jarry rewrote the sketch as a play for puppets, and the
name Ubu derived from Hébert's nicknames, Ebe and Père Heb.
Retaining a great many schoolboy jokes and a good deal of school-

boy smut, the version of 1896 parallels and parodies *Macbeth*, deflating the characters by putting consistently undignified language into their mouths. Jarry, who retained his love for puppets, hated actors, realistic sets and the conventions of heroic theatre. Writing in January 1896 to Lugné-Poë, director of the Théâtre de l'Oeuvre, he made six points: Ubu should wear a mask; for the two equestrian scenes he should wear a cardboard horse's head hanging from his neck, in the style of medieval English theatre; without raising or lowering the curtain, locale could be indicated, as in puppet shows, by placards; an army could be represented by a single soldier; the leading actor should use a special accent or a special voice; costumes should be anachronistic. Though Firmin Gémier, who played Ubu, refused to wear a mask, the production made an enormous impact. 'What more is possible?' asked W. B. Yeats, who was also in the first-night audience. 'After us the Savage God.' Revivals of the play can no longer make any comparable impact because the heroic and realistic conventions are no longer so deeply entrenched, and Ionesco, though indebted to Jarry for many of his ideas, is a superior theatrical craftsman, better at modulating and structuring.

Büchner's *Woyzeck* (written 1835–7) is a still earlier example of caricature and dehumanisation. The suffering soldier in the centre of the action is not caricatured, but his anonymous persecutors are – Doctor, Captain, Drum-Major. Büchner prefigured Expressionism in the same way that Jarry prefigured Dada and Surrealism. In Wedekind's first play *Frühlings Erwachen* (*Spring Awakening*, written 1890; produced 1906) he gained extra sympathy for the adolescents by caricaturing the parents and teachers. An absurdly prolonged argument about whether to open a window anticipates the protracted arguments about trivialities in *La Cantatrice chauve* and in Ionesco's later work. Provocatively, Wedekind went on in later plays to abstract from contemporary reality, making people into grotesque puppets, dangling clumsily on the strings of their own lusts – for money, power, drink, sex. With his abrasively mannered dialogue and his ferociously satirical distortion, he created a closed world which Walter Sokel compares with the autonomous space of the Cubists and the self-contained universe of Kafka.[8]

Georg Kaiser inherited Wedekind's tendency to depersonalise. Kaiser called playwriting 'a geometric problem'. *Von morgens bis mitternachts* (*From Morning till Midnight*, written 1912; produced 1917) showed an anonymous bank cashier in the process of breaking free from a meaningless life by stealing 60,000 Marks. Disconnectedly episodic, the script manipulates the minor characters like puppets. But Expressionist drama was never anti-ideological, as Ionesco's is. The dehumanisation of the figures that represent conformism or authority is a launching-pad for the idealisation of the rebel. Looking at the central conflict in Hasenclever's *Der Sohn*, Kafka suggested that the treatment ought to be comic, as in Synge's *Playboy of the Western World*. In Ionesco's work it is always comic. In the plays which deal most directly (like *Jacques ou la Soumission*) with rebellion against conformism, the rebellious hero is partly exempted from the depersonalisation that is inflicted on the others, though in *La Cantatrice chauve*, as in all his best plays, no one is spared.

But more depends on the actors' personalities than it does in Beckett's plays. Without being able to choose what they express, they are expressing something beyond the words. In the theatre, as in Giordano Bruno's philosophy, extremes meet. In the same way that burlesque can produce a grotesquerie which borders on tragedy, a depersonalising script can bring something of the actors' personalities into abnormally clear focus. Ionesco characterises no more than he would if scripting a Punch-and-Judy show, but the human subsumes the mechanical. 'Hollow, purely social characters: for there is no such thing as a social soul . . . a void in Sunday-clothes, a charming void, a blossoming void, a void of phantom figures, a youthful void, a contemporary void. Beyond the emptiness, there still remained their charm.'[9]

In his second play *La Leçon* (written 1950; produced 1951), Ionesco may seem to be characterising, but he is not establishing personality traits, only moods, and only as a means of showing discontinuity in the behaviour of all three characters. The eighteen-year-old girl is cheerful and lively at the outset, but she becomes more and more morose and sleepy until a nervous aphasia seems to have set in. The Professor starts by being polite and subdued, growing more confident and aggressive until the climax of killing her with an imaginary knife is unmistakably a symbolic rape. The maid, who is at first subservient, becomes dominant, striking him and ordering him about.

In *La Leçon*, as in *La Cantatrice chauve*, Ionesco writes for actors who will not wear masks rather as if they will. Jarry's Ubu seems to stand behind the figure of the Professor. Another source of the nameless Professor was Ionesco's authoritarian father, a Fascist lawyer who was kept on by the Communists when they occupied Bucharest. 'Everything that I've done has been done, as it were, against him.' Ionesco's hatred of dogmaticism – whether political *à la* Brecht or critical *à la* Barthes – is expressed in the action, which shows how the young girl is weakened by the nonsensical teaching which makes the old man stronger. He becomes less and less sympathetic as he puffs himself up with pedantic arguments, launching into a nonsensical discourse about Spanish and neo-Spanish, muddling his own categories, and confusing her. He tells her that the sentence

> The roses of my grandmother are as yellow as my grandfather who was born in Asia

is exactly the same in Spanish, and in neo-Spanish, but when she tries to translate it into both languages, he accuses her of muddling one with the other. Translated into Latin and into Italian, he tells her, the sentence is still exactly the same.

Between the word, the imaginary object and the physical action which will have the theatrical result of killing her, there is a disjunction reminiscent of Magritte's canvas juxtaposing a painting of a horse, a drawing of a horse and a picture of a man saying the word 'horse'. As Magritte reminds us (in a series of eighteen illustrated pronouncements about the relationship between objects, images and names) 'Sometimes the name of an object takes the place of an image . . . An object never fulfils the same function as its name or image.'

In the unreal context of the theatrical action, a word or an image can perform the same function as an object, and the death of the pupil in *La Leçon* is the first of many deaths which Ionesco blames on language. Wanting to expose the danger of trusting

58 *Theatre and Anti-Theatre*

language as if it were a rational system, an articulation of universal order, he shows how easy it is to dislocate it, tie it into self-contradictory knots. But he is enjoying himself in doing so. He is like a champion swimmer, very happy when in the water, fairly happy when talking about the dangers of drowning.

Jacques ou la Soumission (written 1949–50; produced 1955) is, as Ionesco says, 'a kind of parody or caricature of boulevard theatre, boulevard theatre going bad, gone mad'.[10] Like the Bobby Watsons, the members of the family are all given the same name, Jacques, and the stage direction suggests that all should be masked except the central character. As a non-conformist he has many affinities with Expressionist heroes and with Victor Krap in Beckett's 1947 play: he resists the pressures of his family by preserving a stoical silence until he is left alone with his sister, who talks nonsense to him, rather as if she were reciting lessons in a grammar class. The source of his disaffection is revealed later in his love scene with a girl who has three noses. He has been wanting to opt out of life. He was nearly fourteen when he was born, he says, so he realised what it was all about and refused to accept it. But there is no way out:

They've blocked the doors and windows up with ciphers, and ripped out the stairs. Now they've barred the way through the attic, no means of escape from above . . . and yet I've been told they've left trap-doors all over the place . . . If only I could find them . . . I *will* go. If I can't get out through the attic there's still the cellar . . . yes, the cellar . . . Better escape from below than stay here. Nothing could be worse than my present situation.

Sometimes the language moves even closer to surrealist prose poetry:

In my womb there are ponds and swamps . . . I've a house of clay, where I always feel cool . . . where there's foamy loam . . . and fatty flies, beetles, wood lice and toads. Beneath dripping blankets we make love . . . swelling with bliss! My arms enfold you like snakes; and my soft thighs . . . You plunge deep and dissolve . . . in the rain of my streaming hair. My mouth is

flowing, streaming my legs, streaming my shoulders bare, my
hair is flowing, everything flows and streams, the sky's a stream,
the stars strow and fleam . . .

Ionesco does not take much trouble to change gear smoothly
between passages like this and surrealistic visual effects, as when
Jacques removes his hat to reveal green hair, and the three-nosed
girl, Roberta II, turns out to have nine fingers on one hand. What
redeems the play is that less depends on either the prose or the
visual shocks than on the rhythms and animal sounds in the
dialogue. The lovers neigh as their conversation gallops, and at
the frenetic climax, the rhythm spreads to movement when
Jacques clumsily embraces her, kissing each of her noses in turn,
and the family silently returns, swaying about in a weird dance,
surrounding the lovers, silently clapping, pirouetting or rolling
up their trousers. They continue the dance from a squatting
position aimed to embarrass the audience. By the end, before they
disappear, they are emitting miaows, grunts and groans. Language has been defeated.

Acclimatising himself to the medium in the opposite way from
Beckett, Ionesco explores the theatre's pictorial resources more
thoroughly in *Les Chaises* (written 1951; produced 1952), finding
visual correlatives for the disaffection and frustration which are
presented verbally in Jacques's speech about wanting to opt out
of life. As in *Waiting for Godot*, the central isolation is now split
between two characters, but Ionesco goes further than Beckett in
subordinating the human figures to images whose function is to
evoke the void.

I first had the image of chairs, then that of a person bringing
chairs as fast as possible on to an empty stage . . . The chairs
remain empty because there's no one there. And at the end, the
curtain falls to the accompanying noises of a crowd, while
all there is on the stage is empty chairs, curtains fluttering in the
wind, etc . . . and there's nothing. The world doesn't really
exist. The subject of the play was nothingness, not failure. It
was total absence: chairs without people.[11]

By setting the play on an island surrounded by stagnant water,
Ionesco is both creating something of the atmosphere that depends

on locale and establishing a relationship between onstage space and offstage space, though, as in *La Cantatrice chauve*, the indications are partly cancelled by contradictions. Looking out of the window the ninety-five-year-old man talks of seeing boats in the sunshine; the ninety-four-year-old woman tells him it is night-time. (This was written over four years before Beckett began *Endgame*, with its speech about the madman who looked through the window and saw only ashes.)

When Ionesco's old man behaves babyishly, it looks almost like a visual contradiction: he sits in the woman's lap, crying for his mother, while his wife soothes him and sings to him. The emotional effect is quite complex: the sequence is all the more embarrassing and amusing for being moving, especially if we recognise any of our own vanity in his desire to think well of himself.

> OLD MAN: I've a message, you're right, I must fight for it, a mission, I can give birth to a great idea, a message for all men, for all mankind. . . .
>
> OLD WOMAN: For all mankind, my dear, your message! . . .
>
> OLD MAN: It's true, that's really true . . .
>
> OLD WOMAN: (*blowing the* OLD MAN's *nose and wiping away his tears*) That's the way! . . . You're a big boy now, a real soldier, a Quartermaster-General . . .
>
> OLD MAN: (*He has got off the* OLD WOMAN's *knees and is trotting about excitedly*) I'm not like other people, I've an ideal in life. I may be clever, as you say, I am quite talented, but things don't come easily to me.

When the doorbell rings, the old man and woman (like Mrs Smith in *La Cantatrice chauve*) find there is no one there, but this time No One comes in, an invisible lady. When they talk to her, we almost believe in her presence; when the old man fetches her a visible chair, it highlights her absence.

As the stage fills with invisible guests, the writing offers the actors rich opportunities for the kind of inventiveness that the Beckettian text always represses even more stringently than the realistic text. Reacting to non-existent people, miming handshakes, rushing in with chairs, hurrying out to fetch more, answering the incessant doorbell, weaving their way through the invisible crowd, they have to whip up the rhythm of their movements into a flurry of energetic activity, without dispelling the illusion that they are octogenarians. Ionesco's theatre may be more pictorial than Beckett's, but he arrives in a comparably negative way at the composition inside the frame. Instead of giving us spectacular scenic effects, Ionesco denies them at moments when they might be expected. The arrival of the Emperor is preceded by a progressive brightening of the lights and by a fanfare. His entrance consists of nothing. He is as invisible as the milling crowd that surrounds him, but the climax is all the more impressive for forcing the audience's imagination to fill the space left by the minimal theatrical statement.

The play's final sequence is effective in a similar way. The Orator (a real actor made up to look unreal) is about to deliver to mankind the message which the old man has never been able to articulate. Confident that the Emperor and the people will finally hear it, he has nothing left to live for. Before he and the old woman jump into the water, there is another fanfare and a flash of light as they throw confetti and streamers over the invisible Emperor, the impassive Orator and the empty chairs.

The play ends not with the anticlimacteric revelation that the Orator is dumb, but with real sounds from the invisible crowd, and a murmuring of wind and water which 'should be heard for a very long time as though coming from nothing, coming from the void'.[12]

In spite of his belief in the disjunction between discursive thinking and creative writing, Ionesco introduces explicit drama criticism into his next play, *Victimes du devoir* (written 1951–2; produced 1953) which he designates as 'pseudo-drama'. The central character is a writer, Choubert, who maintains that previous playwrights, from the Greeks onwards, have never created anything but thrillers. 'Drama's always been realistic and there's always been a detective about. Every play's an investigation brought to a successful conclusion.'[13] Later on, a poet called Nicolas d'Eu will argue that the theatre is 'not in harmony with the general drift of the other manifestations of the modern spirit'.

Surrealism could still be helpful in so far as it relates to dreams, he says, inspiring him with a different logic and psychology:

> I should introduce contradiction where there is no contradiction, and no contradiction where there is what common-sense usually calls contradiction . . . We'll get rid of the principle of identity and unity of character and let movement and dynamic psychology take its place . . . We are not ourselves . . . Personality doesn't exist.

It is characteristic of Ionesco to make a detective enter within a minute of the complaint about detective drama, and to make him conscious of having an outmoded dramatic function: 'As for me I remain Aristotelically logical, true to myself, faithful to my duty and full of respect for my bosses . . . I don't believe in the absurd.' But he conducts his investigation in a manner which makes this play more Beckettian than Aristotelian.

This is the first of five plays based by Ionesco on ideas he initially developed in stories. In 'Un Victime du devoir', the policeman penetrates to the inside of the narrator's thoughts, reading successfully into memories that remain unspoken. The most inventive writing comes in the sequences of exploring dramatic correlatives for this internal action. Luring Choubert sexily back into his past, the wife, who had been so demure, switches into a different behaviour-pattern, like the characters in *La Leçon*. Her arm serves as a handrail as he goes down an imaginary staircase into the mud. Later he will have to climb a mountain that consists (like the mountain in Brecht's *Puntila*) of chairs piled on a table and in rehearsal Ionesco learned an anti-anti-theatre lesson. 'You really felt he was climbing a steep mountain. This is one of the fairly rare moments when I've understood what the theatre is, what it ought to be: a real, living experience, not just the illustration of a text.' In *La Leçon* he had already been treating actors less like puppets than he had in *La Cantatrice chauve*; here, as in *Les Chaises*, the script encourages the actors to use their imaginations in a way that will stimulate the imagination of the audience. This is the opposite procedure from that of the less pragmatic Beckett, who stimulates the audience by restricting the actors, but there is a Proustian element in Ionesco's nostalgia for the irretrievable past, and the detective serves as a pretext for a *recherche* aimed at uncovering an interior landscape. As Ionesco said of the painter Gerard Schneider,

> You have only to look into yourself never outwards; and then to exteriorize, to give expression to what is inside you, what you have seen and heard there, and allow it free play. In this way it is the world itself, as it is, you will succeed in revealing, authentically, whereas if you only looked outside yourself, you would merely get confused, alienate both aspects of reality and make it incomprehensible to others and to yourself.[14]

In *Victimes du devoir* the main visual effects are created by actors and lighting, the setting is indeterminate; in *Le Nouveau Locataire* (written 1953; produced 1957) the main statement is visual. As in *Les Chaises* the stage is progressively filled with furniture, but this time the dialogue is consistently subordinated to the action. As the new tenant has his furniture moved into the apartment it fills all the available space, dominating him totally. Instead of staying in the background as in Ibsenite parlour plays, the domestic setting spreads like an indoor wilderness until it suffocates the protagonist. Once again social criticism merges with satire on an earlier form of theatre.

The central idea in *Amédée* (produced 1954; based on the story *Oriflamme*, 1953) is similar but this time it is an outsize corpse that progressively encroaches on the living space that the stage represents. From the idea that dead bodies can catch a disease which makes them grow Ionesco develops an amusing series of theatrical surprises. We hear a loud crash as the expanding head breaks the window-pane; we see a huge pair of feet bursting down the door to protrude into the room. Another inconvenient by-product of the corpse's presence is a proliferation of indoor mushrooms, which give off a greenish light. Promising though these ideas are, they do not provide enough material for a three-act play, which is what, for the first time, Ionesco is trying to write. The second act begins effectively enough as we see the stage filled with furniture that the corpse has crowded out of the offstage room, but there is an awkward disparity between the visual effects and some of the dialogue, which ranges between over-extended domestic bickering and attempts at prose poetry. The third act is particularly unsatisfactory, set in the street outside the flat and padded out with irrelevant American soldiers.

The second full-length play, *Tueur sans gages* (*The Killer*, written 1957; produced 1959), was much more successful, disconnected though the three acts are. The physical setting is contrived to express the hunger of the main character, Bérenger, for an external world that corresponds to the internal. The action opens in a radiant city which suggests (and was suggested by) Le Corbusier's *ville radieuse*. When Bérenger – echoing the Symbolists – says that nothing is more real than a mirage, an ornamental pool materialises at the back of the stage, but it vanishes again when he lets the Architect persuade him to look instead at the flowering hawthorn. The movement of the action is more dreamlike than in any of Ionesco's previous plays. Nothing has hard outlines: objects and sequences flow into each other. Bérenger talks about his dreams, and his sudden proposal of marriage to the Architect's blonde secretary is dreamlike, as is her ambiguous refusal to say yes or no. Even when she becomes a victim of the killer who is terrorising the town, the play remains more like a nightmare than like a thriller. There is an enormous policeman who hits people arbitrarily over the head, while another is more interested in directing the traffic than in listening to information that might lead to the arrest of the killer. It is left for Bérenger to track him down, and their confrontation provides an excellent negative illustration of Ionesco's complaint that realism never looks beyond reality, that it ignores our most fundamental obsessions.

The Killer never speaks. The director must choose between making him visible and leaving the audience with the option of thinking that Bérenger is talking to himself, to the darker side of his own nature, which his conscious humanism cannot master. His monologue constitutes a much subtler assault on rationalism than the irrational logic of the early plays: Ionesco shows patient reasonableness tangling itself into confusion and self-contradiction as Bérenger goes on talking into the protracted silence. His initial mistake is to start making assumptions about the Killer's motives. Speculation is the beginning of empathy, and when he has to face the probability that the Killer has no reason for killing, he finds he has no argument for asking him to stop.

The continuity between the suicidal art of the Symbolists and Ionesco's theatre of the grotesque is even more apparent in the next play, *Rhinocéros* (written 1958; produced 1959). It is not so much an anti-humanist play as an exposé of humanity's anti-humanism. Around 1940, watching his anti-fascist friends going one-by-one through the process of conversion to fascism, Ionesco felt like a man isolated among a herd of rhinoceroses, almost wishing that he too could undergo the same mutation. (The first work of Kafka that Ionesco had read was *Metamorphosis*.) Not that the play is any less relevant to the dehumanisation currently being induced by Marxist conformism.

The parallel with *Tueur sans gages* is most evident in Bérenger's attempts to argue with his friend Jean, who is on the point of repudiating his humanity. Bérenger gets nowhere with his appeals to morality, philosophy and civilisation, and the medium emphasises their ineffectuality. The scene's momentum is created by Jean's lumbering charges in and out of the bathroom, more animalised each time we see him.

Le Piéton de l'air (*A Stroll in the Air*, written 1962; produced 1963) contains some dialogue reminiscent of *La Cantatrice chauve*, but of all Ionesco's plays it is the one in which most statements are made for their own sake. Of the four contrasting characters he names Bérenger, this is the one with the most obvious resemblance to himself, and in an interview Bérenger gives to a journalist, he says that he had always known he had no reason to write, that he is a nihilist with nothing to say and cannot go on turning out plays. (*Le Piéton de l'air* broke a four-year silence.)

Oneiric material and references to Ionesco's earlier plays are incorporated in a random, pointless way, while discursive conversation is accompanied by very elaborate visual effects. The stage directions even ask for a miniature train with tiny red passenger cars. Character and dialogue are organised to establish a contrast between those who want to bring themselves into harmony with the world and those who want to bring the world into harmony with themselves – a theme reminiscent of Beckett's *Murphy* – but the discussion is far too much a matter of explicit statement. The play becomes more theatrical when a Visitor from the antiworld appears, with white side-whiskers and old-fashioned clothes. His pipe is upside down in his mouth and the smoke from it goes downwards. His abrupt disappearance cues an explanation from Bérenger, who admits there is no proof that the anti-world exists, but 'You can find it in your own thoughts. The evidence is in your mind. There's more than one antiworld.' There is an unknown quantity of universes, he says, interlocking without touching and co-existing in the same space. Language proves the existence of a negative counterpart to our universe: a phrase like 'the world turned upside down' could have originated only from the anti-world.

Bérenger's argument is illustrated with a series of stage con-juring tricks. When a pink column, covered with flowers, rises out of the ground, he says it has come from the void, and when a tree vanishes, that it has been sucked back into the void. Accord-ing to Ionesco, Pataphysics was now becoming less important to him,[15] but the metaphysics of this play seem to owe a great deal to the mixture of science and nonsense in Alfred Jarry's *Gestes et opinions du Dr. Faustroll Pataphysicien* (written 1898; published 1911). 'Pataphysics will examine the laws governing exceptions,' it says, and 'will explain the universe supplementary to this one'. The sequence in which Bérenger flies and cycles in mid-air on a one-wheeled circus bicycle possibly derives from Jarry's *The Passion Considered as an Uphill Bicycle Race* with its irreverent description of Jesus riding flat on his back on his cross-frame machine in order to reduce the air resistance.[16]

Ionesco has never had greater difficulty in matching his dialogue to his creation of stage pictures than in the last act of this play. After Bérenger has flown out of sight, the action is occupied with the waking nightmares of his wife, Josephine. Characters we have already met reappear as dream figures. Impacts are achieved through blood-red lighting effects, derisive dance music, the gigantic crimson figure of a judge with a solid doll's head, a hang-man in white with a gibbet. When Bérenger reappears, he tries to describe what he has seen, but Ionesco's attempts at apocalyptic verbal imagery are bathetic after the theatrical imagery he has realised three-dimensionally. Bérenger speaks of seeing men with the heads of geese, men licking monkeys' behinds and drinking sows' piss, columns of headless men crossing enormous plains, giant grasshoppers, fallen angels and archangels gone astray. He talks about continents of Paradise all in flames, about blessed creatures being burned alive, about knives, graves, mountains caving in, oceans of blood. The stylistic over-inflation is too great to be countered by attempts at self-deflation. A journalist accuses Bérenger of reading it all in the Apocalypse and another man compares it unfavourably with Dante. We even see Bérenger losing his audience. His listeners drift away, preoccupied with trivialities which to them seem more important than his vision of impending doom.

Something of this vision is carried forward into the next play *Le Roi se meurt* (*Exit the King*, written 1962; produced 1962). As in *Endgame*, there is an impression of ultimate dereliction. Supplies are running out, soil conservation has been neglected; the universe is made to resemble a clockwork toy with no one to wind it up. At the same time, the play is like an anti-ideological *Everyman*. As the central character in the fifteenth-century morality play prepares himself for death, he finds that, except for Good Deeds, none of his friends is willing to go with him; King Bérenger finds that his achievements are of no help to him, although, nonsensically, he is presented as having stolen fire from the gods, written Shakespeare's plays and invented the Zeppelin. Ionesco succeeds very well in blending comedy with serious apprehensions of death. When Bérenger keeps falling over and stumbling to his feet, the stage direction asks that the scene should be played like a tragic Punch and Judy show. In the final sequence (as in Strindberg and Hasenclever) metaphor is translated directly into stage action: we see the load being lightened as Queen Marguerite cuts invisible cords that bind Bérenger to life, and relieves him of an imaginary sack.

La Soif et la faim (written 1964; produced 1964) is more Expressionistic in structure, representing a quest for salvation, almost in the manner of Strindberg's *To Damascus*. Using oneiric and autobiographical material, Ionesco sets the first episode in an oppressively damp cellar. Starved of light and heat, Jean is convinced that the house is sinking. Metaphor is translated into action again: trying to pluck from his heart the love he feels for his wife and baby, he is seen with blood on his shirt and a branch of briar rose in his hand. His wife's remark about seeing through walls is translated into theatrical terms when the back wall vanishes, revealing trees in blossom, luxuriant grass, a blue sky. Then a silver ladder is hanging in the air, its top invisible. Style and substance are both reminiscent of the Expressionist and pre-Expressionist plays in which the hero tests the outer edges of his humanity in a series of adventures; during the second act, the references to the journey ahead recall the allegorical writing of Ibsen and Strindberg. The final episode is set in the refectory of a monastery, but far from being helpers towards salvation, the monks turn out to be malignant persecutors. In a brainwashing sequence their behaviour is suggestive of totalitarianism, but there is no satisfactory answer to the question of what they stand for. This act contains the best individual moments, but the play fails to cohere because the journey fails to acquire any cumulative dramatic significance. Jean at the end is hardly the same character that he was at the beginning, but the changes do not seem to come as a result of the experience he undergoes, and the pattern of changes never comes into focus.

Jeux de massacre (*Killing Game*, produced 1970) is not only more original, especially in its blending of comic and tragic modes, but more successful in sustaining its succession of impacts. Inspired by Defoe's *Journal of the Plague Year* (1722), it depicts a city in the grip of a plague. Needing a huge cast, Ionesco suggests that some of the citizens could be represented by large marionettes or dolls or painted figures. Nonsense makes an early appearance in the dialogue when one of the housewives maintains that unwashed carrots can cause leprosy. Here, as later, much of the effect depends on alternation between stupidity or petty obstinacy or vulgar pleasure and the sudden onset of death. The plague is personified in the tall figure of a cowled monk, who moves in and out, unobserved, among the people who will fall victim to him. The impact of the first death has no time to wear off before it is followed by the second, and the rapidity in the succession of the deaths is at first a major source of tension. There is no central character except the silent monk: no one we meet survives for long, but Ionesco succeeds very well in contriving comedy and variation between scenes that nearly all have the same ending as the characters fall dead.

Macbett (produced 1972) is like *Ubu Roi* in making *Macbeth* into a clown show, but it also represents a further extension of the apocalyptic line that began in *La Soif et la faim*. 'It was as if I was dancing on tens of thousands of corpses,' wrote Ionesco in a programme note, 'and on whole countries that were ravaged by flood and fire as they are all around us.' The play is unlike *Jeux de massacre* in keeping the killing off-stage, but Ionesco succeeds with Macbett's rhetoric where he failed with Bérenger's, infusing a caustic comedy into the holocaustic pronouncements.

> Hundreds of thousands died as they tried in panic to cross the Channel and drowned. Millions died of terror or committed suicide. Tens of millions of others died of anger, apoplexy or grief. Not enough land left to bury them all. The bloated bodies of the drowned have soaked up all the water of the lakes in which they threw themselves. No more water. Not enough vultures to rid us of all this carrion flesh.

Whereas Shakespeare's play was based on an orthodox morality, Ionesco's Duncan, Banco and Macol (Malcolm) are no less obnoxious than Macbett. Or than Ubu. Scotland is no worse off under Macbett's rule than it was under Duncan's, and it will be no better off under Macol's. History repeats itself endlessly as one vicious, unstable tyrant wrests power from his vicious, unstable predecessor. Like Jarry, Ionesco produces considerable theatrical effects with his inversions of Shakespearian points, but it is difficult to integrate the parodistic and the serious elements in production. Unlike the world of *Le Roi se meurt* and *Jeux de massacre*, the world of *Macbett* is patently an artefact, while none of the characters ever becomes real enough to involve or to move us.

Ce formidable bordel (*What a Bloody Circus*, written 1973; produced 1973) is like a version of *La Soif et la faim* in less allegorical terms, and culminating in a more explicitly nihilistic confusion. The anonymous Character begins (like so many Expressionist heroes) by opting out of the monotonous conformism of office life, but (like Victor Krap) he finds no possibility of committing himself positively to an activity or a political cause or a woman.

Ionesco avoids the mistake of using his main character as a mouthpiece for his own ideas and preoccupations, but makes the mistake of using minor characters as mouthpieces, while the Character listens to them. Essentially passive, he is most effective when silent, and in Ionesco's novel, *Le Solitaire* (1973), from which this play is adapted, silence is perfectly viable, but the dramatisation fails most abjectly when it tries most directly to exteriorise the internal pressures that necessitate his withdrawal. The love affair is totally unconvincing. In the novel, the first-person narrative can tell us that the female sex organ has always seemed 'something like a whirlpool but most of all like an open wound, enormous, incurable, deep', or that 'Love was like a jetty into the abyss, a form of despair, a way of dying while accepting death'. In the play Ionesco finds no way of bringing the lovers' non-relationship into focus.

The real subject of both novel and play is nullity, death within life, but the novel ends with Expressionistic visionary optimism. Again the walls dematerialise, and a desert stretches to the horizon under the luminous sky. As in *La Soif et la faim*, a silver ladder seems to descend from just below the sun, and the Character is surrounded by a garden. When all this disappears again, some of the bright light remains. Towards the end of the play, the décor begins to disappear. The concierge removes some of the furniture, the walls are replaced by scrims. The Character will end up alone, on the empty stage, laughing because he has finally realised that it is all a joke. If only he had understood earlier, he wouldn't have taken so much trouble.

4 Genet's
Anti-Worlds

What Genet hates most about the theatre is its frivolity. 'Nothing can be expected from a profession that is conducted with so little seriousness or thought. Its point of departure, its *raison d'être* is exhibitionism ... The Western actor does not try to become a sign charged with significance; he simply wants to identify with a character in the drama or comedy ... I am sure marionettes could do better.'[1]* The kind of characterisation Genet would prefer is typified by Rembrandt's later portraits:

> The more I looked at them, the less these portraits reminded me of anyone. No-one ... No detail, no facial detail denotes a personality, a particular psychology ... It is from the moment that he depersonalises his models, removes from objects all

---

* One of the first playwrights to express a preference for puppets was Kleist. Jarry, Gordon Craig and Artaud all went through periods of wanting to void theatre of the actor's personality.

identifiable characteristics, that he endows both people and
things with the most weight, the greatest reality . . . Rembrandt
does not disfigure painting by trying to confuse it with the
object or the face he has been commissioned to portray: he
presents it as something separate, not ashamed of being what it
is . . . And he presents himself in his crazy enjoyment of daubing
colours.

In 'Ce qui est resté d'un Rembrandt déchiré en petits carrés bien
reguliers, et foutu aux chiottes' ('What Remained of a Rembrandt
Torn Up Neatly into Squares and Thrown into the Shit', *Tel Quel*
No. 29, Spring 1967), the excerpts from a 1958 essay on Rembrandt[2] are printed in a thin column on the right-hand side of the
page. Running parallel on the left-hand side is a slightly longer
narrative about a different sort of identification. Once, on a train,
finding himself looking into the eyes of an unattractive little man
of about fifty, Genet had suddenly felt certain that any man was
identical to any other: 'The world has never contained more than
a single man. He exists quite completely inside each one of us.
Therefore he is ourselves. Each of us is the other person and all
the others.' Rembrandt is mentioned towards the end of this
narrative, when Genet analyses 'the only moments in my life I
could hold to be true, tearing my appearance aside to reveal . . .
what? A solid void which went on continuing me? . . . Rembrandt
was the first to denounce me. Rembrandt! That severe finger
which rips off the fancy wrappings to reveal . . . what? An infinite,
infernal transparency.' The silent encounter on the train had been
mentioned more briefly in an essay published the previous year on
'L'Atelier d'Alberto Giacometti' ('Alberto Giacometti's Studio').[3]
'"Anyone," I told myself, "can be loved on the far side of his ugli-
ness, his stupidity, his wickedness" . . . Giacometti has understood
that for a long time, and he makes a restitution of it . . . The manifest
relationship between his figures seems to be this precious point
where the human being is brought back to his lowest common
multiple: his solitude in being exactly equivalent to everyone
else.' So personal experience has brought Genet to a position not
far from the one Beckett took when he discussed particularities of
time, place, circumstance and personality.

Though Genet had begun writing for the theatre more than ten years before he made these formulations about emptiness, transparency, solitude and equivalence, they help to explain the ritual elements in his drama. Writing *Les Bonnes* (*The Maids*, produced and published 1947) he was hoping 'to achieve the abolition of characters – which usually stand up only by psychological convention – in favour of signs as remote as possible from what they should at first signify, but in touch with it nonetheless, in order to link the author to the audience by this one means . . . The highest modern drama has been expressed every day for two thousand years in the sacrifice of the mass . . . Theatrically I know nothing more effective than the elevation of the host.'[4] A reference in this letter to the Balinese theatre suggests that Genet had been impressed by the writings of Artaud, who got the central idea for his Theatre of Cruelty from seeing a troupe of Balinese dancers in 1931. The performance struck him as being like a holy ritual in excluding 'any absurd aping of reality' and in giving an impression of 'a higher, controlled existence'. A direct contact, it seemed, was being made between the inner life of the performers and the inner life of the audience by means of an 'intense liberation of signs, at first held back, then suddenly thrown in the air'.[5]

These words may have been in Genet's mind when he complained that the Western actor 'does not try to become a sign charged with significance'. He even seems to have been affected by Artaud's anti-verbalism when, in the same letter to Pauvert, he wrote: 'One cannot but dream of an art that would be a profound tangle of active symbols, capable of speaking to the audience a language in which nothing would be said, everything presented.'

If the Catholic mass provides Genet with one model of what theatre ought to be, another is provided by the improvisation that goes on unselfconsciously in children's games. The letter ends with an account of an incident that had been described by another writer. Five or six boys were playing soldiers in a park. In the game, nightfall had to be approaching, so the smallest of the boys was told to be Night – to go away and to come back slowly. When he approached too quickly, he was demoted back into being a soldier. 'The only theatre that could excite me,' says Genet, 'would take this formula as its point of departure.'

For the Catholic it is faith that equates the communion wafer with Jesus's flesh; in children's games the basis of make-believe is unquestioned. But how can a ritual be celebrated in a theatre where the audience's willingness to suspend disbelief can be only a poor substitute for a shared belief? The task Genet sets himself in his plays is to engender belief in emptiness, transparency, solitude and equivalence. Like Rembrandt and Giacometti, he refuses to individualise his characters, stressing the lowest common multiples of humanity, and, in each of his five extraordinary plays (1947–61) he creates an anti-society which he holds up challengingly, provocatively, as a mirror-image to a public which is naturally inclined to deny any resemblance, to withhold all sympathy. How else can a middle-class audience respond when confronted with criminals in a cell? Or with murderous maids plotting against their mistress? Or with prostitutes in a brothel and the fantasy-addicts who dress up fetishistically as a bishop, a judge, a general? Or with militant blacks? Or with Arabs using guerrilla methods against the French forces in Algeria? In each situation bourgeois sympathy would lie on the other side, but Genet uses a combination of shock tactics and insidious stratagems. Some of his stage pictures are violently disturbing. An outsize bishop, mitred and wearing a golden cope, in a brothel. Soldiers farting into the face of a dying lieutenant. But besides antagonising us, Genet woos us, coaxing us into identification with characters who readily identify with each other. He makes the contrasts between them into windows which can easily be wound down. At the beginning of *Les Bonnes*, for instance, we see Solange impersonating Claire, while Claire impersonates Madame with a grotesque exaggeration of her condescension, her intolerably patronising mixture of benevolence and contempt. It is a game, a ritual, which reveals that the three characters are not merely interdependent: they seem to be interchangeable. Each of the three personalities overlaps with the other two, and, in spite of our resistance, we find ourselves overlapping with all three of them.

This would not happen if the rancour on display were unambivalent, but in the envy that makes the maids want to kill Madame, there is something that makes them want to *be* her, or, failing that, to play at being her. This is a kind of love. It is their relationship with her that defines their identity; rebelling against their dependence, they are siding against themselves, and the attempt at murder culminates in suicide. It is apt that the ritual should end in self-sacrifice, because there has been a strong element of self-betrayal in it, as there has in the writing of it. Genet has said:

Perhaps its primary purpose, when I wrote it, was to disgust me with myself by indicating and refusing to indicate who I was. Its secondary purpose was to produce a kind of discomfort in the auditorium . . . I go to the theatre to see myself on the stage (reconstituted in a single character or through a multiple character and in the form of a story) in a form that I wouldn't be able – or wouldn't dare – to see or dream as an image of myself, in spite of knowing that is what I am.[6]

In all Genet's theatre there is an element of self-punishment. *Les Bonnes* is based on the murder committed in 1933, when two maids, Christine and Léa Papin, aged twenty-eight and twenty-one, killed their mistress with an axe. Analysing the crime shortly afterwards, Jacques Lacan wrote that in paranoia the aggressive impulse sometimes implies a wish for self-punishment and expiation. The intellectual content of the murderous delirium, he said, was a superstructure which at once justified and negated the criminal impulse. He felt certain that there was no active Lesbianism between the sisters. 'The homosexual tendency would express itself only through a desperate negation of itself, which would lay the foundation for a conviction of being persecuted and an identification of the persecutor as the loved one.' The hatred is partly an extraversion of self-loathing, the aggression an outlet for guilt. 'Between the sisters there could never be sufficient distance even for them to attack each other.'[7]

Thanks to his technique of making the personalities over-lap, Genet could afford to increase the distance between the sisters. In fact he could not afford not to, since any outbreak of repressed violence would destroy the delicacy of his ritual. The only attempt at murder is gentle and polite: Claire respectfully implores Madame to drink the tea they have poisoned. The final self-immolation is dignified, lyrical, as Claire tries to transform herself into the mistress who has escaped being the victim. The dialogue becomes incantatory, liturgical, when Solange obediently repeats her sister's lines, as if saying responses in a ceremony:

CLAIRE: Repeat after me.

SOLANGE: Go on, but quietly.

CLAIRE (*mechanically*): Madame will have to take her tea.

SOLANGE (*hard*): No, I won't.

CLAIRE (*holding her by the wrists*): Bitch! Say it. Madame will take her tea.

SOLANGE: Madame will take her tea.

CLAIRE: Because she must sleep.

SOLANGE: Because she must sleep.

CLAIRE: And I must stay awake.

SOLANGE: And I must stay awake.

CLAIRE (*she lies down on Madame's bed*): I repeat. Don't interrupt any more. You hear? You'll do as I say? (SOLANGE *nods*.) I repeat. My tea.

SOLANGE (*hesitating*): But . . .

CLAIRE: I said my tea!

SOLANGE: But Madame . . .

CLAIRE: Well? Go on.

SOLANGE: But, madame, it's cold.

CLAIRE: I'll drink it all the same. Give it me. (SOLANGE *brings the tray*.) And you've used the best, the most precious tea-service . . .

With the crowning confirmation of a real death, the ceremonial game attains to an authenticity which has been missing from the day-to-day reality of life with Madame.

In his first novel, *Notre-Dame des Fleurs* (published 1944), Genet had written that if a play of his was ever produced with women in it, he would ask for their roles to be acted by boys. This would have exposed female elements in the male constitution and male in the female. By penetrating as intimately as he did in *Les Bonnes* into the fantasy lives of three women, he revealed something of his own femininity and, when the roles are played by boys, the self-betrayal becomes more complex. As Sartre has put it, 'What appears under the lights is not so much a woman as Genet living the impossibility of being a woman. What is first put on show is the effort, sometimes admirable, sometimes grotesque, of a young male body struggling against its own nature.'[8] Genet had also thought of asking for a placard to be nailed on the set, drawing the audience's attention to the sexual displacement. 'In short,' comments Sartre, 'Genet betrays his actors. He unmasks them, and the performer, seeing his imposture exposed, finds himself in the position of the evildoer reduced to impotence. Illusion, betrayal, frustration: all the cardinal categories which govern Genet's dreams are present here.'

Interdependent with self-betrayal is displacement of reality. Claire will not only be imperfect in impersonating Madame, as Solange will in impersonating Claire, the boys' imperfection in impersonating females would lay extra emphasis on the point that Madame always puts on an act for the benefit of her maids, while they always play roles, not only in their impersonation, and not only when they are with her, trying to impress her with their subservient devotion, but even when they are alone together, not trying to be anything other than themselves. As sisters, they know each other too well to put on acts to impress each other, but the play is written from a negative viewpoint. Everything is defined in terms of what it is not. The sisters know themselves by knowing each other:

> SOLANGE: I'd like to help you, to comfort you, but I know I
> disgust you. I repel you. I know that because you disgust me.
> Loving each other in disgust, that's not loving.
> CLAIRE: It's loving too much. But I'm fed up with this ghastly
> mirror that sends my image back to me like a bad smell.
> You're my bad smell.

And Claire is defining both herself and Madame when, speaking as Madame, she launches into a ritual of insults against maids:

> I hate servants. I hate the whole race. It's odious and vile.
> Servants aren't human. They ooze. They're an effluvium that
> hangs about in our rooms and our corridors, penetrates us,
> enters through the mouth, corrupts us. I spit you out. I know
> they're necessary. Like gravediggers, scavengers, policemen ...
> The look of fear and shame on your faces, your scrawny elbows,
> your unfashionable clothes, your bodies made for wearing

cast-off clothes. You're our distorting mirrors, our safety-valve, our shame, our dregs.

As the play explores the emptiness, the transparency, the solitude and the equivalence of the three characters, violence is being beautified, moral values inverted. As in Genet's other plays, the inversion of values depends on the muting of violence, the lyrical treatment of murder. Even in *Haute Surveillance* (*Deathwatch*), which was written before *Les Bonnes* and extensively revised before it was produced and published in 1949,[9] the killing is quiet, decorous. Yeux-verts, the only one who has committed a murder, is the toughest, the most authoritative, but instead of intervening in what he expects to be no more than a fight between the other two, he tells them to get it over quickly. Lefranc, smiling radiantly, advances on the seventeen-year-old Maurice, who returns the smile. Blocking the boy in a corner, Lefranc strangles him. The body slides between his parted legs.

The least sophisticated of the five plays, *Haute Surveillance*, is the one to make it most obvious that values are being inverted. In this anti-society, there is no justification by bad works. Evil depends on grace. Lefranc would obviously like to *be* Yeux-verts. He has been taking every opportunity to put on the murderer's clothes, and it is not only with the object of rising in the prison hierarchy that Lefranc now proves himself to be capable of murder. But he has not understood the story Yeux-verts has been telling. There was no choice for him. Killing was a misfortune that occurred to him:

> I tried to go backwards. Stop! Impossible! I did everything I could. Ran one way, then the other. Tried to wriggle my way out. Did everything I knew not to become a murderer . . . I wanted to climb back through time, undo what I'd done, live my life again up to the moment of the crime.

It is obvious that both these one-act plays were influenced by Sartre's *Huis Clos* (produced 1944). If we discount the warder in *Haute Surveillance*, both Genet's plays reproduce the claustrophobic single setting in which three characters give each other hell. Sartre's triangle consisted of a heterosexual couple and a Lesbian;

both Genet's triangles are homosexual. But more important than these similarities and this difference are two fundamental contradictions of Sartre, whose point is to equate hell with other people: 'L'Enfer c'est les autres.' Genet is saying that everyone consists of other people, while his doctrine of perverse grace contradicts Sartre's Existentialist insistence on free will. But to say that Sartre's main influence on Genet was negative is not to say that it was unimportant.

The first two plays were the only ones to have been written before the 1952 publication of *Saint Genet: comédien et martyr*, which is mainly about the man and the novels. After collaborating with Sartre in the preparation of the book, Genet could hardly have failed to be affected by it. Between publishing his *Journal du voleur* in 1949 and *Le Balcon* in 1956, he produced nothing of any great substance or length. But if it was a crisis of self-consciousness that caused the silence, the long-term result was that it killed two overlapping compulsions: to write novels and to write autobiographically. *Les Bonnes*, no less than *Haute Surveillance*, is about Genet; the three subsequent plays are not. His first full-length play *Le Balcon* is also impressively free from the defect he had himself diagnosed in *Les Bonnes* when he said, in the letter to Pauvert, that if he had 'invented a tone of voice, a gait, a style of gesture', he might have succeeded better in his attempt to achieve 'a displacement which, allowing a declamatory tone, would make theatre theatrical'.

In *Le Balcon* (produced London 1957, Paris 1960) his use of the medium is at the same time much fuller and much more redolent of anti-theatre. The script does more to impose a style on the production by introducing anti-realistic visual elements – cothurni, outsize costumes and grotesque make-ups.

In both *Haute Surveillance* and *Les Bonnes* some of the stage directions are anti-illusionistic, but they are not so well integrated with the dialogue. In *Haute Surveillance* it is hard for the director to implement Genet's stipulations, and easy for him to ignore them: 'The action develops as in a dream . . . The actors will try to move either with great heaviness or with the incomprehensible speed of lightning. If they can, they will deaden the timbre of their voices.' The most Artaudesque moment of the play depends entirely on the resources of the actor who plays Yeux-verts, and the director. The speech about trying to back-pedal away from the moment of crime is followed by a dance:

> *Here the actor will have to invent a sort of dance which shows Yeux-verts trying to move backwards in time. Silently, he contorts himself. He tries to spiral in on himself. His face expresses great suffering.*

Nor is it surprising that *Les Bonnes* has most often been produced without the alienation effect of casting boys in the three roles. Resigned to having women, Genet asks merely that they should neither be pretty nor have provocative breasts or bottoms. They should appear to be trying, throughout the action, to make themselves beautiful. The dialogue lends itself better than that of *Haute Surveillance* to anti-realistic declamation, but nothing in the action prevents the director from approximating to realism; this could not be said of *Le Balcon*.

While both one-act plays suggest that theatricality permeates life, that role-playing enters even into our relations with ourselves, *Le Balcon* replaces the simple equation of living and acting with a triangular equation: society＝theatre＝brothel. Not that sexuality is treated directly. The only reference to a bed is in the stage direction that asks for a mirror with an ornate frame to reflect an unmade bed which would seem to be situated in the front row of the stalls. The brothel is a house of illusions in which clients act out their fantasies with prostitutes playing the supporting roles.

This time it is only minor characters who are killed, Arthur and Chantal, but death exerts an even stronger tidal pull on the action than in the two earlier plays. The only talk about making love occurs outside the brothel. Chantal, who is no longer on its payroll, is in love with Roger, a leader of the revolution. Inside the brothel the two subjects to arouse the most impassioned involvement are death and dressing up. The man who decks himself out as a bishop has no interest in performing the function, only in enjoying the appearance. Another timid-looking client removes his bowler hat and his gloves to dress up in a cocked hat and a general's uniform. 'Man of war and pomp and circumstance,' he says, admiring his reflection in the mirror, 'there I am in my pure appearance. Nothing, I have nothing contingent in tow.' And he daydreams of being 'close to death . . . where I shall be nothing, but reflected *ad infinitum* in these mirrors, merely an image'. For him, as for Claire and Solange, fantasy and illusion are the only compensations for continuous frustration.

This is like Symbolist literature in its constant tendency to devalue living actuality in favour of the dead image. The brothel is a palace of symbols, and when the Queen is killed during the revolution, she can be replaced by the madame, while the little men who have enjoyed dressing up as Bishop, Judge and General need only the help of costumes and photographers to replace the Bishop, Judge and General. For all four of them, the main function is to animate the image: as the Envoy says, 'The beauty on this earth is all due to masks.' Every living element in the play seems to lust after its own absence, its replacement by an image, a monument, a costume. Carmen's desire to be with her child is not strong enough for her to give up the chance of playing St Teresa in the brothel:

> IRMA: Dead or alive, your daughter is dead. Think of the grave adorned with daisies and artificial wreaths, at the far end of a garden, and think of looking after this garden in your heart . . .
> CARMEN: I'd have liked to see her again.
> IRMA: . . . her image in the image of the garden and the garden in your heart under the burning robe of St. Teresa. And you hesitate? I offer you the most envied of all deaths, and you hesitate? You're a coward?

Even for the man who has power in the world outside the brothel, the Chief of Police, nothing matters so much as to become a hero in other men's fantasies:

> I'm going to make my image detach itself from me, force its way into your studios, multiply itself in reflections. Irma, my function is weighing me down. Here it will bask in the terrible sunshine of pleasure and death.

Nothing tempts him more than the idea of a vast mausoleum that will preserve his memory; posterity matters more than experience.

But the pleasure Genet takes in the idea of death is itself negative. It is not the prospect of extinction that excites him. As in Cocteau's 1949 film *Orphée*, death is imagined as a contiguous counter-world that exists on the far side of a looking-glass. Brought up on public assistance in orphanages and reformatories, Genet had to listen while teachers and priests, using pomp and pomposity, rhetoric and ceremony, exploited the notion of life after death to tighten their disciplinary grip on the boys. But their performances were inadequate. Genet reacted by acquiring criminal habits and a compulsion to create a series of anti-sermons, anti-ceremonies, in which values would be inverted and death would be revealed as the glass in front of the mirror, the transparent membrane that separates us from the void.

In 'L'Etrange Mot d' . . .'[10] he suggests that in modern towns theatres ought to be built only in cemeteries. 'Think how the public would leave after a performance of Mozart's *Don Giovanni*, passing the dead bodies in the earth, before returning to the world of profanity.' Or as he said in the letter to Pauvert, 'If we have chosen to watch ourselves die deliciously, we must be rigorous in arranging the funeral symbols.'

Les Nègres (*The Blacks*, published 1958; produced 1959) is an arrangement of funeral symbols. Like a funeral, the play is a ceremony that depends on the presence of spectators. Our attention, our silence, our failure to intervene, are integral to the proceedings. We have publicly given our consent, acknowledged our impotence in face of the death. We leave the theatre profoundly depressed, our faith in longevity and stability harshly shaken.

During the war Genet had felt 'delighted' and 'avenged' when 'the French army, the most prestigious thing in the world, collapsed against the troops of an Austrian corporal . . . I couldn't help loving the man who had struck a grave blow against French society.'[11] Similarly, in *Les Nègres* Genet looks forward with relish to the disintegration of our moribund civilisation. The relish is again evident in the caricaturing of the archetypal power figures – Queen, Judge, Governor, Missionary (a Bishop *in partibus*) – and in one speech the doomed Queen invokes

Virgins of the Parthenon, angel on the Reims portal, the columns of Valerius, Musset, Chopin, Vincent d'Indy, French cooking, the Unknown Soldier, Tyrolian songs, Cartesian principles, the landscaping of Le Notre, red poppies, cornflowers, a touch of coquetterie, clerical gardens . . .

From Sophocles to Ibsen, dramatists had upheld the values and myths of civilisation; anti-theatre has turned against them. Some attacks on them have been more strident than Genet's, but none more deadly.

In the assault on the audience, the politeness of the language only fortifies the insolence it seems to be restraining. Addressing the spectators, Archibald says:

> This evening we are going to perform for you. But, to make it possible for you to relax comfortably in your seats while faced with the drama which has already started here, to reassure you that there is no danger any such drama will penetrate into your precious lives, we will retain the civility we have learned from you of making communication impossible.

We have already had one visual shock: the curtain was drawn back to reveal a coffin on a catafalque, decorated with flowers, under glaring neon lighting. The black women are wearing spangled evening gowns in bad taste; the black men white ties, tail-coats and yellow shoes. Queen, Judge, Governor, Missionary and Valet, who make their entrance on a higher level, are blacks in white masks. That they are there partly as representatives of the white audience is apparent when the other actors bow ceremoniously to them and to us. The objections and interruptions put into the mouths of the masked Court parody those that we might have been expected to make, and the insult is compounded, half way through the action, when five dolls, dressed exactly like the white characters, are produced from under the skirts of a black man who has put on a white mask and dressed as a woman for a re-enactment of the ritual murder which, we are told, has just been committed. The victim is in the coffin. The eventual revelation that the coffin is empty will not decrease the play's effectiveness as a funeral ceremony for Western civilisation.

The prominence and pervasiveness of ritual in the play camouflage the displacement of story, situation, individual character. As in *Les Bonnes*, superior and inferior define themselves in terms of their opposition, but here the opposition is generalised in terms of colour and continent.

> I order you to be black right into your veins and to circulate black blood in them. Let Africa run through them. Let the Blacks blacken. Let them insist beyond all reason on what they're condemned to be, on their ebony, on their odour, on yellow eyes, on cannibal tastes. Let them not stop at eating whites but cook each other. Let them make up recipes for tibias, knee-caps, skin, thick lips . . .

Though character and attitude are generalised, the generalisation is evolved negatively. There are no whites in the play, but the play is not so much about being black as about the mutual exclusiveness of white and black. If, in *Les Bonnes*, Genet was living out the impossibility of being a woman, here he is now living out the impossibility of being coloured. What he makes his Blacks say about the Whites corresponds more or less realistically to a prevalent attitude. This is feasible because the attitude is negative. What they say about themselves is written not to hide but to emphasise the fact that a white man is putting the words into their mouths. Like Baudelaire celebrating his mulatto mistress, his Black Venus, or like Norman Mailer writing about white jealousy of black potency and dubbing the hipster a White Negro,[12] Genet is making a gesture calculated to cause scandal, implicitly acknowledging his inability to change colour, but going as far as he can to dissociate himself from the norms of white attitudes to Blacks.

At the same time as depending less than his previous plays on story, situation or character, *Les Nègres* depends less on explanation. It was one of the weaknesses of *Le Balcon* that some of the main statements were made by means of discursive prose. Much of the argument was too complex for the audience to digest. In *Les Nègres* the statements are made in other ways. While the arguments are more rudimentary, the shifting between different levels of illusion is more complex than in the earlier plays. In both

Les Bonnes and *Le Balcon*, however volatile personality was, the setting always represented a distinct locale and the action had a defined centre. In *Les Nègres* the stage represents a stage and the black actors represent black actors. 'On this stage,' says Archibald, 'we are like criminals in prison playing at being criminals.'

Though it is more unequivocally a piece of anti-theatre than the previous plays, *Les Nègres* is also more theatrical, generating tension by tapping a wider variety of the medium's resources. Visually, Genet is much more inventive. It is not merely in his word-spinning that he makes skilful use of colour: *Les Nègres* represents a step towards the telling use of costume colours he will make in *Les Paravents*. In both these plays he exploits the possibility of dividing the action between two (or more) levels and he imposes stylised movement on his actors. In *Les Nègres*, for instance, the Queen and her court make their first entrance on the lower level, moving backwards, and there is a sequence of orchestrated trembling. There is also an extremely theatrical use of sound-effects produced by the actors themselves. In one sequence they evoke virgin forest with imitations of toads, owls, hissing, roaring in the distance, branches snapping, and wind.

Genet also succeeds very well in generating and sustaining tension without having more than a sketchy story to tell. Conflict is sometimes evolved out of interruption and apparent disagreement between the performers, sometimes by generalised wrangling between Blacks and pseudo-Whites. There is a fine flyting match between the Queen and Felicity, a Mother Africa figure:

FELICITY: No one would have the strength to deny it. It thrusts, thrusts, my beauty, grows, turns green, shoots out petals, perfumes, and it's the whole of Africa, this fine tree, my crime. The birds have come to nest in it and night is resting in its branches.

THE QUEEN: Every evening, every second, I know it, you abandon yourselves to a preposterous and wicked ritual against me and mine. The smell from the blossom on your tree penetrates to my country, and it's a smell to catch me unawares, destroy me.

FELICITY (*face to face with the* QUEEN): You're a ruin.

QUEEN: But what a ruin! And I haven't finished sculpting myself, making holes, forming myself into a ruin. Eternal. It's not time that corrodes me, it's not weariness forcing me to give up, it's death that compounds me and . . .

FELICITY: If you're dead, what right, what right do you have to accuse me of killing you?

It is sometimes by means of lively language that Genet saves his archetypes from seeming depersonalised into dull abstraction, but the theatrical poetry in this play can safely move into generalisation, as in the litany of insults about the paleness of the Whites. This is recited in a monotone by the prostitute Vertu:

Pale as what comes from the arse of a man with jaundice,
Pale as the stomach of a cobra,
Pale as the men in their condemned cells,
Pale as the god they nibble in the mornings,
Pale as a knife in the night,
Pale . . . except the English, Germans and Belgians. And they're red.

To be complete, a rejection of white culture must renounce white language and white love. In spite of the language it is written in, the play accepts this principle, and makes capital out of it. As soon as Village mentions his father, he is rebuked for letting tenderness creep into his voice when the situation of his people requires only hatred: 'Invent if not words then phrases which cut instead of joining.' No white ideas are admissible unless caricatured. When Village reveals that he is in love with Vertu, Archibald threatens to exile them into the audience: 'And if you succeed in making them like you, come back and tell me. But change your colour first. Get out of it. Go down. Go to them and be spectators.' Even when they are alone together, the lovers have difficulty in expressing themselves without copying the Whites:

VERTU: All men are like you: they imitate. You can't invent anything different?

VILLAGE: For you, I could invent everything: fruits, words even fresher, a wheelbarrow with two wheels, oranges without pips, a bed for three, a non-pricking needle. But expressions of love, that's more difficult . . . Still, if you insist . . .

At the end of the play, the lovers turn their backs on the audience to join the all-black cast, which is now lined up without masks.

Technically, Genet's advance depends partly on his ability to use shifts between levels of illusion as a means of increasing the tension. One of the main climaxes is an anti-climax: the revelation that no white woman has been killed, that the onstage events have merely been a diversion contrived to keep the audience away from the place where a black traitor has been on trial. Not that we believed in the reality of the ritual murder or believe now in the reality of the offstage trial, but despite the layers of illusion there is a connection between the reality of Black Power and the theatrical effectiveness of the moment when the Courtiers take their masks off and the man who has been playing the Valet becomes the most authoritative figure on stage. And as ritual, the final section of the play is all the more effective for its narrative gratuitousness. Ostensibly because they don't want us to overhear their serious deliberations, the actors go back to the charade. When the Courtiers put their white masks on again, it is all the more embarrassing to be forced into accepting them as our representatives in the action, especially when they express the desire to commit suicide rather than allow the Blacks the pleasure of killing them.

Les Paravents (*The Screens*, published 1961; produced Berlin 1961, Paris 1966) is still more deeply penetrated with the principles of anti-theatre. Like Ionesco when he wrote *La Cantatrice chauve*, Genet did not think he was creating something that would be staged. As he wrote to Roger Blin, who directed the Paris production, 'If I had thought the play could be acted, I'd have made it more beautiful – or ruined it completely.' He had obviously been visualising in great detail, but the play has never been given a production of the sort he envisaged – in an open air theatre, with tiers of seats carved out of a hillside, with the stage at the bottom and the screens being moved about in front of a fully grown forest. The natural background would counterpoint the artificiality of the movable white screens, each about ten feet high, on which objects and landscapes are drawn, mostly during the action.

The style is integral to the view taken of the Algerian situation. The opinion of the colonist Sir Harold that a handsome tree is worth more than a handsome man is expressed in a context in which Arabs can produce shade for the French settlers by drawing a palm tree with green chalk, or breeze by simulating the sound of wind in branches.

The characters should all be either masked or unrealistically made up, but the characterisation is extraordinarily vivid and vigorous, while Genet's imagination has never produced more exciting theatrical effects than it does in his exploitation of the screens. In the first scene, the four-panelled screen is hardly more than a backdrop, except that entrances and exits can be made from either side of it: but as the play develops, Genet progressively integrates his décor into his action. There is a stylistically pre-paratory gesture towards the end of Scene Four, when one character, announcing that it's evening, tears up the sun, which is made of yellow tissue paper. This is reminiscent of a moment in Brecht's *Trommeln in der Nacht* (*Drums in the Night*, written 1919; produced 1921) when, complaining that life is just play-acting, a soldier who has returned from the war throws a drum at the lantern which has been representing the moon. Throughout *Les Paravents*, the screens poke fun at the theatrical tradition of painted walls and *trompe l'oeil* landscapes, but at the same time they provide the means for startling theatrical innovations. In Scene Ten, two of the caricatured colonists, Sir Harold and M. Blankensee, who are carrying on a complacent conversation about the lack of discipline among the native labourers, fail to notice when an Arab creeps in to draw yellow flames at the foot of each painted orange tree in the grove on one of the screens. He escapes unseen. Shortly afterwards another Arab is setting fire in the same way to the orange grove on the second screen, and soon a third Arab is sabotaging the trees on the third. Engrossed in their conversation about how much they love their roses, their orange trees, and their cork trees, Sir Harold and M. Blankensee still pay no attention when more Arabs crawl in to blow on the flames or even when the noise of crackling becomes audible. Before the scene ends, ten or twelve Arabs have drawn the flames so big that they reach almost to the top of the trees.

In the first of his letters to Roger Blin,[13] Genet said that the orange trees should look as though they had been painted by a madman. 'I believed a sex maniac who had never seen orange trees or even oranges would invent a better orange grove than anyone else.' The flames should have the brutality of the flames a sadist would draw if he were painting a fire in a brothel full of naked women.

Genet's imagination seems to have worked all the better for the freedom deriving from the assumption that the play would never be staged. He uses the screens even more audaciously when the sixty-year-old Arab woman Kadidja calls on the rebels to describe what they have done to make evil prevail. The one who talks of stealing two revolvers draws them on a screen with a charcoal pencil. Another, who has disembowelled cows, draws horns. One has raped a girl: he paints a red stain. One who screamed out in hatred draws a screaming mouth. New screens are wheeled in, and the pace accelerates as others represent their actions by drawing a bodiless head and two hands chopped off at the wrists.

For the evocation of atmosphere and locale, the screens can work only in a stylised, emblematic way, but this is an advantage, encouraging Genet to develop the non-realistic techniques he was exploring in *Les Nègres* for creating an impression of place through words, movements and sound-effects produced by the actors. At the end of Scene Sixteen, for instance, one of the young Arab prostitutes enters, stumbles and falls. The cabbages and oyster plants are tripping her up, she complains, and the sheets are slapping her. Miming the business of pushing aside washing hanging from a line, she seems to be arriving back at the brothel.

Death is again spliced into the action, and, more clearly than in *Les Nègres*, situated as a contiguous anti-world. 'If we contrast life with theatre,' Genet wrote to Roger Blin, 'it is because we suspect that the stage is an area that borders on death, where liberties can be taken.' No other playwright has ventured beyond the grave in the way Genet does in *Les Paravents*. The possibility of communicating with the dead is introduced in a very funny sequence. When the village women tell Saïd's mother that she is not wanted at the funeral of Si Slimane, a militant who has been killed, she stays away, but afterwards employs a medium at his graveside to ask him whether they were telling her the truth. He says they were. Later we meet him together with other dead characters, and as more and more of the French Foreign Legionaries and Arab rebels are killed, they reappear, sometimes on a higher level of the stage than the living, sometimes on a lower. The indeterminate period of transition is represented by passing through a series of transparent white paper screens arranged behind each other at intervals of about three feet. The moment of arrival is registered by breaking through the paper of the final screen. Each of the new arrivals is amused that during life so much fuss has always been made about something as insignificant as dying.

Just as the maids and the Blacks had defined themselves negatively in relation to the mistress and the whites, the living define themselves negatively in relation to death. Costumes are used, from the outset, in a way which develops the suggestion implanted in *Le Balcon* that function is unimportant in relation to symbol. In the first brothel scene, both the twenty-year-old whore Malika and the forty-year-old Warda wear gold lamé dresses, but whereas Malika is always in a rush to strip when a man arrives with money in his pocket, Warda has learnt to appear very reluctant to take her clothes off. Consequently she is in great demand. It is not her body but her clothes and her style that matter. She has worked for two years to perfect her method of cleaning her teeth ostentatiously with a hatpin. She has also cultivated a spikiness, which adds, like thorns on a rose, to the glamour of her image.

This is a comic development from a Symbolist idea, which emerges in a different way, equally comic, in M. Blankensee's speech about roses, which should be delivered, says the stage-direction, as if he were reciting a poem by Mallarmé:

The stem, straight, stiff. The leaves green, sound, glazed, and between these leaves, thorns. You can't make fun of the rose as you can of the dahlia. The thorns mean that this flower is not a joke. So many weapons to protect it. If you like, fortresses, warriors, demanding the same respect that a Head of State gets. We are the masters of language. To interfere with roses is to interfere with language.

It is not merely with the whores that Genet applies this principle. M. Blankensee pads his stomach and his rump to make himself look more patriarchal. The effect of a grotesque make-up and a bizarre costume on the actor should be liberating, rather like alcohol or a carnival fancy dress. He will feel that he is someone else, not responsible for his own actions, translated out of himself. As Genet wrote to Blin, 'each costume must in itself be a set – backed by the screens – capable of situating the character, but . . . this sumptuousness should not come from a this-worldly beauty . . . Acquart and his wife [the designers] should be capable of inventing terrible adornments which would seem out of place on the shoulders of the living.' The costumes, in other words, will help the characters to look forward to the moment when the core of living reality is squeezed out of existence, when the husk of image is all that survives. In *Le Balcon* Carmen observed that 'emptied of the thighs it contained, a pair of trousers on a chair is beautiful'; in *Les Paravents* that idea is developed into the long speech of the ugly wife, Leila, to the trousers of her absent husband, Saïd. They are better constructed than he is, she says, and seductively, she challenges them to sleep with her. This emphasis on the outer layer, the shell, is highly unusual. The actor is not reduced to immobility, as he is in some of Beckett's plays, but Stanslavski-ish questing for the 'inner truth' of the character is unhelpful when the writer sees the truth as conditioned by the outward appearance. In 1964, when Peter Brook directed RSC actors in the first twelve scenes of the play for a private production at the Donmar Studios, Charles Marowitz, who was working as his associate director, noticed that 'In the space of four hours (the hours during which costumes and design were added), the play was transformed into something bold, brazen, aptly rhetorical and hieratic . . . the costume and décor produced – in one day – two-thirds of the truth, only one-third of which had been evoked in six weeks of rehearsal.'

The screens are not the only visual element that change and get used in different ways. Unless it becomes dirtied or damaged or destroyed, costume cannot change, but the attitude of the whores' clients to their clothes does change. Function becomes more important and appearance less important as the rebellion gains strength. 'It's like working in a steam-bath,' complains Warda, who has to make a slit in the front of her gold skirt. No longer concerned with her image, the men just use her body. In *Le Balcon*, the brothel was the centre of reactionary sentiment. It represented the obsession with image that made it impossible for the rebellion to succeed. In this play the brothel becomes a focus of rebellion, reflecting the change in the spirit of the Arabs. Not that the revolution is unambiguously represented as a success. In throwing off the tyranny of the Europeans, the Arabs fail to avoid the pitfall the Blacks were so wary of – imitating the enemy.

Of all the developments in the play, the one treated in most detail is that of Saïd, who, like Genet himself, moves through abjection towards a form of canonisation which is unacceptable to him. (On one level, *Les Paravents* is an answer to *Saint Genet: comédien et martyr*.) Saïd's cult of humiliation is partly comic. He marries a girl so ugly that she never takes off the black hood which conceals her face. He becomes a thief, a convict and a traitor. He puts out one of his wife's eyes – though this is not made so believable as his other misdeeds. But it is believable that he has become a hero for the women who are goading the men on to greater acts of viciousness. Values have been inverted again, and in the world of the dead, as Genet represents it, there is no judgment. Nor does the judge have any function among the living as the rebellion progresses. The Cadi, seen presiding over his courtroom in Scene Seven, is himself taken to prison in the final scene, boasting of his thefts. It is through his mouth (in Scene Fourteen) that Genet makes a Proustian point about beauty: things cease to belong to those who have enhanced their attractiveness.

The main function of Saïd and Leila in the play is to enhance the attractiveness of abjection. The play is self-defeating to the extent that, in doing so, they make themselves redundant. As evil triumphs, the action disintegrates. The final scene, with screens on three levels of the stage, is brilliant in its use of space, but there can be no satisfactory ending because Leila, who has disappeared, does not reappear among the dead, and neither does Saïd, when he is shot by the Arab soldiers after he has refused their offer of forgiveness for his betrayal. After achieving perfection in the art of failure, his final apotheosis must be absence. Genet knew there was no solution to the artistic problem he had set himself. The Academician in the final scene asks whether a new art can possibly be born to enshrine the facts that people would like to forget.

'Usually plays are said to have a meaning,' wrote Genet to Roger Blin. 'Not this one. It is a feast-day with components that don't fit, a non-celebration.' By producing only the first twelve scenes, Peter Brook evaded the slide into non-meaning, but this is essential to the play's nihilism. The justice that the Cadi administers in his first scene is reminiscent of Azdak's judgments in Brecht's *Der kaukasische Kreidekreis* (*The Caucasian Chalk Circle*, written 1944–5; produced 1954) but Azdak's final verdict has the wisdom of Solomon in it, whereas in Genet's Algeria, as Amer says in the last scene, there are no more judges, only thieves, murderers, arsonists.

That the drift towards anarchy can be given a certain theatrical beauty is proved by the lyricism in the relationship between Saïd and Leila. She loves him in spite of or because of his maltreatment of her, and he finally confesses that had it not been for the presence of his mother, the stirrings of tenderness he felt towards his wife might not have been abortive. But the mother is formidably potent, even after death. When he seems to be hesitating between the Arab soldiers, who want him to join them, and Ommu, the Arab matriarch who wants him as a symbol of viciousness, the mother intervenes from among the dead, speaking to him as if she were a voice inside his consciousness, persuading him to say no to both.

What is most unsatisfactory about the ending is the lack of clarity. The inversion of values works to good comic effect in such lines as the mother's claim that she would have the strength to divide the Red Sea in order to clear a path for the Pharaoh. Leila and Ommu make powerful speeches dedicating themselves to evil, while the overall construction is extremely skilful. Ambitiously, Genet takes a great diversity of elements into his picture, and, despite what he says himself, they do not remain disparate. He also succeeds in relating the private fantasies of the characters to the political realities of the situation, and, with extraordinary insight, he reveals improbable connections, exposing, for instance, a genuine affinity between the handsome, brutal sergeant and the predatory whores, who recognise him as one of them. The Lieutenant, ignorant of his own homosexuality, is shown sublimating it into patriotic fervour. In both its positives and its negatives, the play is phenomenally rich, but the ending is a double negative which generates neither a positive nor a vacuum. Some kind of anti-climax is needed, but the non-appearance of Saïd among the dead is not sufficient. Or not sufficiently insufficient.

Les Paravents is not primarily a play about Algeria. As Genet wrote to Blin, it is 'not an apologia for treason'. It takes place 'where morality is replaced by an aesthetics of the stage'. The failure to solve the aesthetic problem cannot, therefore, be condoned, even if it was inevitable.

With his two one-act plays and his three full-length plays, Genet is among the least prolific of great dramatists, but it cannot be said that the silence he has maintained since 1961 (both as playwright and novelist) is integral to his achievement. The plays are themselves so powerfully negative that no subsequent act of negation could either add to them or subtract from them.

5 Peter Handke and the Sentence

Wim Wenders, who directed the film of Handke's 1970 novel *Die Angst des Tormanns beim Elfmeter* (*The Goalie's Anxiety at the Penalty Kick*), has said he was attracted to the book because 'it is more the sequence of sentences than the sequence of the plot that is interesting'. In 1966, when Handke made his début as a playwright with *Publikumsbeschimpfung* (*Insulting the Audience*,[1] written 1965), no play had ever depended more on the sequence of sentences and less on plot. Nor has any play ever depended less on character. If it is a play – Handke uses the word *Sprechstück*, literally 'speech-piece', though *Stück*, as a shortening of *Theaterstück*, is the word most commonly used in German for *play* – it is the most abstract, most non-figurative play ever to become an international success.

The normal expectations of theatregoers are misleadingly encouraged by backstage noises and movements against the

curtain calculated to suggest that a set is being positioned. But the
curtain goes up on an empty stage. Four speakers – Handke avoids
the word actors – come forwards, casually dressed, apparently still
rehearsing their lines. The script provides sentences and sequence,
but, apart from suggesting that each of the four is given about the
same quantity of lines, Handke makes no stipulations about who
says what. Even when there are contradictions, he does not mind
whether the speakers are contradicting themselves or each other.

> You will hear what you have usually seen.
> You will hear what you have not usually seen here.
> You will not see a play . . .
> You will see a play without pictures.

Nor does he specify the age or sex of the speakers. In the German
première, they were all male; in the English, there were two men
and two women. Handke even invites the director to depart from
the sequence of the script, though it is unlikely that any major
rearrangements would seem desirable. What distinguishes the
play from Dadaist experiments in insulting the audience is the
architectural expertise of the long, elaborate and subtle sequence
of sentences. An hour of outright insults would be intolerable,
mainly because it would be so boring. Handke's play is entertaining because there is always sufficient suspense about what will be
said next, in spite of long stretches in which the style borders on
that of a thesaurus as he catalogues what is not on offer.

> Here the potentialities of the theatre will not be exploited. The
> extent of the potentialities will not be surveyed. The theatre will
> not be unchained. The theatre will be chained. References to
> fate will be ironic. Our comedy is not subversive. Your
> laughter cannot be liberating. We are not playful. The play
> does not represent a world. It is not half a world. We are not
> making two worlds.

Probably most members of the audience had anticipated neither
an ordinary play nor a mere string of insults, without knowing
how far between the two extremes to pitch their expectations.
Having predicted this uncertainty, Handke plays with it, adding
to the provocation by presenting a phenomenon that seems to

invite classification but vigorously eludes it. The form in which he casts his sentences, the strong rhythms, the approximation to aphorism, the repetition and near-repetition are all reminiscent of something, but what? A poem? A litany? A statute-book? Wittgenstein's *Tractatus Logico-Philosophicus*? Are we being involved in some kind of ceremony or anti-ceremony? Are we being led up a garden path towards a nasty smell? Perhaps the elaboration and the avoidance of unpleasantness are intended to put us off our guard, so that the insults, when they come, will be all the more hurtful. Our confusion is itself a source of theatrical tension.

There is a stage direction to tell the speakers not to look anyone in the eye, but they are not only talking to us directly, they are drawing attention to the fact that they are overriding the theatrical convention by which the performer pretends the audience is not there: 'You are no longer eavesdroppers behind a wall.' They are talking about us and about the situation we have involved ourselves in. Having come to the theatre, we have temporarily forfeited our separateness. 'You sit in rows. You form a pattern. You sit in a certain order. Your faces point in a certain direction. You sit at the same distance from each other. You are an audience. You form a unity.' There is an unmistakable pressure against the norms of the entertainments that draw theatregoers together, but it is worryingly difficult to gauge how much hostility there is behind it.

In order to disillusion you we need no illusions . . . This is no slice of life. We aren't telling you a story . . . When we say 'we', we can also mean you. We are not representing your situation. In us you cannot recognise yourselves . . . These boards do not signify a world. They belong to the world. These boards serve for us to stand on them. This is no other world than yours. You are no longer intruders. You are in focus. You are the centre of focus in our world.

Ironic compliments alternate with reassurance: 'We are not making side-swipes against you . . . You are our partners in the scene.' Are we going to be treated like the guinea-pigs who are submitted to a series of progressively unpleasant shocks? 'You are not symbolical. You are an ornament . . . You are discovered. You are the discovery of the evening.'

The more playful the provocation becomes, the more serious are the covert insults. We remain uncertain of how much resentment we ought to be feeling. Tantalisingly interwoven with the contradictory indications are reiterations of the implicit challenge to categorise the entertainment we are passively participating in. The speakers keep providing negative hints. It does not fill an evening, is not true to life, not theatrically effective, does not transport us into another world. Even when the hints are phrased positively they have a great many negatives in them:

> You have recognised that we are saying no to something. You have recognised that we repeat ourselves. You have recognised that this play (*Stück*) is a confrontation with the theatre. You have recognised the dialectical structure of this play. You have recognised a certain spirit of contradiction. You have made your minds up about the play's intention. You have recognised that we are mostly being negative . . . You have not yet understood the dialectical structure of this play.

This passage is immediately followed by one complimenting us on our appearance, and then by one criticising us as if we were a play. We do not fill an evening. We are not true to life, not theatrically effective. We are not playful. We have no feeling for theatre. We have nothing to say. Our début is unconvincing.

It is almost a relief when we are given direct commands which are either impossible to obey or self-contradictory. We are told to stop moving our eyelashes, our tongues, to stop swallowing, not to hear, not to smell, not to collect saliva, not to sweat, not to shift in our seats or to breathe. Then we are told to swallow, collect saliva, blink, hear, breathe. Unmistakably, we are now being treated with less respect and more aggression. An overt reference to insults comes soon afterwards. We will be insulted, we are told, because insults too are a way of talking to us:

> With insults we can be direct. We can strike a spark. We can destroy the acting area. We can tear down a wall. We can pay attention to you . . . When you are insulted, your immobility and passivity will finally fall into place. But we will not insult you. For the moment, we will use insulting words that you use. With the insulting words we will contradict ourselves.

The final climax of insults is very well judged. It is neither too much of an anti-climax nor too subtle to be theatrically powerful, but neither is it crude. Like the rest of the text, it is ritualised by the reiteration of the same words at the beginning of each phrase, while the impact is muted by the impression that, as in a thesaurus, we are being offered a choice of not quite synonymous words and phrases, not all of which can possibly be applicable to our particular case:

> Oh you cancer-victims, oh you TB-germ spitters, oh you multiple sclerotics, oh you syphilitics, oh you cardiac cases, oh you people with swollen livers, oh you dropsicals, oh you apopleptics, oh you carriers of terminal diseases, oh you candidates for suicide, oh you potential victims of peace, oh you potential victims of war, oh you potential victims of fatal accidents, oh you potential dead.

The final words spoken are polite: 'You were welcome here. We thank you. Good night.' The curtain falls and, regardless of the audience's reaction, immediately goes up again. The speakers stand staring into the auditorium, while an ecstatic ovation is played over the loudspeakers. Handke suggests a recording of audience reaction at a Beatles' concert. This continues until the auditorium is empty. As a final provocation, we have been deprived of the silence in which we could have expressed our reaction.

Though Handke rejected the description 'anti-theatre', the play is directly in the anti-theatre tradition, using the medium against the medium, not in order to destroy it but to reform it by exposing what is bad about the way it has been used. The basic intention, he has said, was to make people

> aware of the world of the theatre – not of the outside world . . .
> The stage is an artifact; I wanted this play to point out that every word, every utterance onstage is dramaturgy. Every human utterance the theatre presents as natural is not evolved, but produced. I wanted to show the 'producedness' of theatre.
> . . . I wanted to show that the dramaturgy of the old plays did not satisfy me any more (that, indeed, it bores me, in the sense

that the conventional events on stage are far removed from
me). I couldn't stand the pretence of reality anymore. I felt as if
the actors were under a glass bell. My point was to use words to
encircle the audience so they'd want to free themselves by heckling; they might feel naked and get involved. What is said
doesn't really matter. I reduced the play to words because my
words are not descriptions, only quotations, and because the
only possibility they point to is the one that happens while the
words are spoken on the stage. . . . My theatrical plan is to have
the audience always look upon my play as a means of testing
other plays . . . Most normal plays disappoint the spectator
because they really have nothing to do with his situation in the
outside world: they only refer to specific individuals . . . This
dramaturgy is a hundred years old; it runs behind the reality of
the day like a rusty bicycle, a tandem.[2]

Though *Publikumsbeschimpfung* was Handke's first play to be
produced, the first to be written was *Weissagung* (*Prophecy*), which
he completed the previous year, 1964. This was the first of four
Sprechstücke, the other two being *Selbstbezichtigung* (*Self-Accusation*,
written 1965; produced with *Weissagung*, 1966) and *Hilferufe* (*Cries
for Help*, produced 1967). In his 'Bermerkungen zu meinem
Sprechstücken' ('Remarks on My Speechplays') he described
them as

plays without pictures in that they provide no picture of the
world. The world is shown not in the form of pictures but in
the form of words, and the words of the speechplays do not
show the world as situated outside the words: they show the
world in the words themselves. The words . . . provide a concept of the world. The speechplays are theatrical in so far as they
make use of natural forms of expression in reality . . . The
natural forms of expression they use are insult, self-accusation,
confession, declaration, question, justification, excuse, prophecy,
cry for help.

It is likely that Handke's term *Sprechstück* derives from Wittgenstein's *Sprechspiel* (language game). Wittgenstein had already
suggested in the *Tractatus* that 'the introduction of elementary

propositions provides the basis for understanding all other kinds of proposition'. In *The Blue Book*[3] he uses the word *Sprechspiele* for

> ways of using signs simpler than those in which we use the signs of our highly complicated everyday language . . . If we want to study the problems of truth and falsehood, of the agreement and disagreement of propositions with reality, of the nature of assertion, assumption, and question, we shall with great advantage look at primitive forms of language in which these forms of thinking appear without the confusing background of highly complicated processes of thought. When we look at such simple forms of language the mental mist which seems to enshroud our ordinary use of language disappears.

Weissagung might almost have been written as an extended footnote to this suggestion. The four speakers start with a series of statements most of which depend tautologically on similes which repeat a word that has already been used:

> The flies will die like flies.
> The dogs on heat will nuzzle like dogs on heat.
> The stuck pig will squeal as if stuck.
> The bull will bellow like a bull.

Sometimes two, three or four voices speak in unison, sometimes several sentences are grouped together with no change of speaker or speakers, but there is little variation in either the length or the structure of the sentences. Going on like this for about fifteen minutes, the play becomes extremely irksome and, on internal evidence alone, it would be hard to understand its purpose. But the epigraph is a quotation from Mandelstam, which complains that 'the air shudders with similes', and in an essay called 'Theater und Film: Das Elend des Vergleichens' ('Theatre and Film: the Wretchedness of Comparison')[4] Handke suggests that our mania for comparison arises from an incapacity to respond to an individual object without measuring it against something else and therefore making a value judgment. 'Objects seem to be there only so that they can be played off against each other, abstracted into potentialities for comparison.'[5]

In the *Tractatus* Wittgenstein wrote, 'It is self-evident that identity is not a relation between objects.' He categorises elementary propositions as true or false according to whether the state of affairs they describe exists or not. 'The world is completely described by giving all elementary propositions, and adding which of them are true and which false.' The two extreme cases among possible groups of truth-conditions (*Wahrheitsbedingungen*) are tautologies and contradictions. 'Propositions show what they say: tautologies and contradictions show that they say nothing. A tautology has no truth-condition because it is unconditionally true: and a contradiction is true on no condition . . . Tautologies and contradictions are not pictures of reality. They do not represent any possible situations. For the former admit *all* possible situations and the latter none.' In his linguistic games with tautologies and contradictions, Handke was not merely avoiding the pictorial function, he was experimenting with the possibility of saying nothing.

Selbstbezichtigung is more interesting both as a play and as a language game, abstracting confessions from their situation. This time there are only two speakers, male and female, but, as in *Publikumsbeschimpfung*, it is for the director to decide who says which lines, and which, if any, are spoken in unison. It does not even matter whether we assume that the recurrent 'I' refers to a single character or to two. The confessions are not primarily autobiographical, though there is some residue from Handke's Catholic education in the suggestion of Original Sin. The play's first sentence is 'I came into the world', and, couched in confessional terms, the ensuing account of development implies that each step forward was sinful, though Handke may merely be testing the effect of the implications:

> I moved my mouth. I came to my senses. I made myself noticed. I cried. I spoke. I heard noises. I distinguished between noises. I produced noises . . . I saw. I saw things I had seen before. I became conscious.

In the sequence dealing with the acquisition of language, the tone is not so much that of apologia as of complaint about a victimising system:

I learnt the difference between good and evil. I learnt the words that designate possession. I learnt the difference between mine and yours . . . I became the object of sentences. . . . I became a movement of the mouth. I became a series of letters.

Many of the sentences are about learning rules for the avoidance of danger, evil, social injustice and abuse of sexual powers. The theatrical tension again depends very much on the sequence of sentences, and though the syntax is always simple, they vary in length and pattern. A leavening of satirical comedy combines with surprising juxtapositions and contradictions to keep the audience on the alert, while the regularity of rhythm throws the surprises into greater relief.

I have acted as though I were alone in the world.
I have not been well-behaved. I have been obstinate.
I have been weak-willed . . . I have been alone too much.
I have been alone too little.

According to Handke, the play, like *Publikumsbeschimpfung*, 'came out of an ever greater reduction of means. I had been planning a play with a genuine plot, with a story, a kind of confession – there was constant confessing onstage, in dialogue form. Then this plan was gradually reduced to words, which don't refer to any objects or problems on stage; they merely quote, and what they do least is give the appearance of another reality – rather, they create their own reality of words.'[6]

The last of the four *Sprechstücke*, *Hilferufe* (*Cries for Help*, produced 1967), is similar in abstracting sentences from situations, but dissimilar in divorcing words from their usual sense. The play is a game in which at least two speakers try to point the way to the word HELP by means of the tone they adopt for a number of sentences in which they have to ignore the normal meaning of the words:

breakfast is included in the price: NO. You are treading on forbidden ground: NO. the train is likely to arrive a few minutes late: NO.

The word NO should be spoken in different ways, indicating how inaccurate the guess is, and, at the end of the play, the correct guess, 'Help', repeated several times, is greeted with YES. Here too, of course, word and meaning diverge. Having arrived at the solution, the speaker is not in need of help and is no longer trying to sound as if he were.

Kaspar (produced May 1968) was Handke's first full-length play, his first not to be designated as a *Sprechstück*, and his first to have a named character in it. Kasperle is the German for Mr Punch, but the main reference is to Kaspar Hauser, who in 1828 was found wandering the streets of Nuremberg, having spent the first sixteen years of his life cooped up in a wooden compartment. Linguistically he was still almost a virgin, having only one sentence at his disposal: 'I want to be a horseman like my father once was.' Handke is not attempting to dramatise the story told in Hauser's autobiography, but to analyse a comparable loss of linguistic innocence, and, as in Ionesco's early plays, the underlying assumption is that language can be an instrument of oppression and depersonalisation. *Kaspar*, says Handke, 'shows how someone can be led into speaking by speaking. The play could also be titled *Speech Torture*'. To formalise the torture, Handke suggests a kind of magic eye should be visible, blinking to register the ferocity of the assault on Kaspar's consciousness.

The voices that bear down on him are all partially depersonalised. They are heard through loudspeakers, and their manner – regardless of what the lines mean – should be that of voices speaking through public address systems, megaphones or telephones. As in *Publikumsbeschimpfung*, the stage represents nothing but a stage, and though there are props on it this time, Handke wants it to be apparent that they are objects which have a theatrical function but no other past or future. As the audience comes into the theatre, it hears the stage directions (which I am summarising) read over and over again through loudspeakers.

Kaspar wears a lifelike mask which expresses astonishment and confusion. His costume is theatrical. His movements are uncoordinated. His sentence (unlike Kaspar Hauser's) contains no clues about period or family background: 'I want to be someone like somebody else once was.' He is at first like the speakers of

Hilferufe in using language with no sense of the words' normal meaning.

Not so much an anti-play as the *Sprechstücke*, it not only has more narrative content, it is concerned more with making a statement about language and less with criticising the medium or the way it is normally used. But *Kaspar* is revolutionary in its use of the stage, and it represents a continuation of the work done in the *Sprechstücke*, picking up a great many threads from them and developing the technical experiments. The first linguistic game is a kind of battle between Kaspar's sentence and the sentences aimed at him by the invisible speakers. Trying 'not to make sense but to show that they are playing at speaking', they talk to him about his sentence. He can use it to make himself noticeable, they say, or to tell himself everything he can't tell other people. He can use it to assert himself against other sentences. He can make all objects into it.

The realistic question of how he would understand what they are saying to him is not relevant. What matters is whether he can retain his sentence in face of their calculated and concerted attempts to prod him into speaking other sentences. Like Wittgenstein, Handke is constantly concerned with the discontinuity between objects and words. He told Artur Joseph that the play 'consists primarily of sentence games and sentence models dealing with the impossibility of *expressing* anything in language . . . I think a sentence doesn't mean something else: it means itself.'

Some of the speakers' pronouncements echo and parody Wittgenstein's:

You talk things through to the end: you think things through to the end: if you could not talk them through to the end you could not say 'I think them through to the end'.

In the *Tractatus* Wittgenstein wrote: '*The limits of my language* means the limits of my world' and 'Everything that can be thought at all can be thought clearly. Everything that can be put into words can be put clearly.' But while propositions can represent the whole of reality, he says, they cannot represent what they must have in common with reality in order to represent it – logical form. To represent logical form we should have to station ourselves somewhere outside the world. 'Propositions *show* the logical form of reality. They display it . . . What *can* be shown *cannot* be said.' In Handke's play, speaking in unison with the voices, Kaspar says: 'To represent conditions in general does not correspond to the facts; not to represent conditions at all corresponds to them far better. It is not true that conditions correspond to facts.'

The action of the play pivots on the relationship between the habit of orderliness in arranging words and the habit of orderliness in arranging objects. Furniture and props are initially positioned on the stage with no obvious relationship to each other, while Kaspar is initially in no state to impose order on them by rearranging them. Clumsily, uncomprehendingly, he moves about examining them, fiddling with them, becoming entangled with them, while the torturers continue their verbal bombardment. It is one of their stratagems to promise him that the sentence he owns will exorcise all disorder. Every impossible order will become possible for him, every real disorder impossible.

As in *Selbstbezichtigung*, Handke wants to expose societal pressures that condition the learning process, and to suggest that the learning of language is a discipline which depersonalises by imposing self-consciousness and feelings of guilt. In linguistic games, as in all games, there have to be rules, while the relationship between the players must in some way be analogous to social relationships, at least in so far as individuals have different and interdependent functions. In the series of games that constitute this play, Kaspar has to learn both the rules of the games and the rules of language as he goes along. Theatrically the first game is all the more effective for the fact that he starts by trying not to play. While he concentrates on keeping his sentence intact, other sentences confuse him by forcing comparisons on him. Unable to keep the sentences he hears away from his own sentence, he produces variations on it and fragmentations of it. Other sentences become indispensable to him, but before he can pronounce them he is reduced to silence, forfeiting his own sentence. Then he begins to speak – single words first, then awkward phrases:

'Because me already at least here. Into the hands. Further and wide. Or there. Fallen out. Eyes beaten. Nobody is. Goes neither home. To the hole. Goat's eyes. Watercatch. Left for dead. If I already here at least go on telling myself.' The first syntactically correct sentence he utters expresses nostalgia for the linguistic innocence he has lost: 'In those days, when I was still away, I never had so many pains in my head, and I was not tortured as I have been since being here.' The line is followed by a blackout.

In Handke's second novel *Der Hausirer* (*The Pedlar*, 1967) – his first, *Die Hornissen* (*The Hornets*), had been published the previous year – we are presented at the beginning with an extreme, quasi-ceremonial orderliness, which will be disrupted by the murder. The resolution of the plot will restore order. In *Kaspar* orderliness is equated with linguistic potency. A table is no longer a source of horror when one has the word 'table' not only to keep it in its place but to keep other objects out of the way. Apply the word 'table' to a wardrobe and you are left with the reality of the wardrobe and the possibility of a table. Arranging words in order, according to the rules of grammar, in order to form a sentence is cognate with arranging objects in a room or articles of clothing, according to society's rules, in order to conform with the norms. As the speakers say, the orderly sentence becomes a model: 'With the model sentences you have you can push your way through . . . everything that seems to be disorderly can be set in order: you can declare it to be orderly; each object can be whatever you designate it to be; if you *see* it differently from the way you speak of it, you must be in error.' The object, which can be described, becomes 'an orderly object which poses no problems'. No stories need to be told about it. As Kaspar rearranges the furniture, moving spot-lights show him where to position the sofa, the chairs, the little table, the broom and the shovel. So the theatrical machinery is involved in the conspiracy to inflict torture, as in Beckett's two *Actes sans paroles* (*Acts Without Words*, produced 1957 and 1964) in which the protagonist is tormented by a palm-tree which closes up like a parasol to prevent him from enjoying its shade, a pair of scissors which is whisked out of the way before he can cut his throat with it, and a goad which prods at him, manipulated from the wings.

When a second Kaspar makes his entrance, wearing an identical mask and costume, sweeping the stage with a broom, we get the impression that the man no longer belongs to himself. 'In my unconscious,' said Antonin Artaud, 'it is always other people that I hear.' Kaspar can no longer hear his own sentence, no longer distinguish between himself and other people's precepts. A third Kaspar appears, accompanying a fourth, who walks on crutches. Others appear, and in a sequence of short silent scenes, punctuated by blackouts, we see them involved in different kinds of movement. The long, climacteric speech which comes just before the interval presents an antithesis to *Selbstbezichtigung*. Instead of accusing himself, Kaspar makes a series of claims, accepting the values implicit in what has been said to him:

> I'm healthy and strong. I'm honest and easily satisfied. I'm conscientious. I'm hard-working, reticent and modest. I'm always friendly. I make no troublesome demands. My behaviour is natural and winning. Everyone likes me. I can cope with anything. I'm available for everybody . . . Once it seemed to me that I didn't even exist. Now I exist almost too much and if there were too many objects at that time, it seems to me now that they have become almost too few.

It is essential to the first half of the play that the speakers are invisible and that Kaspar is alone on stage. So Handke is renouncing all possibility of interaction between visible characters. But it is the second half which is theatrically the less effective half. Once the impact of the other Kaspars' appearance is over, their presence on stage seems to be more of a liability than an asset: the activities Handke contrives for them neither successfully counterpoint the theme nor contribute to developing it. Having shown how Kaspar is brought to full articulacy and to full contentment with his new powers, Handke wants to show him using them in his attempt to establish a satisfactory relationship with the surrounding world of objects. When the attempt fails, his pronouncements begin to disintegrate into nonsense.

The Kaspar who reappears after the interval is not quite the same character: he is wearing a different mask, with a contented expression on it and, as he speaks through the down-stage microphone, his voice begins to sound like those of the speakers. In very short lines, some of which rhyme, he talks about phases of development. He used to feel as though objects were interrogating him. He felt lost among them, confused. The pain of falling into the world, he says, drove a wedge between him and objects. But now he begins, optimistically, to formulate rules, while the other Kaspars try to sabotage what he is saying by making disorderly noises – stylised sobbing, giggling, imitations of the wind, grumbling, croaking, lamenting, falsetto singing, hooting, laughter, warbling, singing, shouting, a single scream. In one sequence he prescribes social rules:

> Everyone must concern himself about other people.
> Everyone must come to table with his hair combed . . .
> Everyone must cut his fingernails.

The heckling from behind him becomes more obstreperous. The other Kaspars clear their throats, groan, twitter. Even the off-stage voices enter into the game of baiting him, joining in, canon-fashion, when he breaks into song. They do not sing words but hum, screech, yodel. The Kaspars produce nailfiles to create distracting noises.

Though the rudimentary conflict cannot fail to make an impact, the introduction of rhyme and song would be almost incomprehensible if it were not for the notes Handke provides under the heading 'Kaspar's 16 phases'. Each phase is represented by a question. For the twelfth phase it is 'Can rhyming sentences bring Kaspar to the point of making a rhyme out of the objects of the sentences?' The fourteenth question is 'Can Kaspar, by applying unprejudiced sentences to his old, prejudiced sentences, correct the inversion in those sentences?' The fifteenth is 'With an inverted world of sentences can Kaspar at least maintain his ground against inverted sentences about the world? Or: by inverting inverted sentences, can he at least avoid the false appearance of rightness?'

It is this last formulation which makes it most obvious that Handke is using Kaspar as an embodiment of his own dilemma. Like Beckett in *Eleuthéria* and Ionesco in *Jacques, Rhinocéros* and most of his other plays, Handke is attacking the language of conformism without having anything but negative proposals to

make. Here too Handke's position is similar to the one Wittgenstein adopts in his *Tractatus*. The famous final sentence, 'What we
cannot speak about we must pass over in silence', is preceded by
'My propositions serve as elucidations in the following way: anyone who understands me eventually recognizes them as nonsensical, when he has used them – as steps – to climb up beyond
them. (He must, so to speak, throw away the ladder after he has
climbed up it.)' Handke, too, claims that he can help people to see
the world more clearly. His aim, he has said, is 'to make myself
and other people more attentive, more sensitive, alert and precise'.[7]
But while *Kaspar* arguably alerts the audience to ways in which
language is conditioning consciousness, the theatrical failure of
the second act must be computed against the achievement. After
being bewildered by the rhyming and singing, the audience is
enervated by the variety of sounds produced by the rival Kaspars,
who go on trying to obstruct Kaspar's long monologue by singing, scraping nail-files noisily against brown-paper parcels,
barking, squealing, laughing and giggling. They succeed in
making Kaspar forget what he has said, but while it was clear in
the first act that the voices represented societal pressures, it is not
at all clear what the obstruction represents. Is it, as one critic
suggests, his repressed spontaneity struggling to be felt?[8] Handke
is forced back into giving Kaspar a long monologue to explain
what has been going on. But this fails too, partly because it contains too much information for the audience to digest.

Nor is the final collapse into nonsense as compelling as the
comparable climax in *La Cantatrice chauve*. Having shown interaction and communication of a sort, Ionesco can develop it into
disintegration: having dramatised only indoctrination and
obstruction, Handke can present Kaspar's loss of faith in words
only by means of statement and fragmentation of monologue.
Kaspar finally tells us that he is only goats and monkeys.

In the next one-act play *Das Mündel will Vormund sein* (*My Foot
My Tutor*,[9] produced 1969), there is a great deal of interaction
between the two characters, but not a word is spoken, though the
play lasts more than an hour. With his distrust of language and his
strongly reductive instincts, Handke proves that action can be
developed and theatrical tension sustained without dialogue.

Again the characters are masked and anonymous. The relationship between them is not developed in terms of personal psychology; it is a generalised relationship between a man in a position of authority and his younger dependant.

Though the silence and the depersonalisation are highly anti-traditional, the play proves they can be conducive to extreme theatricality and it is remarkable that a man with no training in mime or theatre – Handke studied Law for four years at the University of Graz in his native Austria – should have developed such a keen eye for the observation of human movement, and such an extraordinary sensitivity for the theatrically telling gesture. Many of the effects produced in *Das Mündel will Vormund sein* are effects that might well have been produced – unrepeatably – in an actors' improvisation. Handke conjures them out of his visual imagination, choreographs them with immaculate precision in a script which consists entirely of stage directions, and creates a satisfying play by structuring them into a sequence of interrelated incidents separated by blackouts. The game of action and response is fascinating to watch.

The ward: stands up; stands there.

The guardian runs: the ward begins to walk.

The guardian jumps up and down: the ward begins . . .

The ward climbs up on a chair and now stands on the chair: the ward does not jump but remains standing; stands.

The guardian climbs on the table: the ward climbs on the chair.

The guardian places the other chair on the table and climbs on to the chair on the table: the ward – how could it be otherwise? – climbs on to the table.

The guardian holds on to a dangling rope and suspends himself: the ward climbs on to the chair on the table . . .

The guardian lets go. He lands with bent knees; straightens himself slowly up to his full height.

The ward: quickly clambers down from the chair on to the table, from the table to the other chair, from this chair to the floor, at the same time lifting the first chair off the table, putting it back in its place and quickly squatting down . . .

The guardian slowly squats down.

The ward: sits on the floor.
The guardian: also sits, slowly.
The ward: scarcely has the guardian sat when he lies down quickly on the floor, on his back.

Handke seems to be widening the theatre's vocabulary by removing words from it. In Beckett's two *Actes sans paroles* the only relationships of the protagonist were with props and stage machinery, but this is unquestionably dialogue, and the impossibility of seeing any change of expression on the men's faces makes their actions seem all the more expressive. We lose sight of such questions as whether the ward, exerting himself to remain on a lower level, is hoping for love or trying to avoid punishment, and whether there is any element of playfulness or irony in the initiatives that the guardian takes. Drama is aspiring to the condition of semi-abstract painting.

For the first time in a Handke play there is a set. It represents the façade of a farmhouse with a view of a beetroot field on one side and a corn field on the other, but the corn field backdrop consists of small movable parts, and the guardian makes his first entrance by walking through it. This indication of contempt for theatrical illusion is not the only piece of audience-provocation. There is a protracted period of inaction at the beginning of the play, when the ward eats an apple, unobserved at first, later watched by the guardian. And there are other anti-theatre jokes, as when the guardian lights an oil-lamp and the whole acting area becomes disproportionately brighter. Handke seems to be critical not only of theatrical conventions but of the theatre's more facile methods of raising laughter. He is aware that an audience is liable to find it amusing when a man cuts his toenails on stage. He specifies that the guardian must cut his toenails slowly and that the sequence must be sufficiently prolonged for it to become unfunny.

Not that Handke contents himself with parodying the overfamiliar and the over-facile; he is also capable of producing theatrical effects that are highly original. The most memorable of these comes at the climax of the crockery-throwing sequence, and it is characteristic of his constructional skill that this sequence is placed shortly after the burr-throwing. While the guardian, in a series of movements that will remind us of a schoolmaster, keeps turning his back on the ward to write in chalk on the door, the ward throws burrs, which stick to the guardian's shirt, but the scenario insists that the actor must express nothing by the way he throws them. Later, when the guardian grabs the ward's shoulder, the action must not be violent enough to express anything, and when he turns the ward around and around, we should not be aware of what either of them is feeling. Both behave as if they were thinking of something else. But at the end it will be obvious that the ward is giddy, and when the guardian starts to throw bottles, plates and glasses to him, he is unable to catch them. Some of them smash as they fall to the floor. When, unexpectedly, he succeeds in catching one, the lights black out quickly. The noise of smashing glass and crockery has been all the more enervating because most of the previous action has gone on in silence, broken only by the background music – a track from a record by Country Joe and the Fish. The noise emphasises the bullying; the ward's final success is very welcome.

From his successful experiment in muteness, Handke proceeded to an unsuccessful experiment in inaudibility. Having proved that he could dispense with the spoken word in a complex hour-long play, he went on in *Quodlibet* (produced 1970) to test the assumption that, if the characters were speaking, it would be viable for most of their dialogue to remain unscripted and for much of it to be inaudible. The linguistic game in this play depends on tricking the audience into misinterpreting the fragmentary phrases it is allowed to hear. The actors have to improvise most of what they say, but the scenario makes detailed suggestions about how to fabricate misunderstandings. A series of partially audible sentences will incorporate the words 'gold-tooth', 'shower-room', 'electrified wire', 'platform', 'soap' and 'towers'. If there is any remaining doubt that the actors are discussing concentration camps, it is likely to be dispelled by the word 'ausschwitzen' (to sweat) which will probably be mis-heard as Auschwitz. The whole play could be taken as a jokey theatrical warning that any interpretation is liable to be a misinterpretation. But the play deprives us of nearly all the usual theatrical pleasures, leaving us in no mood for resisting the inclination to make as much as we can of the few scraps that are on offer. Handke has gone beyond reductionism into perversity.

The curtain goes up on an empty stage. The characters who drift on are what Handke calls figures of world theatre – a uniformed general, a bishop in vestments, a university chancellor, a Knight Hospitaller, a cadet with peaked cap and ceremonial belt, a Chicago gangster in a double-breasted suit, a politician with two armed CIA bodyguards, a pair of ballroom dancers, a lady in evening dress with a fan, another lady with a poodle on a lead. As in the *Sprechstücke*, the script does not specify who is to say what, but it does make suggestions for dealing with the hostility that a mainly inaudible performance is liable to provoke. Hecklers can be answered with quips like 'Shouting is a sign of having nothing to say', 'No-one has taught him that it's rude to interrupt', 'You don't prove you're in the right just by having dirty fingernails'.

More than most dramatists, Handke depends visibly, in every play he writes, on the whole of his previous work. His second full-length play *Der Ritt über dem Bodensee* (*The Ride across Lake Constance*, produced 1971) was conceived as a continuation to *Kaspar*. In an Author's Note, he says that his original aim was twofold: to portray the forms of human behaviour prevalent in our society by observing such haphazard phenomena as loving, working, buying and selling; and to measure them against their theatrical counterparts which are no less haphazard and no more immune to the economic forces of an oppressive society. The conception of this new full-length play preceded the writing of *Das Mündel will Vormund sein*, which brought postures into close-up by abstracting action from narrative context. Highlighting the artificiality of theatrical performance, Handke also highlighted the element of performance in everyday behaviour. By the time he came to start writing *Der Ritt*, he needed, as he says, to move further away from his original conception than in any of his other plays, and it is proportionately less didactic. But he applies the microscope to elements of theatricality in everyday behaviour, and instead of teasing the audience, as in *Quodlibet*, by courting misinterpretation, he makes the actors misinterpret each other and tease each other with actions and questions that are liable to be misunderstood. The two hours of continuous action involve eight people, without telling a story, and without using blackouts (as he did in *Kaspar* and in *Das Mündel*) to separate the sequences. In fact, discontinuity becomes one of the themes. We see the actors having to cope with it without being able to stop. As in the other plays, the fact of performance is in focus.

The actors are required to be and to play themselves; but, in the script, to avoid calling them by numbers or letters, he gives them the names of well-known actors: Emil Jannings, Heinrich George, Elisabeth Bergner, Erich von Stroheim, Henny Porten, the Kessler twins. The famous names probably helped him, during the process of writing, to feel estranged from the characters he was creating, and in so far as the play is still didactic, its intention is to introduce a wedge of estrangement between us and remarks, reactions, polite answers, stock responses in social behaviour we normally take for granted. It is by no means a Brechtian play, but it applies a lesson he learned from Brecht. The Brechtian model of contradictions, he says, exposes the whole of reality as artificial. Its functioning, which most people take to be natural, is revealed as subject to changes imposed by human agency. It is possible, therefore, that further changes can be made, and that further changes are desirable.

Handke's title refers to a legend about a traveller who rides his horse over a frozen lake in the belief that he has not yet come to it, only to die of fright when he learns of the danger he has survived. The implication is that we all depend for our survival on ignoring the fragility of our systems – language, logic, love and manners. *Der Ritt über dem Bodensee* is a comedy of manners in which the manners are plucked away from situation. In most plays behaviour is conditioned by situation; in this play the fluid series of situations is created only to illustrate social behaviour. But the fluidity is dreamlike, which reinforces the suggestion that we are all behaving like sleepwalkers. It is dangerous to let us go on sleeping, but would it be more dangerous still to wake us up?

In Handke's 1972 novel *Der kurze Brief zum langen Abschied* (*Short Letter, Long Farewell*) the narrator reminisces about the boarding schools which cut him off almost completely from the outside world. There were so many vetoes that he was alerted to

possibilities of experience he might never otherwise have discovered. And because the prohibitions formed a system, he was
later able to enjoy the sinful experiences systematically. Or at least
anti-systematically. But how was it possible for those without a
system to avoid the confusion that would have led to either
suicide or madness? If the reminiscences are partly autobiographical, it could be said that Handke's experiences as a law
student must have extended his negative experiences, as he became
hypothetically aware of innumerable possibilities of crime, innumerable possibilities of punishment. He has described how he
was affected by reading about executions under martial law. 'The
consequentiality of the sentences, which, basically were each con-
ditional clauses for a concrete imaginable reality, that is, usable,
if the conditions occurred in reality, seemed to me extremely
sinister and oppressive. The abstract sentences, which did not tell
the story of any specific death, nevertheless pointed to a new
possibility of looking at death.'[10]

The theatrical tension in *Der Ritt über dem Bodensee* depends
neither on plot nor merely, as in the *Sprechstücke*, on a sequence of
sentences, but on a sequence in which sentences, actions, poses,
silences, misinterpretations are equally important.

In *Kurze Brief* the writer-narrator considers the possibility of
introducing a character who would be the anti-type of the
raisonneur. Instead of holding the narrative together with understanding comments, he would be inaccurate in all his predictions,
absurd in all his interpretations. There is no such anti-*raisonneur* in
Der Ritt, but all the characters perform this function for each
other. Some of the misinterpretations are extremely minor.
Jannings points to the cigar box wanting George to pick it up;
George inspects it, thinking he is being asked to look at something on the box. A pause in the middle of a sentence makes it
seem to mean something different from what it is intended to
mean. Later, misinterpretation will be made into a game, a com-
petition in which each of the five main characters can score points
over the others. The technique of *Das Mündel* is developed into
something much more complex, with more characters competing
and more ways in which superiority can be won, but again the
progression is abstract, and again, though there are no blackouts,

the action is divided into short sequences. But the games are much more sophisticated. The characters play at domination and subservience, which is not to say that success or failure in the game has no effect on the balance of power between them. They play at refusing to interpret:

HENNY PORTEN: Someone keeps looking round while he's walking along: has he got a bad conscience?

ELISABETH BERGNER: No, he just keeps looking round.

Which is not to say that no inferences are being drawn by the other characters or by the audience about the behaviour of these two at this instant.

Not that there is any continuity or consistency in their behaviour. Inference can be valid only for the moment. One disadvantage the play has over *Das Mündel* is that inevitably a certain amount of commentary and analysis is built into the dialogue; with silent action, any interpreting we did was entirely at our own risk. One advantage *Der Ritt* has over *Kaspar* is that it is generally more playful, while devices such as having the characters break into song are made to work in a more comic vein. But sometimes the playfulness is sacrificed in favour of the compulsion to make analytical statements about oppressive human behaviour:

HEINRICH GEORGE: Why do they do that? Why do they listen to you? . . .

EMIL JANNINGS: Because it's natural to them. They did it once without my saying anything, either when they were half asleep or because it just happened. Then I said it, and they did it again. Then they asked me: 'May I do that for you?' And I said: 'You should!' From then on, they did it without my needing to say anything. It had come to seem natural . . . People began to have dealings with each other, and it became the practice . . . an order emerged, and to continue in their dealings with each other, they made this order explicit, formulated it. . . . In the same way that trains have to obey a timetable, to obviate disorder, you must obey me.

This provides the cue for one of several Genet-esque passages. The speech ends with Jannings's boast that he thinks about

women in the categories of *hors d'oeuvre* and main dish. Talking
as if by rote, Henny asks whether she was good. Are her knees too
bony? Is she too heavy? Are her breasts too small? Does he think
she's too fat? 'You see,' says Jannings, 'she uses the same categories one thinks of her in.'

A great deal of the dialogue consists of stories the characters tell
each other, mostly about trivial or trivial-seeming events. When
the stories invite illustration in the form of action, the transition
into game-playing is easy. But unlike Genet's game-playing,
Handke's has nothing to do with identity. Even when Heinrich
George puts on Emil Jannings's rings, it is not in order to play at
being Emil Jannings, it is to savour the idea of owning them,
and this provokes a discussion of whether there is such a thing as a
'born owner'. If life is a game, he suggests, a born winner must be
a born owner. Sometimes Handke seems to be primarily interested in the analytical discussion, sometimes in the gestures,
movements, verbal reactions he can isolate for examination
under the microscope.

He makes his five main characters highly articulate, highly
sensitive and highly nervous. Though the scraps of behaviour he
isolates for investigation are all relevant to normal everyday life,
the atmosphere comes to seem rarefied and dreamlike, so that an
abrupt change of emotional temperature is produced by the
breezy irruption of the two girls Handke designates as the
Kessler twins. They are not representatives of wakefulness, or
orderliness or politeness or cheerfulness, but by presenting an
appearance of living in accordance with a different set of rules from
the others they give indications of a negative definition of themselves, rather as the dead do *vis-à-vis* the living in Genet's *Les
Paravents*. In the absence of norms, a negative definition is the best
available, but what is most valuable in what the play has to
offer is not definitions, analyses or warnings, but fragments of
experience which can be appreciated in their full flavour
because they are being isolated. Abstraction is making them
more concrete.

On the surface, at least, Handke's next play *Die Unvernünftigen
sterben aus* (*The Unintelligent Ones are Dying Out*[11], produced 1974)
is more conventional than any of his previous work. It tells a

coherent story, and though unrealistic elements will be introduced into the décor, the stage represents a specific locale, a room belonging to a business tycoon, Hermann Quitt. What would immediately seem odd to the theatregoer with no experience of Handke's previous work is the detail in which characters analyse their feelings:

> I saw my wife in her dressing-gown and her lacquered toes and felt suddenly lonely. It was such objective loneliness that I can quite easily talk about it. It relieved me, I disintegrated, melted into it . . . Everything turned its back on me, softly harmonious. While shitting I heard my sounds as if a stranger was making them in an adjacent cubicle.

But there is also a plot, a consistency in the characters, and a progression of changing relationships between them. Not that we are ever allowed to forget that what we are watching is a play. There may be nothing anti-illusionistic in the first reminder about the theatricality of everyday life: Quitt complains to his assistant, Hans, that he is playing his daily part too much as if he had learnt it by heart. But when Hans, left alone on stage, goes on talking, it is clear that we are not watching a realistic play.

The richness of the texture shows how much Handke has gained from his experimental experience. He writes with precision, economy and the sort of relaxation an actor needs to preserve an appearance of spontaneity and effortlessness while taking considerable risks. Even in this, the least experimental of his plays, Handke is constantly testing his own ability to sustain tension and continuity while interpolating analytical discussions about the themes that preoccupy him – the dangers of interpretation, for instance, or contemporary alienation from the nineteenth-century view of nature. Sometimes the discussion is too protracted, but the tension slackens only briefly.

The least successful sequence is the boardroom sequence, when a minority shareholder, Kilb, tries to sabotage the discussion between Quitt and three rival businessmen who are making a pact with him about future collaboration. The dialogue deteriorates into a slanging match, punctuated by such gestures as sticking the tongue out, but there is a startlingly violent climax. A woman is stripped to the waist, champagne glasses are smashed, Quitt spits into the face of everyone present, attacks Kilb with a fragment of glass and finally, gripping him in a headlock, butts his head against everybody else. What Handke has learnt from *Der Ritt* is the possibility of substituting a montage of disconnected speeches and actions for a facsimile of organic development. Climaxes no longer have to grow plausibly out of what preceded them. Quitt's actions are no less expressive for the improbability that a man of his type would behave in this way under this degree of provocation.

Handke's treatment of Quitt's relationships with Paula and with his wife is similarly jerky, but the jerks are themselves expressive. This is not how people behave, but it depicts behaviour in a revealingly unrealistic way. In the second act, the set no longer looks like a room, but the unrealistic changes prepare us for the developments in the action. The punch-bag, which Quitt was belabouring when the lights went up on Act One, has been replaced by a huge balloon which is slowly losing air. The sofa and armchairs have been replaced by a large block of ice, which is visibly melting. There is a glass trough with dough rising in it, and a large boulder with phrases which appear and fade away. 'Our greatest sin – the impatience of concepts' and 'The worst is over – The last hope'. The dialogue too goes on to present a premonition of holocaust which is sometimes reminiscent of Shaw's *Too True to Be Good*, though the quality of Handke's writing is vastly superior, and the focus is constantly shifting back to the theatre. Talking to Hans about the characters in a play he saw recently, Quitt says:

> With their apparently dehumanised way of carrying on, they wanted in reality to be as nice to each other as we spectators – who all live in a more human environment – have been for ages. They too want tenderness, marital life and so on – only they can't say so and that's why they rape and murder each other. These who live in sub-human conditions are the stage representatives of the last human beings.

Handke is patently writing about his own characters, who are far from inarticulate but resort to violence partly because they fail in all their attempts to articulate their emotions. This inability to put them into order is indistinguishable from the inability to put them into words. And their most expressive moments occur when, transported by rage, they find themselves inarticulate, as von Wullnow does after Quitt has betrayed the agreement he made with the cartel of businessmen:

> Now I'm really not going to say anything else. I'll just stick my finger into my throat in front of you. (*Does so, and and goes, but comes straight back.*) What's more, I was devoted to you. (*Goes, and comes back.*) You with your frog's body. (*He goes and comes back.*) My spit is too good for you. At most I'd spit from the back of my mouth to the front. (*Does so and goes, comes back, out of control, pulls a fearful grimace and makes a final exit.*)

Where Handke sometimes fails is in dovetailing serio-comic effects like this, which do not depend primarily on words, with the long speeches. Another businessman, Koerber-Kent, has a long tirade: as a listing of the cartel's grievances against Quitt, it is relevant to the plot, and, as a listing of Handke's grievances against commercial malpractice, it is relevant to the theme, but it still fails to sit comfortably in its context. The failure is one of style, but it may be only a temporary failure: if Handke goes on writing plays that tell stories, he may find better means of juxtaposing monologues with sequences in which words count for very little.

The rift in the play is most obvious in the second half of the second act, where, as so often in Genet's plays, death exerts a strong tidal pull on both monologues and action. Koerber-Kent's speech about the painter who sketched his dying wife is grafted only perfunctorily into the developing action, and some of the subsequent talk about death is only partially justified by the threats – veiled at first, overt later – that Lutz and Koerber-Kent are making against Quitt's life.

The love that Paula Tax professes to feel for him is shown to be potentially no less lethal. When verbal sparring flares into action, she tries to choke him, and he submits for a while before shaking her off. When she then wants to take his head in her hands, he kicks her off balance, but Handke is not merely showing how hatred is intertwined with the love or lust between them: he also shows how their desire for each other exists only in the interstices of business relationships.

> QUITT: The way your eyeballs are jerking about! And the spittle in your mouth will overflow in a minute. (*He turns away. Pause.*)
> PAULA: I'm going now. It's no use. I'll sell then.
> QUITT (*scrutinising her*): And I'll decide about the fine print.
> PAULA: Just promise me not to tidy up after me the moment I'm gone.
> QUITT: Buy yourself a hat. It's comforting.
> PAULA: Now I know why I like you. It's so nice to think about something else when you're talking.

Effective though exchanges like this are, there is a certain arbitrariness about them, as there is about the development of the action. If Handke goes on writing narrative drama, one of the main technical problems he will have to resolve is the relationship of discontinuity to organic development. Having written so many abstract plays, he is uncertain how much nonsequentiality is admissible to the narrative and logic of a play like *Die Unvernünftigen sterben aus*. Though the final climax does not altogether misfire, it is not altogether successful, partly because the jerks, tangents, irrelevances and non-sequiturs are more effective separately than cumulatively, while moments of extreme violence seem either arbitrary or over-prepared in an over-verbal way. That the killing of Kilb is unmotivated is part of the point, but the fact that his death is quite unnecessary to Quitt makes it almost unnecessary to the action; the suicide of Quitt provides the final resolution to the theme which has been almost over-developed in his monologues – the feeling that he no longer has anything to do with his face, that the outer layers of his self are dead and that there is only a feeble twitching in the innermost centre, that he feels like a sole survivor, that he feels a need to stutter, instead of talking fluently.

After he has killed himself by running his head against the rock, a fruit crate hurtles on to the stage, and a long grey carpet rolls out from behind the rock, with snakes writhing on it, as they are in the fruit crate. The gear-change into Surrealism is only partly prepared by the anti-realistic elements in the décor. The image is undeniably powerful; the question is whether the powerful theatrical effects are too disparate.

6 Pinter and Stoppard

In the work of Beckett, Ionesco, Genet and Handke, strong anti-theatre impulses have clashed with strong theatrical instincts, generating a tension which has produced highly original writing. But for their aversion towards the existing theatre, they would not have written for it so well. Their ideas and innovations have diverted the mainstream of Western drama, which means that they have influenced the work of playwrights totally devoid of anti-theatre impulses. Pinter, for instance, was earning his living as an actor before he became a playwright, and Stoppard feels more committed to the 'showbiz' element in theatre than to the literary element. But in examining the work of Pinter, Stoppard, Albee and Sam Shepard, it will be important to analyse not only the flow of energy that gives life to their work, but the relationships between its separate surges. Reductionism is, on the whole, less important in their plays than in those of our first four playwrights, and – far from functioning only negatively – it helps to provide a unity of drive and a framework of discipline.

I would be oversimplifying my thesis if I said that only an artistic revolutionary – with his painful mixture of love for the medium and hatred for the way it has been used – has the stamina to generate the kind of creative drive that leads to a continuous flow of first-class work, but in the work of Pinter and Albee it is worth analysing the reasons for certain discontinuities within individual plays and in the progression from play to play. Diagnosis of motive for writing must always be tentative: we have only the finished result to judge by. But some defects (such as mannerism and emotional self-indulgence) seem to result from inadequacy in the motive, and often there seems to be a discontinuity between the motive for starting it and the motive for completing it, as in Pinter's *No Man's Land*.

Harold Pinter was trained as an actor, and in 1957, when he wrote his first play, he was working in weekly repertory. He had discovered the novels of Samuel Beckett in 1949, when an extract from *Watt* was published in *Irish Writing*. Enthused, Pinter went on to steal a copy of *Murphy* from Bermondsey Public Library, and, when *Watt* was published in 1953, he read the whole book. The second section contains the account of the piano tuners' visit to Mr Knott's house. Instead of ending when the two men leave, the event goes on reverberating in Watt's mind, unfolding endlessly, but becoming more and more indefinite as 'it developed a purely plastic content, and gradually lost, in the nice processes of its light, its sound, its impacts and its rhythm, all meaning, even the most literal . . . The incident ceased so rapidly to have even the paltry significance of two men, come to tune a piano, and tuning it, and exchanging a few words, as men will do, and going, that this seemed rather to belong to some story heard long before, an instant in the life of another, ill-told, ill-heard, and more than half forgotten.'

It would be difficult to prove that Beckett's influence on Pinter has been more than catalytic, but the first three plays – *The Room* (written 1957; produced at Bristol University 1957, professionally produced 1960), *The Birthday Party* (written 1957; produced 1958) and *The Dumb Waiter* (written 1957; produced in Germany 1959, in England 1960) – are strikingly insistent in their refusal to define or specify. Beckett's characters are vague about time and place, but the vagueness is apparently involuntary. They seem genuinely unable to provide each other with information about their present situation or about recent events in their experience or current events in the world outside. Pinter's characters are equally vague and uncommunicative, but it does not always seem that ignorance is their reason for withholding information. They tend to be less benevolent, more competitive, aggressive, perverse. They are liable to provide misleading information for the sake of causing confusion and anxiety, disturbing the audience at the same time as they disturb each other. Pinter constantly violates the theatrical convention by which audiences can assume that characters are truthful unless clear indications are given to the contrary. In Pirandello's plays, when the testimony of the characters cannot be resolved into a coherent situation, the inconsistencies are always brought into the foreground; in Pinter's work the contradictions are casual and incidental. It is taken for granted that the characters are unreliable witnesses, even of their own behaviour. They are forgetful or dishonest about the past, vague or secretive about their intentions, ignorant or biased about their motivations. Their behaviour is liable to be inconsistent both with their explanations of it and in itself.

In *The Birthday Party* it is apparent that Stanley is not telling the truth either about his past career as a pianist or about his relationship with his father. But it is pointless to speculate (as we need to in Pirandello's plays) about how the facts are being distorted. In a Pinter play there are no offstage facts: nothing is either true or false except what happens in front of us. Goldberg is the incarnation of his dialogue and his actions. Some of his remarks may remind us of people we have met, but he is not realistically characterised. There is no attempt to cultivate the illusion that his life began before his first entrance and went on after his final exit. The words, the rhythms and the pauses tell the actor all he needs to know about how to play the part, but the role would present almost insuperable problems to a Method actor in the habit of constructing an imaginary biography for each character he plays. When Goldberg is talking about his past, it is not even necessary for the actor to make up his mind how much 'truth' there is in what he says, while the audience, knowing virtually nothing about the man, will be unable to picture him in any other situations than the ones it sees him in. He is a character in a play who is not being presented as anything more than a character in a play. The same could be said of McCann, but not of Meg and Petey, though their solidity is partly undermined by the presence of non-realistic characters. Stanley starts as realistic but the pressure exerted on him by Goldberg and McCann tends to negate his reality. On his final appearance, he is, for the first time, neatly dressed, but the clothes seem to contain nothing. He has become a figure, a cipher, a sign that does not signify.

To interpret stage events is to impose significance. Goldberg and McCann have been interpreted as representatives of society's conformist pressures, brainwashing Stanley into respectability and, as midwives, forcing him out of his pre-natal lethargy. For Martin Esslin, Stanley is 'the *artist* whom society claims back from a comfortable, bohemian "opt-out" existence', though he also suggests that at the end, Goldberg's black car could 'represent a hearse, while Stanley's correct dress, his speechlessness, and his blindness would be an image of him laid out and lying in state as a corpse'.[1] So the play's interpreters are not in agreement about whether the final images represent birth or death: the fallacy is in the assumption that a play must have a meaning which can be translated into an expository summary. But often the kernel of what a playwright is trying to articulate derives primarily from the residue of an experience or of a mixture of experiences, one of which may be the experience of seeing or reading another play. The reduction of Stanley to speechlessness echoes the final climax of Ionesco's *Les Chaises* (1952) in which the Orator turns out to be incapable of uttering anything more than incoherent sounds. Whether Pinter had Ionesco's scene in mind or not, the final climax of *The Birthday Party* should not be interpreted as if Stanley's speechlessness were something to be explained in terms of events that have caused it. The sequence makes a strong theatrical effect which is to be appreciated and judged in relation to the series of theatrical effects which have preceded it.

Pinter has made good use of the ideas he has taken over from

Beckett and Ionesco, but the anti-theatre impulse that is basic to their work is missing from his, which is suffused with an actor's instinct for theatrical effect. Acting in plays about murder and detection in weekly repertory companies at Bournemouth, Torquay, Worthing and Colchester, he had learned that mystification and suspense are powerful weapons, that audiences have a masochistic love of being kept in ignorance, that the puzzle matters infinitely more than the solution. The more unreliable characters seem, the more they push us into playing the game of 'True or false?' with every piece of evidence that they produce. If *Waiting for Godot* and *Endgame* consist partly of games that the characters play with each other, Pinter's plays consist partly of teasing games he plays with us. Watching *The Collection*, for instance, we may go on reminding ourselves that there is no point in trying to solve the problem of whether Bill and Stella slept together in Leeds, that there is no such thing as offstage facts, that in a play, as in a novel, statements about the past are not verifiable. But, as in reading a thriller, we can't help making efforts to evaluate each piece of testimony as if it were either true or false. However, it is obvious enough that what matters are the present insecurities of Stella's husband and of the man who lives with Bill, and that Stella and Bill are more interested in their partners' suspicions than in their memories of what happened in Leeds. Sadistically, they both add to the mystification by producing contradictory and self-contradictory versions of the past, but as they tease and tantalise both partners and rivals with truths, half-truths and fictions, we are teased and tantalised too. Unlike an ordinary thriller, though, the play ends without solving the mystery. Unlike Beckett, Pinter usually works his theatrical action towards a major climax, but, as in Beckett, the central questions remain unanswered.

In Beckett's plays the stage setting is invariably subject to reductionist simplification and generalisation – a low mound with one tree, an almost unfurnished room with windows where the eyes would be if the room were a head, three unlocalised urns. The décor never reminds us of a place we have seen, whereas in Pinter's earlier plays the setting is nearly always a realistic representation of a room, even if we are to be left uncomfortably uncertain about the size of the house and whereabouts in it the

room is. The living-room of the seaside boarding house in
The Birthday Party and the junk-filled room in *The Caretaker* may
remind us of rooms we have seen, but the appearance of specific
actuality is only superficially reassuring. In *The Room*, Rose's fear
that she may be evicted is exacerbated by contradictory information about who the landlord is and how many storeys there are in
the house. In *The Dumb Waiter* Gus and Ben do not know who is
operating the food-lift in the house they had thought was empty;
in *The Caretaker* Davies does not know whether the house belongs
to Mick or Aston.

There may be a connection between these sources of terror and
a neurasthenic assumption voiced in *The Dwarfs*, which was
started as a novel, then produced as a radio play in 1960 and as a
stage play in 1963. Objects, says Len, cannot be counted on to
retain the same shape.

> The rooms we live in . . . open and shut. (*Pause.*) Can't you see?
> They change shape at their own will. I wouldn't grumble if
> only they would keep to some consistency. But they don't.
> And I can't tell the limits, the boundaries, which I've been led
> to believe are natural. I'm all for the natural behaviour of
> rooms, doors, staircases, the lot. But I can't rely on them.
> When, for example, I look through a train window, at night,
> and see the yellow lights, very clearly, I can see what they are,
> and I see that they're still . . . insofar as the earth itself is still,
> which of course it isn't. The point is, in a nutshell, that I can
> only appreciate such facts when I'm moving. When I'm still,
> nothing around me follows a natural course of conduct. I'm
> not saying I'm any criterion, I wouldn't say that. After all,
> when I'm on that train I'm not really moving at all. That's
> obvious. I'm in the corner seat. I'm still. I am perhaps being
> moved, but I do not move. Neither do the yellow lights.

The character's paranoia could be called Einsteinian. Following
Proust and Beckett, Pinter works from a relativistic premiss. It
does not, finally, matter whether it is the observer who is constantly shifting his position or the object which is constantly
changing its appearance. Nothing, in either event, is stable, and it
could be said of Pinter (as it has been of Stoppard) that it is the

plurality of contexts which concerns him: 'ambiguities are just
places where contexts join.'[2] Both playwrights create a theatrical
equivalent of the space-time continuum; their representation of
reality 'exists to be ungraspable, its creator having discovered that
no readily appreciable scheme can possibly be adequate to the
complexity of experience'.[3]

But whereas Stoppard usually concerns himself only obliquely
and comically with the uncertainties of the individual psyche,
Pinter's early plays are full of young men who have not succeeded
in coming to sexual maturity. In return for the security of shelter
within the household, they resentfully sacrifice their independence
on the altar of a nagging matriarch. In some of the plays, possession of a room is presented as if it were an alternative to possession
of a woman and as if the hero were being denied free choice
between the alternatives. *Kullus* (1949), one of Pinter's earliest
published works, is a fragment of Beckettian dialogue which
anticipates Pinter's 1967 television play *The Basement* (staged 1970)
in suggesting that it is possible for the central character to be in
possession of either the room or the girl but never of both. Bringing a woman into the room, Kullus appropriates it, settling her
into the bed. She is subsequently quite amiable towards the
narrator, but he fails to seize his opportunity of moving back in,
taking possession of her at the same time. In *The Basement*, Law,
losing his room to Stott, at least acquires Stott's girl. In *The
Birthday Party* Stanley appears to be more interested in continuing
his partly filial relationship with the landlady of the squalid boarding house than in having an affair with Lulu, a girl of about his
own age. He lets himself be worsted by an older man, Goldberg,
who both takes the girl and puts an end to Stanley's long stay in the
boarding house. In *A Night Out* (broadcast and televised 1960;
staged 1961) Albert rebels against his nagging mother to seek
comfort with a prostitute, who turns out to be just as tiresomely
fussy and just as overbearing. In *Night School* (televised 1960)
Walter returns from a stretch of imprisonment to the house of his
two aunts, who have let his room to a girl. Missing his opportunity to take possession of it and her at the same time, he turns for
help to an older man, who, like Goldberg, gets the girl for himself.
Without exception, the women in these plays are presented nega-

tively, from the male viewpoint. Either they are exorbitantly talkative mother-figures, so overwhelmingly possessive that the man's sanity is in danger, or they are flirtatious poppets who can be possessed like objects. None of the young men in these plays ever arrives at self-confident stability, and the uncertainty affects the framework of the drama. Fluidity of character and relationships merges with the apparent fluidity of objects and houses, which ought to be solid.

In *Happy Days* and *Play* Beckett stabilises his characters by immobilising them, and in several of his plays, as in plays by Ionesco, Genet and Handke, there is a reductionist and abstractionist tendency to cut down on the free expression of the actor's personality. In Beckett's trilogy of novels the dwindling mobility of his narrators had its advantages. Their thought-processes were so slippery, their identity so volatile, that a firm base was needed. In his early plays he loved to paralyse characters in dustbins, urns, heaps of sand. Concealing part of the body was a first step towards erosion of facial individuality through heavy make-up or through concealing part of the face. Beckett has never used masks, but in *Play* he asks for the three faces to be 'so lost to age and aspect as to seem almost part of the urns'. In *Not I* we see nothing of the actress but her mouth. In the plays of Ionesco, Genet and Handke, reductionist and abstractionist inclinations tend similarly towards the depersonalisation of the actors, whether through grotesque make-ups (as in *Les Paravents*), through masks (as in *Jacques, Les Nègres, Kaspar* and *Das Mündel*) or through total concealment of the face (as with Leila in *Les Paravents*): drama approximating to puppet drama. Though Pinter never has recourse to any of these de-individualising stratagems, there is a sense in which Peter Hall – midwife at the birth of all his full-length plays since they co-directed *The Collection* – is quite right to say: 'all Pinter's characters have masks'.[4] What he means is that there is an unusually pronounced dichotomy between behaviour and emotion. Not that characters in the traditional Ibsenite play necessarily reveal all they are feeling. Hedda Gabler and Judge Brack, for instance, conceal more than they reveal in their scenes together, in which each is playing an elaborate game. But Beckett raised game-playing to a power it had never previously had in the theatre, and

Pinter's games depend more than Beckett's do on preserving a poker face. From *The Birthday Party* to *No Man's Land* (produced 1975) the plays contain sequences in which one speaker is implicitly asserting superiority over the other by taking the initiative in a blustering series of claims, some of which go beyond the frontier of plausibility. But the listener is usually in no position to call the speaker's bluff.

> GOLDBERG: All my life I've said the same. Play up, play up, and play the game. Honour thy father and thy mother. All along the line. Follow the line, the line, McCann, and you can't go wrong. What do you think, I'm a self-made man? No! I sat where I was told to sit. I kept my eye on the ball. School? Don't talk to me about school. Top in all subjects.
>
> (*The Birthday Party*)

> MICK: If you want more space, there's four more rooms along the landing ready to go. Bathroom, living-room, bedroom and nursery. You can have this as your study ... So what do you say? Eight hundred odd for this room or three thousand down for the whole upper storey. On the other hand, if you prefer to approach it in the long-term way I know an insurance firm in West Ham'll be pleased to handle the deal for you. No strings attached, open and above board, untarnished record; twenty per cent interest, fifty per cent deposit; down payments, back payments, family allowances, bonus schemes, remission of term for good behaviour, six months' lease, yearly examination of the archives, tea laid on, disposal of shares, benefit extension, compensation on cessation, comprehensive indemnity against Riot, Civil Commotion, Labour Disturbances, Storm, Tempest, Thunderbolt, Larceny or Cattle all subject to a daily check and double check.
>
> (*The Caretaker*)

> BILL: I'm expecting guests in a minute, you know. Cocktails. I'm standing for Parliament next season.
> JAMES: Come here.
> BILL: I'm going to be Minister for Home Affairs.
>
> (*The Collection*)

LENNY: Well, this lady was very insistent and started taking liberties with me down under this arch, liberties which by any criterion I couldn't be expected to tolerate, the facts being what they were, so I clumped her one. It was on my mind at the time to do away with her, you know, to kill her, and the fact is, that as killings go, it would have been a simple matter, nothing to it. Her chauffeur, who had located me for her, he'd popped round the corner to have a drink, which just left this lady and myself, you see, alone, standing underneath this arch, watching all the steamers steaming up, no one about, all quiet on the Western Front, and there she was up against this wall – well, just sliding down the wall, following the blow I'd given her.   (*The Homecoming*)

DEELEY: I had a great crew in Sicily. A marvellous cameraman. Irving Shultz. Best in the business. We took a pretty austere look at the women in black. The little old women in black. I wrote the film and directed it. My name is Orson Welles.
(*Old Times*)

As Peter Hall says, the actor often needs to adopt a tone which is disconnected from the character's emotions: 'If you really are feeling very heavy, it's almost axiomatic in Pinter that you play very light.' To reveal the heaviness would be to expose a vulnerability that might be exploited by one of the other players in the game.

The work in which subtext is most savagely at odds with text is *The Homecoming* (produced 1965). Its dialogue is full of insults, but the most dangerous threats are all made politely or even amiably, as at the ominous ending of Act One:

MAX: You want to kiss your old father? Want a cuddle with your old father?
TEDDY: Come on, then. (TEDDY *moves a step towards him.*) Come on. (*Pause.*)
MAX: You still love your old Dad, eh? (*They face each other.*)
TEDDY: Come on, Dad. I'm ready for the cuddle. (MAX *begins to chuckle, gurgling. He turns to the family and addresses them.*)
MAX: He still loves his father!

Though it is clear enough that neither of them means what he is saying, that each is threatening the other, the audience is not sure why they are challenging each other, or how battle can be joined. Later, when the family plans to set Ruth up as a prostitute, Teddy is careful not to seem proprietorial about his wife – having come back to sleep in the family home, he has lost her. Her reaction to the family's plan for her is equally guarded:

> TEDDY: Ruth ... the family have invited you to stay, for a little while longer. As a ... as a kind of guest. If you like the idea I don't mind. We can manage very easily at home ... until you come back.
> RUTH: How very nice of them. (*Pause.*)
> MAX: It's an offer from our heart.
> RUTH: It's very sweet of you.
> MAX: Listen ... it would be our pleasure.

Like the behaviour of the family, the setting is less realistic in *The Homecoming* than in the earlier plays. Written for the wide stage of the Aldwych Theatre, the action is set in a very large room, very sparsely furnished. Peter Hall said: 'The area they were fighting over, which was the father's chair and the sofa where the seduction takes place, and the rug in front, was an island in the middle of antiseptic cleanliness – that scrubbed lino, acres of it. And the journey from that island where the family fought each other, across to the sideboard to get the apple, was very perilous, and this was all quite deliberate – a few objects in space, and a feeling of absolute chilliness and hostility ... If the set for *The Homecoming* is a naturalistic representation of a house in North London, then the glass of water makes almost no impression, because it's one glass among many knick-knacks.' The glass of water provides the fulcrum for a non-realistic sexual confrontation between Lenny and his brother's wife at their first meeting:

> RUTH: If you take the glass ... I'll take you. (*Pause.*)
> LENNY: How about me taking the glass without you taking me?
> RUTH: Why don't I just take you?

Again, the masks are in place: the tone is divorced from the intention.

The Birthday Party and *The Dumb Waiter* are the most obviously Beckettian of Pinter's early plays, following the pattern of the novels *Molloy* and *Malone Dies* in showing two men, one with authority over the other, apparently working for an organisation, but without knowing much about it. In both novels and both plays the two men, on behalf of the organisation, are hunting down a third. In all four works, a good deal of the comedy hinges on the discrepancy between the gravity of the mission and the triviality of the incidental distraction.[5]

In *The Homecoming* there is relatively little evidence of Beckett's influence. *Play* appears to have inaugurated not only a new phase in Beckett's development – immobilising all three characters in urns and relegating all action to the past – but also a new phase in Pinter's. *Landscape* (broadcast 1968; staged 1969) and *Silence* (staged with it in a double bill) also immobilise the actors and relegate most of the action to the past. Like Beckett, Pinter is now repudiating the resources that the medium is putting at his disposal, approximating to the condition of radio drama. (Though *Landscape* was broadcast before being staged, it was written for the theatre.) In a March 1969 interview on BBC Television, Pinter said: 'I felt that after *The Homecoming* ... I couldn't any longer stay in the room with this bunch of people who opened doors and came in and went out.' In *Landscape* the two characters are placed not in urns but in the kitchen of a country house. Duff talks of Beth as 'you' but the text consists not so much of dialogue as of two interwoven monologues. The speakers are both more alive than the three characters in *Play* – they have a present and a future as well as a past; they have desires, needs, moods – but the action consists entirely of words and sounds. As in Handke's early work, more depends on the sequence of sentences than on sequential action. There is more of a story than in most of Handke's plays, but it is presented impressionistically as flotsam from the two characters' past relationship, washed up on the shores of their present consciousness. While *Landscape* has no movement in it, *Silence* has very little, and the characters are less often talking to each other than to themselves about themselves. The relationships they have had are not dramatised, only evoked by the words, as are the locales. The stage setting provides no more than a generalised background. The play is like a dramatic poem, spoken by three voices, in which the relationship between three styles is clearer and more important than the relationship between the three characters.

Without having written *Landscape* and *Silence*, Pinter could not have written *Old Times* (produced 1971), which explores new kinds of fluidity in and between the characters, new ways of circumventing the tiresome business of opening doors and coming in and going out. As the lights go up at the beginning on Kate and Deeley in their converted farmhouse, a third figure, Anna, is in the background, dimly lit. They talk about her as if she is not there, but when she comes downstage into the brighter light, it is clear that the movement does not signify an entrance. She has heard part of their conversation. There are also casual shifts in time, forwards into the period immediately after dinner, and twenty years backwards to the time when Kate and Anna were both secretaries, sharing a flat. Re-enactment of the past alternates with reminiscence about it, but though the experiences of all three seem to have overlapped, their memories are inconsistent and irreconcilable. In Deeley's mind memories of the girls seem to merge. Sometimes the two of them appear almost interchangeable. Anna seems, in some sense, to have wanted to *be* Kate, and (as in Genet's *Haute surveillance*) wearing another person's clothes represents an attempt at identification, but the two girls have conflicting memories about who took the initiative. 'She was pretending to be you at the time,' says Deeley to Kate. 'Did it pretty well.' The critics disagreed about whether Anna was 'actually' present in the room or just a presence in the memories of the other two. But a playwright can swing rapidly between two such alternatives or even have it both ways at the same time.

As a game in which the players try to outmanoeuvre each other, *Old Times* has some affinities with *Der Ritt über dem Bodensee* and *Die Unvernünftigen sterben aus*. Plays and gambits make their effect independently, without having to grow organically out of a situational context, and climaxes move jerkily into unexpected violence, though in *Old Times* the violence is all verbal. At the end,

Kate, in effect, kills Anna by talking about memories of her dead body.

Not that Handke has influenced Pinter: if anything, it is the younger playwright who is more likely to have been influenced. As early as *The Birthday Party* , with his actor's instinct for isolated theatrical effects, Pinter was separating actions from dialogue and cultivating climaxes that did not have either to grow organically out of situations or to be subject to logical explanation. As the lights go up on Act Two of *The Birthday Party*, McCann is tearing a sheet of newspaper into five equal strips. Stanley is watching, but they talk about other things until Stanley touches one of the strips and McCann tells him not to. Part of the sequence's impact depends on mystification, but the only answer to the question 'What does it mean?' is that the meaning is in the effect. Certainly the effect depends partly on what has been established about Stanley's anxiety and about McCann's commission to intimidate him. The newspaper-tearing may constitute a new phase in the relationship between the two men, but Pinter is not trying to make the development seem organic or autonomous.

In *No Man's Land*, the affinity with Handke is still more striking. There is a marked discontinuity between the sequences in which Hirst, a rich man of letters ensconced in a Hampstead mansion, and Spooner, a penurious poet, play a series of variations in the roles of host and guest, house-owner and visitor at pains not to outstay his welcome, or at least not to appear to. In one sequence Hirst seems not even to recognise the man he has been entertaining, and in another he greets him like an equal who has only just arrived: 'Charles, how nice of you to drop in.' As in *Old Times*, reminiscence becomes a weapon, each man using his own version of the past to oust the other's. The discrepancies go even further than they did in *Old Times*: there are contradictory indications about whether the two men have met before. At first it looks as though they haven't; later Hirst is claiming to have seduced Spooner's wife. As in *The Collection*, the offstage action can consolidate no reality, but we still cannot help being drawn into the 'True or false?' game as the two men duel with rival versions of the past.

.　　.　　.　　.　　.

The influence of Beckett is hardly less important in Tom Stoppard's work. Without *Waiting for Godot, Rosencrantz and Guildenstern Are Dead* (written 1964–5; produced by undergraduates
1966, by professionals 1967) could not have been conceived. The
main action is waiting: like Vladimir and Estragon, Rosencrantz
and Guildenstern have to fill the vacuum created by inaction. Each
pair of men is on stage for virtually the whole of the play's
duration. Vladimir and Estragon are waiting for Godot; Rosencrantz and Guildenstern have been under orders since a royal
messenger called them. Not being free to go away, they pass the
time by tossing coins or fabricating arguments or playing verbal
games. Both playwrights use enforced idleness as a trampoline for
conversational bounces: what Stoppard had learned from Beckett
was that it was possible to dispense with the old machinery for
generating suspense by means of plot, conflict and non-stop action.
As Stoppard said, *Waiting for Godot* 'redefined the minima of
theatrical validity'.[6] If the audience is persuaded into feeling a
modicum of sympathy for the characters, it can be entertained
quite sufficiently with a free-wheeling conversation, which can
even contain a certain amount of abstruse philosophical argument, provided that it doesn't continue for too long on one tack.
Nor does sympathy for the characters depend on knowledge
about their background. We know no more about Rosencrantz's
or Guildenstern's previous experience than we do about Vladimir's or Estragon's.

Hamlet is a Copernican play: the throne is as central to it as the
earth was to the current view of the universe. Stoppard's change
of perspective pushes the royal hero out to the periphery, centring
on two men who are more passive and more ordinary – more
nearly representative of the Common Man. While other playwrights were writing about working-class anti-heroes, and while
directors were casting working-class actors as noblemen, Stoppard found his own way of turning heroic tragedy inside out,
concentrating on two figures in whom Shakespeare had little
interest. Like Beckett, Genet and Handke – and like Shakespeare –
Stoppard draws attention to the theatricality of his play, using a
troupe of players as one of his pivots. As the leader of the troupe
says, 'We keep to our usual stuff, more or less, only inside out.

We do on stage the things that are supposed to happen off. Which is a kind of integrity, if you look on every exit being an entrance somewhere else.'

In *Hamlet* the actors who play Rosencrantz and Guildenstern have to spend most of the evening in their dressing-room, waiting for cues. In Stoppard's play, most of Shakespeare's *Hamlet* happens offstage in so far as it happens at all, and what happens onstage bears a strong resemblance to what the actors might have been doing in their dressing-rooms, playing games to pass the time, chatting alternately about trivialities and about the meaning of life. The premiss is exactly the same as in *Waiting for Godot*: that a play of inaction is more realistic than a conventional heroic drama, at least in bearing a closer resemblance to the way most of us pass most of our time. Theatrically, both *Godot* and *Rosencrantz* succeed partly because, on the stage, action will always flood in to fill the vacuum created by inaction, but neither play could have been written without a profound *Angst* about the human condition. Though he is less *Angst*-ridden than Beckett, and more inclined to take his bearings from existing literature and existing cultural trends, Stoppard has always been preoccupied by the problem of accident and design. In his 1966 novel *Lord Malquist and Mr Moon*, he grapples with it amusingly but explicitly:

> The rest of the world intruded itself in a cause-and-effect chain reaction that left him appalled at its endlessness; he experienced a vision of the billion connecting moments that lay behind and led to his simplest action, a vision of himself straightening his tie as the culminating act of a sequence that fled back into prehistory and began with the shift of a glacier.

In *Rosencrantz and Guildenstern Are Dead* the plot of Shakespeare's play represents a line of action which is predetermined and quasi-deterministic. The freedom of the characters exists only in its interstices. Whether this freedom, or any freedom, is real or illusory depends on the viewpoint from which you look at it. Stoppard comes close to Estragon's 'Nothing to be done' when he makes Lord Malquist say 'Nothing is the history of the world viewed from a suitable distance'.

Some of the best moments in *Rosencrantz and Guildenstern Are Dead* depend on the dizzying shifting of perspective as the stage is suddenly filled with characters we know from *Hamlet*, and we move abruptly from Stoppard's dialogue to Shakespeare's. The change of style is all the more disconcerting because two characters we have come to like are suddenly caught up in somethingthing they cannot control. As the title reminds us, they are being carried so rapidly towards death, they might just as well be dead already.

The changes of perspective in Stoppard's plays nearly always cause vertigo. In the 1966 radio play *If You're Glad I'll Be Frank*, Gladys, who provides the voice for the Post Office's speaking clock, complains that 'the scale you live by' is upset when you look down from a great height, 'reducing the life-size to nothing'. This feeling is crucial to the 1967 radio play *Albert's Bridge*. Albert is happy only when he is alone, high above the confusion of the city, working as a bridge-painter. His solitude is disturbed by Fraser, who intends to throw himself off the bridge. Suicidal because there is no design in the chain of accidents, he finds that seen from above, 'the idea of society is just about tenable'. But when he goes down again, he wants only to come back up. In both the 1967 television play *Another Moon called Earth* and in *Jumpers* (produced 1972) a woman is demented by the moon landings:

> PENELOPE: I tell you, he's smashed the mirror – finally, broken through – he has stood outside and seen us whole, all in one go, little. And suddenly everything we live by – our rules – our good, our evil – our ideas of love, duty – all the things we've counted on as being absolute truths – because we filled all existence – they're all suddenly exposed as nothing more than local customs – nothing more – Because he has seen the edges where we stop, and we never stopped anywhere before –
>
> BONE: Penelope –
>
> PENELOPE (*intensely*): I'm telling you – when that thought drips through to the bottom, people won't just carry on.
>
> (*Another Moon Called Earth*)

DOTTY: Not only are we no longer the still centre of God's universe, we're not even uniquely graced by his footprint in man's image ... Man is on the Moon, his feet on solid ground and he has seen us whole, all in one go, *little – local* ... and all our absolutes, the thou-shalts and the thou-shalt-nots that seemed to be the very condition of our existence, how did they look to two moonmen with a single neck to save between them? Like the local customs of another place. When that thought drips through to the bottom, people won't just carry on. (*Jumpers*)

The vertigo is comparable to the confusion felt four centuries earlier by the Metaphysical poets. In response to the new science and the doubt it was casting on all the old systematised relationships, they took refuge in verbal conceits, forging linguistic chains as if to replace the interconnections that had previously seemed intrinsic to the cosmos. Calling his irresistible mistress 'Oh more than Moone',[7] John Donne revelled in the illusion of creating his own cosmogeny; ordering the sun not to disturb him when he was in bed with her, or with another girl, he invented a cosmic triangle with a narrow human base and two very long sides. Dr Johnson complained of the Metaphysicals that 'the most heterogeneous ideas are yoked by violence together'. Violence was to become a matter of policy for the Surrealists. 'For me,' said Breton, 'the only real evidence is a result of the spontaneous, extra-lucid and defiant relationship suddenly sensed between two things which common sense would never bring together.'

Stoppard's plays are full of relationships between things which common sense would never have brought together. Sometimes the connections are made through wordplay. *Jumpers* is structured around the multiple meanings the title word acquires. We first hear it at the beginning, when Archie's voice announces 'And now! – ladies and gentlemen! – the INCREDIBLE – RADICAL! – LIBERAL!! – JUMPERS!!' and four of them come on from either side of the stage, jumping, tumbling and somersaulting. Already coupled with the name of a political party, the word soon acquires an overtone of expediency, and George, the unheroic moral philosopher, becomes almost heroic in his refusal to 'jump along with the rest'. Unfashionably, he is a deist in the materialist university which serves as a microcosm for the new society, and he is temperamentally incapable of 'jumping through the Vice-Chancellor's hoop'. Sir Archibald, the opportunistic Vice-Chancellor, whose surname turns out to be Jumper, refuses to give George the vacant Chair of Logic, preferring to look for 'someone with a bit of bounce'. The vacancy has occurred because the previous professor has been murdered – and murder was integral to the theatrically spectacular idea which was Stoppard's starting point. 'I thought: "How marvellous to have a pyramid of people on a stage, and a rifle shot, and one member of the pyramid just being blown out of it and the others imploding on the hole as he leaves." '[8] But, as he says, 'there's more than one point of origin for a play . . . while thinking of that pyramid I knew I wanted to write a play about a professor of moral philosophy, and it's the work of a moment to think that there was a metaphor at work in the play already between acrobatics, mental acrobatics and so on.'[9] So the fulcrum of the whole structure is a pun, a verbal association between two unassociated activities.

In championing George's refusal to jump along with the rest, Stoppard is developing the theme of nonconformism which has occurred in several of his earlier plays, as it has in the work of Beckett, Ionesco and Handke. In Stoppard's 1966 television play *A Separate Peace*, John Brown follows the example of Beckett's early heroes, opting out of the fuss and bustle for the sake of inaction. In *If You're Glad I'll Be Frank* both Gladys and her bus-driver husband are in rebellion against the tight world of schedules and time-tables. In *Albert's Bridge* when the hero becomes a bridge-painter, refusing to step on to the treadmill of business and industry, his decision serves as an analogy for the detachment of the artist:

> I saw the context. It reduced philosophy and everything else. I got a perspective. Because that bridge was – separate – complete – removed, defined by principles of engineering which make it stop at a certain point, which compels a certain shape, certain joints – the whole thing utterly fixed by the rules that make it stay up.

Every artist is concerned, pragmatically, to find the rules that make the work of art stay up. The Stoppardian play is not so much removed as caught in the process of removing itself from another play, as *Rosencrantz and Guildenstern* does from *Hamlet* or as *The Real Inspector Hound* (1968) does from the half-written thriller at its core. Whether the new play is spliced into *Hamlet* or into a pastiche of Stoppard's invention, the component halves are brought into intimate relationship. *Travesties* is rather like a new version of *The Importance of Being Earnest* with all the original dialogue rubbed out.

In Stoppard's rearrangements of existing literary artefacts, some elements of chance are allowed to operate, though not quite as in Tzara's cut-up poems. He starts writing without knowing how the strands will eventually come together. Sometimes he goes out of his way to make it difficult for himself. In his novel *Lord Malquist and Mr Moon* he starts the narrative with a montage of episodes which look as though they will defy integration into a story. The 1970 play *After Magritte* opens with a tableau more suggestive of a modernist painting than of a situation likely to occur. An old lady in a bathing cap is lying on an ironing board with a white bathtowel over her body and a black bowler hat on her stomach. Standing on a chair is a half-clothed man wearing evening-dress trousers under thigh-length green rubber fishing waders. He is blowing upwards into the metal lampshade which is on a pulley, counter-weighted by a basket overflowing with apples, oranges, bananas, pineapple and grapes. An attractive woman in her thirties is on her hands and knees, wearing a full-length ballgown. The furniture, including a settee, a television set and a gramophone with an old-fashioned horn is all stacked against the street door. Looking in through the window is a helmeted police constable. But the subsequent development provides quasi-realistic explanations for everything. The man, Harris, is trying to cool the bulb, which is too hot to handle. The furniture has been piled up to clear space for some last-minute ballroom dancing before a professional appearance. He is bare to the waist because his dress shirt has to be ironed. He has been wearing waders to replace a bulb in the bathroom while the bath was full. The wife is on her hands and knees because she is looking for her shoes. The mother-in-law has been lying on the ironing-board for a massage. The policeman is there because the Harrises' car has been traced as having been parked in Ponsonby Place near the Victoria Palace at 2.25 this afternoon. Stoppard even manages to steer the action towards a closing moment that yields an equally improbable tableau.

What attracts him towards Magritte is an affinity with the painter's sense of humour, and an interest in his argumentative insistence that object and image are not identical, that similarity can never be taken as proof of identity, that there is no logic of causality to map the relations between things, images and names. The principle behind Stoppard's 1971 play *Dogg's Our Pet* is partly Magrittean and partly Wittgensteinian. As the Preface explains, a man engaged in building a platform may be shouting out the words 'Plank', 'Block', 'Brick', 'Cube' and 'Slab', and another man may be throwing him bits of wood that correspond to his words. An observer would assume that they both speak the same language. But suppose the second man knows in advance exactly what the first needs. It is conceivable that he is speaking a different language in which

Plank = Here!
Slab = Ready!
Block = Next!
Brick = The thrower's name.
Cube = Thank-you!

And if life for Charlie and Brick consisted only of building platforms in this manner there would be no reason for either of them ever to discover that they were each using a language which was not understood by the other. But this happy state of affairs would end when a third person begins to use the language in a way which is puzzling to either Charlie or Brick.

Stoppard proceeds to test out the implications of his hypothesis in a way that yields considerable amusement. It is a more abstract play than *After Magritte*, with less delineation of a situation and less narrative, but it uses combinations of words and actions to create rhythms which arouse audience expectations. As in music, these are sometimes satisfied, sometimes satisfyingly frustrated.

Like Handke, and like many modern painters, Stoppard was exerting himself to discourage interpretation by showing how inaccurate it could be, but at the same time, in beginning to explore the possibility of dichotomy between sound and action, he was launching himself on a process that would yield different results in later plays. The plot of the 1972 radio play *Artist Descending a Staircase* pivots on an ambiguous sound preserved by a tape recorder. Against the background of snore-like buzzing, we hear stealthy footsteps and a creaking board. Both sounds stop before Donner is heard saying 'Ah! There you are'. Two quick steps are followed by a thump, a cry, and the noises he makes as he falls through the balustrade to land, dead, at the bottom of the stairs. Assuming the footsteps to be those of a murderer creeping up on the sleeping man, each of the two other artists who lived with him, Beauchamp and Martello, suspects the other. Eventually the footsteps are revealed to be those of Donner himself as he stalked up on the fly that was buzzing stertorously near the microphone.

Another misinterpretation is pivotal to the story that is told through the flashbacks. Seeing the three young artists at an exhibition of their work, Sophie, a beautiful girl on the verge of blindness, falls in love with one of them when she sees him posing for a photographer against what she takes to be a snow scene. Beauchamp, who had painted a border fence in the snow, becomes her lover, but after their unhappy affair has culminated in her death, it is revealed that Donner was possibly the man who attracted her. With her failing sight, she may have mistaken his painting of white posts for a snow scene: when Beauchamp mentioned his fence, she probably misconstrued her memory of the dark gaps between the posts.

Like Tristan Tzara, Beauchamp takes the view that art has nothing to do with expertise. Doing something well is no excuse for doing the expected. In Stoppard's 1974 stage play *Travesties*, Tzara, appearing as one of the characters, carries on the same argument: 'Nowadays an artist is someone who makes art mean the things he does. A man may be an artist by exhibiting his hindquarters. He may be a poet by drawing words out of a hat.' The opposite view, represented in *Artist Descending a Staircase* by

Donner, is put forward in *Travesties* by Henry Carr, who uses exactly the same words as Donner: 'An artist is someone who is gifted in some way that enables him to do something more or less well which can only be done badly or not at all by someone who is not thus gifted.' Not concerning himself deeply with Tzara either as an artist or as a man, Stoppard stylishly uses his belief in chance to attack the idea of design:

> The clever people try to impose a design on the world and when it goes calamitously wrong they call it fate. In point of fact, everything is Chance, including design. . . the causes we know everything about depend on causes we know absolutely nothing about. And it is the duty of the artist to jeer and howl and belch at the delusion that infinite generations of real effects can be inferred from the gross expression of apparent cause.

In the Copernican universe, everything had been design, including chance.

7 Albee
and
Shepard

Like Tom Stoppard, Edward Albee is visibly affected by his reading. When he was asked whether there were elements of *Faust* in *Tiny Alice* (produced 1964), he said: 'The only way you can avoid having any of these things creeping in is to be a self-conscious illiterate.'[1] Stoppard has found a way of leaning lightly on the shoulders of writers from whom he borrows heavily; Albee is liable to let literary indebtedness push his plays off balance. He has a fine ear for prose rhythms, and at his best, in *The Zoo Story* (written 1958; produced 1962), he can distil a powerful rhetoric which is entirely his own. His other plays are less unflawed, less self-consistent, and they often reproduce rhythms he has picked up from Eliot and Beckett, while the influence of Genet and Ionesco is sometimes only partially digested.

In one way or another, nearly all his plays have been provocative.

At almost every performance of *The Zoo Story* and *The American Dream* [written 1959–60; produced 1961] people used to get up and walk out and yell at the actors saying, 'Goddamn you, how dare you talk this way, how dare you do this, how dare you offend me.' . . . But you have two alternatives: you either affect people or you leave them indifferent. And I would loathe to leave an audience indifferent.[2]

Most of the New York critics were hostile to *The American Dream*; one of them was so infuriated by it that he refused to review Albee's next play. As Albee had said in the same 1963 interview, 'Some of the things people see on Broadway aren't plays at all but manufactured *artifices*. They confirm and put to sleep rather than disturb and keep awake.'

Albee's first full-length play, *Who's Afraid of Virginia Woolf?*, which was written for Off-Broadway but presented on Broadway with phenomenal success, provoked the audience by embarrassing it. We had the feeling of being shut up in a room with four people who were intent on stripping themselves and each other psychologically naked, relentlessly exposing secrets and private fantasies. The vicious games George and Martha were playing with each other soon came to depend on having Nick and Honey as their audience, but from their first entrance, the younger couple was partly standing in for us, and the more deeply they were drawn into the marital games, the more we had to take over the role of onlookers from them, knowing that our discomfited presence was indispensable to the ritual being celebrated on stage. Albee aptly titles his second act *Walpurgisnacht*.

Apart from the adaptation of Carson McCullers's novel *The Ballad of the Sad Café* (produced 1963), *Tiny Alice* was Albee's next play to be seen on Broadway. It provoked by mystifying. After it had been running for twelve weeks, he called a press conference, which he addressed from the stage. After insisting that 'it is a fairly simple play and not at all unclear, once you approach it on its own terms', he went on to explain it.

His adaptation of James Purdy's novel *Malcolm* flopped when it was produced in 1966, but the next original play, *A Delicate Balance* (produced 1966), won a Pulitzer Prize. In most ways it is the least provocative of his plays. The next adaptation (produced 1967) was potentially more offensive. A reworking of another play, Giles Cooper's *Everything in the Garden* (produced in London 1962), it centres on a group of suburban housewives who turn to prostitution as an easy means of improving their income, but Albee's version is less mordant and *risqué* than the original.

Box and *Quotations from Chairman Mao Tse-Tung*, a double-bill staged in 1968, is more experimental than any of his previous work. *Box* is one of the most abstract plays ever written. There is no action and no actors are visible. The stage is empty except for the outline of a large cube, while we hear nothing but sound effects and a disembodied voice speaking a prose poem, which is like a meditation on the word 'box'. Without plunging the stage into darkness it would not be possible to pare down much further on the visual content of theatre. As in Handke's *Sprechstücke*, the effect has to be made by the words and the spaces between them.

Quotations from Chairman Mao Tse-Tung is not quite equally devoid of story, but, as in Beckett's *Play* and in Pinter's *Landscape* and *Silence*, the characters are static, while the action is all in the past. The full-length play *All Over* (written 1970; produced 1971) is similar in its repudiation of action and developing relationships. It is like a version of Ionesco's *Le Roi se meurt* with the dying man kept off stage, so that conversational approaches to death have to be made by the wife, mistress, friend and family who are hovering around the deathbed. *Seascape* (produced 1975) is equally static, equally a conversation piece. The main provocation (which may derive partly from Ionesco's *Rhinocéros*) is that two of the four characters are lizards.

The writing in the plays is consistently stylish, but stylistically they are remarkably discontinuous. If they had been performed anonymously, no one would have guessed that they were all the work of one man. Though Albee never repeats himself, the discontinuity is also a symptom of his inability to profit (as Peter Handke profits) from each phase of his writing experience. Handke develops by remembering everything he has done; Albee moves forward by forgetting.

His first play, *The Zoo Story*, is still, arguably, his best and there is no visible debt to any other playwright in the rhythm or in the dynamic by which the action moves unhurriedly, idiosyncratically, ineluctably forward through abrasive dialogue and one enormously protracted monologue towards its violent climax.

Confrontation between two strangers on a park bench is one of the clichés of drama school improvisations. The territorial claim they both make on the bench is reminiscent of Pinter; the contrast between the middle-class conformist (Peter) and the drop-out (Jerry) is reminiscent of Expressionism, of Beckett's *Eleuthéria* and of Ionesco's *Jacques* plays. But Albee's treatment of this unpromising material is brilliantly original. The analogy between human isolation and the loneliness of caged animals and domestic pets is articulated through criss-crossing strands of action: Jerry's story about his attempt to make contact with his landlady's dog while keeping the woman at bay is set off against his efforts to achieve contact with Peter. The long speech about his relationship with the dog is extremely well written, but the success of the play depends more on the liveliness and spikiness of the dialogue. Jerry uses aggression, humour, wit, charm, effrontery and acute intelligence in a series of assaults on Peter's conventional reserve:

JERRY: And you have children.
PETER: Yes, two.
JERRY: Boys.
PETER: No, girls . . . both girls.
JERRY: But you wanted boys.
PETER: Well . . . naturally, every man wants a son, but . . .
JERRY (*lightly mocking*): But that's the way the cookie crumbles.
    (*Jerry crosses up centre.*)
PETER (*annoyed*): I wasn't going to say that.
JERRY: And you're not going to have any more kids, are you?
    (*Jerry crosses L., round up stage bench to D.L. – L. of bench.*)
PETER (*a bit distantly*): No. No more. (*Peter turns to Jerry. Then back, and irksome.*) Why did you say that? How would you know about that?
JERRY: The way you cross your legs, perhaps; something in the voice. Or maybe I'm just guessing. Is it your wife?

PETER (*furious*): That's none of your business! (*A silence.*) Do you understand? (*Jerry nods. Jerry crosses in two steps to Peter. Peter is quiet now.*) Well, you're right. We'll have no more children.

The dialogue generates an exciting sense of danger in exchanges like this, and in moments of forced physical contact, when Jerry is tickling Peter or punching him on the arm, telling him to move along the bench. We get the impression that Jerry will stop at nothing in his determination to make contact. Is Jerry mad? Rhythms in the prose, repetitions of particular words (zoo, animals, people), circling movements of the dialogue as it shifts away from a subject and returns to it – all these contribute to the sense of impending disaster. It is not altogether surprising when Jerry pulls out a knife, but it is surprising when he tosses it to Peter and when the placid bourgeois paterfamilias lets himself be provoked into holding it out aggressively. It is more surprising still when Jerry impales himself on it.

There is nothing in the text of *The Zoo Story* to enforce a departure from realism. The action has a specific location – Central Park, New York – and the stage directions prescribe foliage, trees, sky, while the dialogue presents no problems of stylisation. In the next play, *The Death of Bessie Smith* (written 1959; produced Berlin 1960, New York 1961), there is a variety of locations in and around an unnamed Southern town during the thirties. The stage directions ask for the scenic detail to be minimal and for the sky to fill the whole back wall, varying symbolically from hot blue to an angry red-orange sunset. Apart from Bessie Smith and her coloured manager, Jack, the characters are all known Expressionistically by their functions – Nurse, Orderly, Intern, Father. The car-crash in which Bessie Smith dies is staged through indications. Jack's voice is first heard talking to her calmly, then screaming at her to watch out. We hear the noise of the crash and see the beams of the car's headlights, which swing across the stage before going out abruptly. And in the same way that the action varies between realism and stylisation, the dialogue varies between realism and literary rhetoric:

INTERN: Here am I – here am I tangential – while all the while I would serve more nobly as a radiant, not outward from, but reversed, plunging straight to your lovely vortex.

NURSE (*laughing*): Oh, la! You just keep your mind off my lovely vortex – you just remain – uh – tangential.

The Sandbox (written 1959; produced 1960) and *The American Dream* (written 1959–60); produced 1961) are much less realistic. The most important influences seem to have been Ionesco on the surface and Beckett deeper down, but there is a stronger grain of social criticism in these two plays than in either Ionesco or Beckett. In *The Sandbox*, as in *The Death of Bessie Smith*, the skycloth is used symbolically, darkening slowly from bright daylight to blackness. Throughout the action, the Angel of Death is represented by a young man who goes on doing arm exercises 'which should suggest the beating and fluttering of wings'. When Mommy and Daddy dump Grandma in the child's sandbox, as if she were already dead and about to be buried, we are reminded of how Hamm had consigned his parents to dustbins. It is the old lady who strikes up the most direct relationship with the audience. She also makes friends with the anonymous Young Man, who tells her that the studio has not yet given him a name, and with the Musician, who starts and stops playing when she tells him to. When she shouts to someone offstage that it should be getting dark, the lighting dims. Later it goes off altogether, except for a spot on the young man. When it comes up again we see her lying on her side in the sandbox, shovelling sand over herself and complaining about the toy shovel. When she can no longer move, the play draws ironical attention to the fact that it is a play. Abandoning his exercises, the Young Man delivers his key line, hesitating like a bad amateur actor. 'I am the Angel of Death. I am . . . uh . . . I am come for you.' He kisses Grandma on the forehead and she compliments him on his performance.

The play's social comment is made mainly through Mommy and Daddy, who are both materialistic and heartless in the way they dispose of the old woman. Mommy is hard, selfish, overbearing; he is feeble, dependent, lacking in initiative. Unlike Hamm, they emerge as representatives of a society.

Both characters are developed in *The American Dream*, which also brings back the Young Man and the eighty-six-year-old grandmother who has outstayed her welcome on earth. This time Mommy and Daddy are shown to be ruthless not only towards her but towards the boys they adopt, being apparently incapable (like so many characters in Albee's plays) of having their own children. About twenty years ago they bought a child from the Bye-Bye Adoption Society, but they were unsatisfied with it, first of all because it did not look like either of them, and then because it only had eyes for its Daddy. Mrs Barker, one of the society's officials, is no more tolerant than they are:

MRS BARKER: Why, any self-respecting woman would have gouged those eyes right out of its head.

GRANDMA: Well, she did. That's exactly what she did. But then, it kept its nose up in the air.

MRS BARKER: Ufggh! How disgusting!

GRANDMA: That's what they thought. But *then*, it began to develop an interest in its you-know-what.

MRS BARKER: In its you-know-what! Well, I hope they cut its hands off at the wrists!

GRANDMA: Well, yes, they did that eventually. But first, they cut off its you-know-what.

Himself the adopted child of very rich parents, Albee is cantilevering out from private preoccupations into satire on the emasculating effects of matriarchal family life. Writing about dehumanisation, he finds himself drifting towards the style of Ionesco, who for different reasons, had reduced his characters to puppet-like automatism. The beginning of the sequence with Mrs Barker is full of echoes from *La Cantatrice chauve*. When the doorbell rings, Daddy hesitates about whether to answer it, Mommy first encourages him by praising his masculinity, and then prods him by calling him womanish and indecisive. When Mrs Barker comes in, she is invited to sit down, to have a drink, to have a cigarette, to cross her legs, to take her dress off. After Mommy has folded it neatly over the back of the sofa, they reveal that they do not know who she is. When they ask her, she says she is the chairman of the women's club.

MOMMY: Don't be ridiculous. I was talking to the chairman of my women's club just yester –. Why, so you are.

Unfortunately the comedy in the manner of Ionesco has the effect of blunting the social satire, and the style changes again when, with the character of the Young Man, Albee tries to make points explicitly through a kind of rhetoric which seems anomalous in the mouth of a character who has just made his first entrance, though it had been acceptable enough when Jerry was intruding on Peter's privacy:

> From time to time, in the years that have passed, I have suffered losses . . . that I can't explain. A fall from grace . . . a departure of innocence . . . loss . . . loss. How can I put it to you? All right – like this; Once . . . it was as if all at once my heart . . . became numb . . . almost as though I . . . almost as though . . . just like that . . . it had been wrenched from my body . . . and from that time I have been unable to love. Once . . . I was asleep at the time . . . I awoke, and my eyes were burning. And since that time I have been unable to see anything, *anything*, with pity, with affection . . . with anything but . . . cool disinterest. And my groin . . . even there . . . since one time . . . one specific agony since then I have not been able to *love* anyone with my body.

The idiom is Albee's own, but it fails to blend with Ionesco's, rather in the way that the private preoccupations in the play are failing to blend with the social satire. An acute sense of loss is a recurrent theme in Albee's work: sometimes, instead of dramatising it, he is content to let characters talk about it.

In both *The Sandbox* and *The American Dream* behaviour is sometimes discussed – not without distortion – and sometimes indicated by action which is surrealistically representative of it, but it is never mirrored realistically. In the full-length play *Who's Afraid of Virginia Woolf?* Albee returns to the technique he had used in *The Zoo Story* and *The Death of Bessie Smith*, directly dramatising the effect that personalities can have on each other through nervous friction. But it is not merely a play about personal relationships. The whole of American civilisation is implicated in the charge of emotional and spiritual sterility, and it is no accident that George and Martha are given the same Christian names as the Washingtons.

The theme of conformism has not been absent from any of the plays. It was treated more subtly and more obliquely in *The Death of Bessie Smith* than in *The Zoo Story*. In the two unrealistic plays, *The Sandbox* and *The American Dream*, it was suggested by Daddy's meek submissiveness to Mommy's ruthless leadership. In *Who's Afraid of Virginia Woolf?* George is like the Intern in having rebel inclinations, but better able to subdue them. As a university lecturer, he is the employee of an Establishment institution; as the husband of the President's daughter, he has sacrificed his creative vitality on the altar of his father-in-law's wishes: the novel to which the old man objects has remained unpublished. Though highly critical of the offstage father-figure, George, unlike Jerry, calculates what gestures of protest he can afford. In contrast to the younger lecturer, Nick, a scientist, he has too much self-respect to become an abject conformist, but too little to rebel.

Martha is partially descended from the monstrous Mommies of *The Sandbox* and *The American Dream*, but she is not only more realistic, she is also more subtle. She is unlike them in being revealed as vulnerable, able to feel both fear and pain. This is the first play since *The Zoo Story* in which Albee has made full use of his talent for writing dialogue that shows each speaker changing gear very quickly in a taxing series of efforts to measure up to an opponent who is quick to see any chink in the defences, and equally quick to attack it.

MARTHA: Hello, C'mon over here and give your Mommy a big sloppy kiss.

GEORGE: . . . Oh, now . . .

MARTHA: I WANT A BIG SLOPPY KISS!

GEORGE (*preoccupied*): I don't *want* to kiss you, Martha. Where *are* these people? Where are these *people* you invited over?

MARTHA: They stayed on to talk to Daddy . . . They'll be here . . . Why don't you want to kiss me?

GEORGE (*too matter-of-fact*): Well, dear, if I kissed you I'd get all excited . . . I'd get beside myself and I'd take you, by force,

right here on the living-room rug, and then our little guests
would walk in, and . . . well, just think what your father
would say about *that*.

MARTHA: You pig!

GEORGE: Oink! Oink!

MARTHA: Ha, ha, ha, HA! Make me another drink . . . lover.

GEORGE (*taking her glass*): My God, you can swill it down, can't
you?

MARTHA (*imitating a child*): I'm firsty.

GEORGE: Jesus!

MARTHA (*swinging around*): Look, sweetheart, I can drink you
under any goddam table you want . . . so don't worry about
me!

These are two hardened marital warriors, thoroughly accustomed
to each other's methods of fighting, adept at varying their
own.

The desperation of George and Martha to involve Nick and
Honey in their internecine conflict parallels Jerry's desperation
to make contact with Peter. Nick, like Peter, says that he does not
wish to become involved in other people's affairs, but again the
frontier of polite conventionality is easily crossed, and in the process of making the characters goad each other beyond it, Albee
imbues the dialogue with a rhetorical intensity which previously
he had introduced only into long monologues. When Nick is provoked into rejecting George's offer of advice with the phrase 'Up
yours', George answers:

You take the trouble to construct a civilization . . . to . . . to
build a society, based on the principles of . . . of principle . . .
you endeavour to make communicable sense out of natural order,
morality out of the unnatural disorder of man's mind . . . you
make government and art, and realize that they are, must be,
both the same . . . you bring things to the saddest of all points
. . . to the point where there is something to lose . . . then all at
once, through all the music, through all the sensible sounds of
men building, attempting, comes the *Dies Irae*. And what is it?
What does the trumpet sound? Up yours. I suppose there's
justice to it, after all the years . . . Up yours.

The rhythms in the prose Martha speaks are similar, but not identical, corresponding to her different sense of humour and her different way of making threats

> You know what's happened, George? You want to know what's
> really happened? (*Snaps her fingers.*) It's snapped, finally. Not me
> . . . *it*. The whole arrangement. You can go along . . . forever,
> and everything's . . . manageable. You make all sorts of excuses
> to yourself . . . you know . . . this is life . . . the hell with it . . .
> maybe tomorrow he'll be dead . . . maybe tomorrow *you'll* be
> dead . . . all sorts of excuses. But then, one day, one night,
> something happens . . . and SNAP! It breaks. And you just
> don't give a damn any more. I've tried with you, baby . . .
> really, I've tried.

The next play, *Tiny Alice*, moves very much further away from realism. Robert Brustein was quick to notice the indebtedness to Genet in the way religious ritual is explored and exploited as a form of play-acting, but he was possibly unfair in alleging that Dürrenmatt's 1956 play *Die Besuch der alten Dame* (*The Old Lady's Visit*) was the source of the story about the rich woman who buys a man's life. This theme of buying a man is almost obsessional in Albee's work: even in *Who's Afraid of Virginia Woolf?* there is the hint that the university President wanted to buy George for his daughter.

Again several of the characters remain unnamed – Cardinal, Lawyer, Butler – except that the Butler is ironically and superfluously given the surname Butler. But the first scene, which is between the Cardinal and the Lawyer, tends towards characterising them as individuals. Albee even introduces details from their past: having been classmates at school they have kept hostile memories of each other. The barbed brilliance of their dialogue makes the scene intensely enjoyable, but it is not a good preparation for the less realistic, densely symbolical action which ensues. The main character, Julian, a lay brother, seems pallid, making his first appearance after these two minor characters have brought their scene to such vivid life, while the interest we develop in their personal antagonism does not predispose us towards taking the kind of interest Albee needs us to take in the central question of the relationship between abstraction and reality. The idea is fascinating, but his treatment of it is fouled up by uncertainty, about what degree of abstraction he wants. Having succeeded so well in sustaining tension through the quadrilateral battle of personalities in *Who's Afraid of Virginia Woolf*, he set himself a different task, rejecting that kind of friction and that kind of tension, but not dispensing altogether with the realistic reflection of personal behaviour. For everything Julian does, he is provided with elaborate – perhaps over-elaborate – motives, and his explanations of them involve exposition about his past life; Alice functions quite differently. Like the pairs of characters in Beckett and Pinter, who receive orders from a mysterious organisation, Alice and the Lawyer are not always doing what they personally want to do. But the conflict between duty and desire, like their conflict with Julian, is confused by a conflict of styles.

A Delicate Balance (written 1965–6; produced 1966) is similar in containing brilliant speeches and powerful sequences, and in lacking unity. The creative energy seems to have come in spurts, not in a sustained flow. There are sequences – mainly passages of verbal aggressiveness – written in Albee's distinctive idiom, but there are also sequences that seem to have been written inside a literary echo chamber where the voices of Eliot and Beckett were predominant. There are references to the plague which may have been inspired by Artaud's 'Le Théâtre et la peste', there is a territorial battle for a room which is reminiscent of Pinter; and Albee even echoes himself with a narrative about a cat, which parallels the dog narrative in *The Zoo Story*.

The cadences of the opening speech echo Winnie in Beckett's *Happy Days*:

What I find most astonishing – aside from that belief of mine, which never ceases to surprise me by the very fact of its surprising lack of unpleasantness, the belief that I might very easily – as they say – lose my mind one day, not that I suspect I am about to, or am even . . . nearby . . . for I'm not that sort; merely that it is not beyond . . . happening: some gentle loosening of the moorings sending the balloon adrift – and I think that is the only out-weighing thing: adrift; the . . . becoming a stranger in . . . the world, quite . . . uninvolved, for I never see it as violent, only a drifting.

Later, she will pick up Eliot's rhythms:

> I haven't time for the four-hour talk, the soothing recapitula-
> tion. You don't go through it, my love: the history. Nothing is
> calmed by a pat on the hand, a gentle massage, or slowly, slowly
> combing the hair, no: the history.

When she says: 'We become allegorical, my darling Tobias, as we
grow older' we recognise the signal that Albee is aware of the
literary danger, but the problem is not solved by imposing a literary self-consciousness on his characters.

At the same time, the influence of Genet seems to be at work in
the way Albee lets the characters overlap with each other. With
her drunken insights and her penchant for unpalatable truths,
Claire is sometimes reminiscent of the Fool in *Lear*; with her
self-indulgence and her yodelling she sometimes seems, like
Falstaff, to be a representative of Riot, of the disorderly forces
latent in all the other characters. Edna and Harry, the
friends who are running away from a nameless plague-like terror,
taking refuge in the house of Agnes and Tobias, are not altogether separate from Agnes and Tobias. Not only do Edna and
Harry voice insecurities that their friends suppress, they take
over some of the parental functions within the family. But, as in
Tiny Alice, the blending of realistic and unrealistic elements is
awkward. The fear that drives Edna and Harry out of their own
house does not need to be explained, but it does need to be integrated into the action. It remains not only a mystery but an anomaly,
and when Edna talks about it, she sounds like a rather poor parody
of Agatha in Eliot's *The Family Reunion*:

> If we come to the point . . . if we are at home one evening, and
> the . . . terror comes . . . descends . . . if all at once we . . .
> NEED . . . we come where we are wanted, where we know we
> are expected, not only where we want; we come where the
> table has been laid for us in such an event . . . where the bed is
> turned down . . . and warmed . . . and has been ready should we
> need it.

Later on, we are reminded of the choric quartet of uncles and
aunts in *The Family Reunion*: during a long speech of Tobias's,

the four women in the play appear, each carrying a coffee cup, to stand watching, like a silent chorus. In a stage direction Albee describes Tobias's speech as an aria and he notates it very meticulously, telling the actor where to shout and where to speak softly, where to laugh and where to make 'great breathing sounds'. But the actual speech is feebly written, and not nearly substantial enough to provide a dramatic development of the sort needed at this juncture. Though none of the points have been made to Harry before, they have all been made to the audience.

You come in here, you come in here with your . . . wife, and with your . . . terror! And you ask me if I want you here! (*great breathing sounds*)
YES! OF COURSE! I WANT YOU HERE! I HAVE BUILT THIS HOUSE! I WANT YOU IN IT! I WANT YOUR PLAGUE! YOU'VE GOT SOME TERROR WITH YOU? BRING IT IN! (*pause, then even louder*)
BRING IT IN!! YOU'VE GOT THE ENTREE, BUDDY, YOU DON'T NEED A KEY! YOU'VE GOT THE ENTREE, BUDDY! FORTY YEARS!
(*soft now; soft and fast, almost a monotone*)
You don't need to ask me, Harry, you don't need to ask a thing; you're our friends, our very best friends in the world, and you don't have to ask.
(*a shout*)
WANT? ASK?
(*soft as before*)
You come for dinner don't you come for cocktails see us at the club on Saturdays and talk and lie and laugh with us and pat old Agnes on the hand and say you don't know what old Toby'd do without her and we've known you all these years and we love each other don't we?
(*shout*)
DON'T WE? DON'T WE LOVE EACH OTHER?
(*soft again, laughter and tears in it*)
Doesn't friendship grow to that? To love? Doesn't forty years amount to anything? We've cast our lot together, boy, we're friends, we've been through lots of thick OR thin together.

Which is it, boy?
(*shout*)
WHICH IS IT, BOY?!
THICK?!
THIN?!
WELL? WHATEVER IT IS, WE'VE BEEN THROUGH IT,
BOY!

Always interested in the possibility of applying musical form to writing in the theatre, Albee did not, in his early plays, keep form in the front of his mind. In *A Delicate Balance*, he was able to disguise the shapelessness of Tobias's 'aria' by including instructions about tempo and volume in the stage directions. In *Box* and *Quotations from Chairman Mao Tse-Tung* he goes much further in subordinating the normal priorities of theatre to the attempt at musical structuring. In *Box* Beckett is the principal influence. The cadences seem to drive from those of *Happy Days* and from the radio plays, while the stage directions are even more specific than Beckett's, laying down the exact duration of the main pauses, which are very long, sometimes three or five seconds. The monologues may have been conceived as an alternative to music: the voice says that it is now impossible to hear it 'When the beauty of it reminds us of *loss*. Instead of the attainable. When it tells us what we cannot have . . .'. Motifs and images are introduced individually and developed in relationship to each other; mood and structure are what matter most.

Though *Quotations from Chairman Mao Tse-Tung* is less abstract, little depends on the exiguous story and a great deal on the contrapuntal relationship between the components. Chairman Mao addresses his political homilies directly to the audience; while an upper middle-class lady of sixty talks long-windedly to a silent clergyman about her life while they both sit in deck chairs, and a shabby old woman quotes Will Carleton's 'Over the Hill to the Poor-House'. We also hear brief reprises from *Box*. Though the attitude of the Long-Winded Lady is very different from that of Winnie in *Happy Days*, the tone is very similar:

Oh, what a treasurehouse! I can exclude his dying; I can not think about it, except the times I want it back – the times I

want, for myself, something less general than . . . tristesse.
Though that is usually enough.

The method of constructing a play out of interlocking monologues derives directly from Beckett's *Play*.

All Over (written 1970; produced 1971) moves back towards
realism, though none of the characters is named and the action
tends to avoid the specific. In so far as the dialogue explores the
characters, the exploration is almost entirely verbal and retrospective. In fact the play is mainly a threnody, not on the death of
the man in the bed, but on the lives of the others who will survive
him. Again, the structure is almost musical. The seven voices are
like instruments in a septet, developing each other's themes as one
dominates one section, and another the next. The music is a carefully cadenced rhetoric, with clearly notated pauses and prolonged
parentheses containing rubato stresses. Apart from occasional outcrops of violence, the only action is the inaction of waiting for
death, but unlike the inaction of *Waiting for Godot*, it does not
make a point of focusing on the fact of passivity. The play
might be better if it did.

The disadvantage of the method Albee has adopted in his recent
work is that conversations tend to become inordinately distended.
This happens in *Seascape* (written 1974; produced 1975) where
most of the first act is devoted to a static chat between husband
and wife on a Beckettian sand dune. Certainly there are poignant
moments as they chew painfully over what they have shared and
what they have failed to share during so many years of marriage.
But there is less comedy than in either *Waiting for Godot* or
Rosencrantz and Guildenstern Are Dead, while the play depends
more on the interest we take in the personalities of the characters,
and in the personal relationship between them. The appearance of
the two talking lizards provides an effective climax to the act, but
though the quadrilateral conversation that fills the second act is less
personal, touching as it does on such general questions as evolution, the dynamic is insufficient. The play's only momentum is the
momentum of a conversation which Albee is patently manipulating.

Counting the Ways (written and produced 1976) is a short play

which he describes as a vaudeville. Though he divides the action
into twenty brief sequences, punctuated by blackouts, this merely
disguises the shapelessness of the conversation and the fact that,
once again, the action is incidental to a conversation which cannot
provide enough momentum to carry the play interestingly forward.

When Albee fails, it is not because he borrows too much from
other writers, but because he does not borrow imaginatively
enough. Sam Shepard is no less eclectic. He not only draws freely
on the fund of theatrical ideas accumulated by Beckett, Ionesco,
Genet, Handke, Pinter and Albee, he imports elements from
cinema, rock music, science fiction, pop painting, cartoon strips,
sport, and the chatter of radio disc jockeys. But the differences
between Albee's borrowings and Shepard's correspond to the
distinction Coleridge drew between Fancy and Imagination.
Fancy 'is indeed no other than a mode of Memory emancipated
from the order of time and space; while it is blended with, and
modified by that empirical phenomenon of the will, which we
express by the word CHOICE'. But the Imagination 'dissolves,
diffuses, dissipates, in order to recreate; or where this process is
rendered impossible, yet still at all events it struggles to idealize
and to unify'.[3] Though it is 'first put in action by the will and
understanding', the Imagination

> reveals itself in the balance or reconciliation of opposite or
> discordant qualities: of sameness, with difference; of the
> general, with the concrete; the idea, with the image; the
> individual, with the representative; the sense of novelty and
> freshness, with old and familiar objects; a more than usual state
> of emotion, with more than usual order; judgment ever awake
> and steady self-possession, with enthusiasm and feeling pro-
> found or vehement; and while it blends and harmonizes the
> natural and the artificial, still subordinates art to nature.[4]

Shepard, in fact, has the best claim of any writer since Beckett and
Genet – both his seniors by about thirty-five years – to being a
poet of the theatre.

He thinks penetratingly about current conditions in America, and he thinks in theatrical terms. It is not a matter of translating the ideas into theatrical imagery: they are conceived as moving three-dimensional metaphors, and the presentation of an exciting succession of theatrical images is inseparable from the development of the ideas. It occurred to him, for instance, that in Duarte, California, where he grew up, and in Azusa, the neighbouring town he uses as a setting for his play *The Unseen Hand* (produced New York 1970, London 1973), the accumulation of population was an accidental process. In each place people settled without knowing what they were doing. 'They fall into it from outer space. They find themselves in the middle of nowhere. They even come back from death.' The notion sprouts into the creation of a weird character called Willie, who claims to have travelled through two galaxies to meet up with three gangsters, two of whom have been dead since an eighteen-seventies shoot-up and now have to be revived. It seems to Shepard that the citizens of these towns are no more aware of what is happening to them than they were when they decided to settle there. 'Something unseen is working on them. Using them.' Willie, therefore, is in the power of the Unseen Hand. There is a black hand-print burned into the hairless crown of his head. The sorcerers who have gained power in his country, Nogoland, do not allow his thoughts to go beyond the circumference of a prescribed circle, or the Hand will squeeze down, forcing them back. The Unseen Hand is 'a muscle contracting syndrome hooked up to the will of the Silent Ones'. We see his whole body shaking in spasms of agony.

A town like Azusa or Duarte consists of 'a collection of junk. Mostly people'. Shepard makes the point theatrically by centring the action on the abandoned wreck of a 1951 Chevrolet, surrounded by garbage, tin cans, Coca-Cola bottles. An ancient drunk, Blue Morphan, the only survivor of the three gangsters, has been living in it for years. At the end of the play he will move on, and one of his resurrected brothers will take over not only his living quarters but also his way of speaking, and, with it, his theatrical identity.

Shepard is unrivalled among contemporary playwrights for inventive energy, and he uses it imaginatively – in Coleridge's sense. Sweeping aside the norms of realism, logic and plausibility, he presents a compellingly watchable series of stage events. In *The Unseen Hand*, before the main lighting comes up on the acting area, the first visual impact is made as the headlights of a passing diesel truck illuminate the derelict Chevrolet; the second when Blue Morphan emerges out of the back seat; the third when the space freak, Willie, staggers on stage, dressed in orange tights, pointed shoes and a Vinyl vest with a black shirt that comes up like a hood over the back of his head. The materialisation of the two dead gangsters has been predicted in the dialogue, but each entrance is contrived at an unexpected moment, when it will make the most impact, and the appearance of the Kid, a cheer leader, is also surprising. He is drunk, with his trousers around his ankles, and he is yelling abuse through a megaphone at an unseen gang from a rival high school. He has noticed the armed men on stage.

Shepard makes good use of moments when they threaten each other with guns, or shoot at each other, but he also capitalises on the theatrical possibility of making characters immune to bullets. Neither Willie nor the dead gangsters are vulnerable.

Visually, the most imaginative and exciting sequence in this play occurs when Willie rejuvenates Blue. They sit facing each other, with their feet out, soles touching. 'You'll feel an interior shrinkage,' warns Willie, 'as your organs rearrange themselves and grow stronger, but don't panic.' He then goes into a seizure. Both men's bodies quake violently as if a rapid series of high voltage electric shocks were passing from Willie to Blue, who gradually becomes younger. Eventually, he can speak and move like a man of about thirty.

At the end of the play language is used as a weapon, as in Ionesco's *La Leçon*, but Shepard's sequence is scenically more spectacular. The Kid, who has learnt about urban guerrilla tactics, is threatening the others with a gun, and, making a passionately jingoistic speech, backed by rock and roll chords, about his love for Azusa, for his car and for his Mom:

And you creeps aren't going to take that away from me. You're not going to take that from me because I'll kill you first! I'll kill every one of you if it's the last thing I do!

Willie then goes into a trance, speaking what he believes to be a strange ancient language. In fact it consists of the Kid's words, reversed:

Od i gniht tsal eht sti fi uoy fo eno yreve llik lli. Tsrif uoy llik lli esuaceb em morf yawa taht ekat ot gniog ton eruoy

After trying to shut him up, the Kid empties the gun into him, but Willie survives, 'accumulating incredible power from the language he speaks'. The Kid is reduced to screaming for mercy, writhing and twitching on the floor as Willie had when he was gripped by the Unseen Hand, while pingpong balls coated with luminous paint start to fall from the flies, bouncing on the stage. Believing that the ancient language of Nogoland must still have been alive inside his brain, Willie has the power not only to defeat an armed adversary but to liberate his people from the sorcerers.

The Tooth of Crime (produced London 1972, New York 1973) is another play in which language is used as a weapon. The established pop star, Hoss, has to face a challenge from an outsider, Crow, and the climacteric duel is fought with words, backed, some of the time, by music. The verbal battle in Genet's *Les Nègres* between the Queen and Felicity is comparable,[5] and there are similar exchanges of insults in some Elizabethan tragedies. There are also non-literary precedents:

In Alaska and in Greenland all disputes except murder are settled by a song duel. In these areas an Eskimo male is often as acclaimed for his ability to sing insults as for his hunting prowess. The song duel consists of lampoons, insults, and obscenities and the disputants sing to each other and, of course, to their delighted audience. The verses are earthy and very much to the point; they are intended to humiliate, and no physical deformity, personal shame, or family trouble is sacred. As verse after verse is sung in turn by the opponents the audience begins to take sides; it applauds one singer a bit longer and laughs a bit louder at his lampoons. Finally, he is the only one to get applause, and he thereby becomes the winner of a bloodless contest. The loser suffers a great punishment, for disapproval of the community is very difficult to bear in a group as small as that of the Eskimo.[6]

But Shepard gives his duel of styles an aura of decadence by taking images and jargon from the contemporary subculture, using rock music and the language of science fiction, cowboy and gangster films, astrologists, disc jockeys, sports commentators and guerrilla warfare manuals.

Language is not only the ammunition used by the duellists, it is also the matrix in which the play is conceived. In the same way that Stoppard's structure for *Jumpers* depends on the multiple meanings of the title word, *The Tooth of Crime*'s structure depends on the double or triple meanings of 'hit', 'big killing' and 'contract' in the worlds of rock music, crime and big business.[7] By extending the idea of killing into business and rock music, Shepard points at the quasi-criminal ruthlessness in both. Like Brecht's 1941 play *Der aufhaltsame Aufsteig des Arturo Ui* (*The Resistible Rise of Arturo Ui*), which materialises out of a comparison between Nazism and Chicago gangsterism, *The Tooth of Crime* builds by making its pop stars as aggressive, as ruthless and as calculating as gangster-businessmen. Not that the three worlds are separate in reality: the Mafia plays a large role in American business life, while pop music is nothing if not commercial. Shepard is merely presenting a Surrealistic-seeming close-up of strands that overlap.

Like Willie – and like Shepard – Crow wins because he can derive strength from the words he has in his head.

> Can't get it sideways walkin' the dog. Tries trainin' his voice to sound like a frog. Sound like a Dylan, sound like a Jagger, sound like an earthquake all over the Fender. Wearin' a shag now, looks like a fag now. Can't get it together with chicks in the mag. Can't get it together for all his tryin'. Can't get it together for fear that he's dyin'. Fear that he's crackin' busted in two. Busted in three parts. Busted in four. Busted and dyin' and cryin' for more. Busted and bleedin' all over the floor. All bleedin' and wasted and tryin' to score.

Unlike the battle between Willie and the Kid, the duel in *The Tooth of Crime* is wholly verbal. Both men fight with words, winning or losing according to the style they choose. Each has many options open to him. Before the referee arrives and the scoring starts, Hoss shows his strength by using a Cowboy-Western idiom which makes Crow nervous, though he regains confidence when he notices that Hoss has switched to a Twenties-Gangster language. On the surface, *The Tooth of Crime* could hardly be more dissimilar to *Travesties*, but both are plays about style, and, like Stoppard, Shepard is skilful, resourceful and witty in his use of pastiche. He also recycles cinematic clichés, renewing their vitality as he integrates them into the conflict.

Before he started writing for the theatre, Shepard was a drummer in a rock band, and if his plays aspire to the condition of rock music, it is not only that he weaves songs and passages of strongly rhythmic prose into the dialogue. He has a predilection for writing sequences in which one instrument takes over, regardless of logic or plot development. After the referee has been murdered by the defeated Hoss, his girl, Becky, has an effective but irrelevant solo section, talking straight out to the audience. Marcel Marceau's technique of playing a silent love-scene with himself, hands creeping up his own back, is piquantly verbalised into a striptease: coyly slapping her hand away from the breasts she has bared, she protests to an imaginary male that he is going too far. The sequence is not helping to characterise her by adding to our knowledge of her past experience or her present intentions; it is like a jazz riff.

Incidentally and almost accidentally the play also works as a variation on the myth of the dying god, which gives tragedy its pattern. As the inevitability of the old king's death becomes more apparent, the younger man moves ineluctably closer to the throne. The cycle of replacement is like the progression of the seasons: summer cannot last; winter must eventually be replaced by spring. The element of fatality in Hoss's defeat is amusingly introduced through the astrologer, Star-man, whose references to charts and stars are usefully ambiguous. 'The wrong move'll throw you back a year or more. You can't afford that now. The charts are moving too fast. Every week there's a new star.' Though Shepard is using ingredients quite unlike those of tragedy, a partly unconscious impulse seems to be at work, reconciling discordant qualities, harmonising new images with old ideas. Hoss and Crow are not so much individuals as representatives of a generation gap. In Shepard's plays, as in Pinter's and Handke's, climaxes do not grow organically out of what has preceded them, but his ability to combine intense emotion with steady self-possession makes it possible for him to organise potentially anarchic material into a satisfying pattern, simultaneously satirising the sixties pop scene and generalising it into very wide relevance.

To a limited extent, his plays are *about* language.

I feel that language is a veil hiding demons and angels which the characters are always out of touch with. Their quest in the play is the same as ours in life – to find those forces, to meet them face to face and end the mystery. I'm pulled toward images that shine in the middle of junk.[8]

He has also said:

Every play is a discovery. You create a framework ... and leave something open in the hope you will discover something. Whether it has a name to it I don't know, but with a really great writer like Samuel Beckett every time he writes he is approaching a certain kind of secret. As he approaches it the audience is approaching it too. As soon as you name it you kill it. There is no question of naming and having it at the same time.[9]

This corresponds with the Symbolist idea that to name an object is to evoke its absence, not its presence.[10] Instead of appearing in all its particularity, it disappears into generalisation and abstraction. But Shepard has also said: 'The fantastic thing about theatre is that it can make something be seen that's invisible.' Sometimes, especially in the early plays, he achieves this by making the characters talk very vividly about the invisible thing, while reacting emotionally or even hysterically. In *Red Cross* (produced New York 1968, London 1972) we may have the illusion of seeing the bugs that Jim picks out of the skin on his bare legs, crushing them underfoot. In *4-H Club* (produced New York 1965) the boys battle against imaginary mice, kicking at the garbage and dirty paper on the floor, alternately yelling threats and talking in whispers, so that the mice will not be afraid to come out of their hiding-places.

Sometimes the audience is kept in a state of uncertainty about the 'reality' of the invisible thing. In Shepard's plays, as in Pinter's, we cannot take it for granted that what the characters are saying is 'true', while often the surrounding story is so loose or so vague that the question of whether to 'believe' them is of secondary importance. In *Icarus's Mother*, which was produced in New York in 1965, when Shepard was twenty-two (and in London in 1971), three boys and two girls are lying on their backs, belching at random and talking about a jet plane, which is leaving a trail in the sky above them. We hear birds chirping, and, later, the noises of fireworks exploding and of a watching crowd reacting to them. But we hear no sound from the jet, and it is questionable whether it is ever more than the subject of a fantasy which is first shared, later disputed. They argue about whether the trail is a signal. They pretend that the pilot is married to one of the girls, Jill. Pat then claims to be his other wife. In the quarrel that ensues between her and Howard, he attacks her with a description of what it is like to be a pilot. Here, too, words are weapons. After the boys have been left alone on stage, the girls come back with a story about crouching 'like desert nomads' on the beach with their pants down, trying to pee, while the plane flew backwards and forwards, very low, above their heads. Howard counters this narrative by telling them that Frank claims to have seen the plane crash into the sea. What Howard says is patently untrue because Frank, who went for a walk, has not yet come back. When he does come, his vivid description of the crash gains theatrical amplification from the sounds and flashes of the firework display. Even if the plane was no more real than the son in *Who's Afraid of Virginia Woolf?*, Frank, like George, achieves a verbal victory in finishing it off.

Shepard's more recent plays succeed in hooking language firmly into the action; in his early work, as he has said, the characters are liable to be 'physically marooned by their speaking', even when the imagery comes out of the situation.[11] He has given up neither long monologues nor the habit of letting events sheer off at unpredictable tangents, but there is more co-ordination between what is said and what is seen to be happening. In *The Curse of the Starving Class* (produced London 1976) the father, Weston, has a speech, rather like a souped-up Tennessee Williams monologue, about castrating lambs and throwing the testes on to the roof of a shed for an eagle, which keeps flying down to peck them up. The speech is not written merely for its immediate effect. The mention of lambs links with the lamb which has been brought inside the house because it has maggots, with the news we hear later that Wesley, the son, has butchered it offstage, and with the skinned carcase that is later carried into the room.

Some of Shepard's most effective three-dimensional images are realistic, like this one, and like the blindfolded, barefoot man bound with steel contacts to the electric chair in the monologue *Killer's Head* (produced New York 1975). He also uses unrealistic images such as the computer in *Operation Sidewinder* (produced New York 1970). It looks and sounds like a six-foot rattlesnake with flashing eyes and darting tongue, and it can move on its own initiative. After swaying, blinking and hissing at the man and woman who appear in the first scene, it coils itself around the screaming woman, soon bringing her to an orgasm. We know we are not watching a real snake, but we do not yet know that it does not represent a real snake.

In *Angel City* (produced San Francisco 1976) it is more immediately obvious that the key images are unrealistic. The skin on the arm of the film magnate, Wheeler, is turning green: 'The city is eating us alive . . . It's turning us into snakes or lizards or something.' By the end of the play the skin of the man called in to cure him, Rabbit Brown, has also turned green and slimy; he has acquired fangs, long black fingernails, and a long thick mane of black hair. Shepard may be indebted to Kafka, Ionesco, and possibly Albee, but he is also developing an idea he had used in an earlier play, *Black Bog Beast Bait* (produced New York 1971), which culminates in the regression of all the characters to an animal state. One woman starts hooting and fluttering like an owl, while another screams and prowls like a wildcat. The man who has already undergone an identity-change from preacher to poacher becomes an alligator, slithering across the stage to attack a cowboy, who starts behaving like a bull, pawing the ground and trying to gore the alligator. The other cowboy becomes a coyote, howling at the moon. The play ends in a furore of animal movements and noises.

In another scene of *Angel City* Shepard may be indebted to
Genet's *Le Balcon* and to Japanese Noh Theatre. Wearing long
silken robes, which not only cover their heads but seem to extend
them, while making their shoulders look huge, two figures duel
with sticks, like Samurai warriors, shrieking against the accompaniment of saxophone and percussion. But the overall progression of the action is not reminiscent of any other writer; Shepard
has his own way of straddling narrative and abstraction. Is a particular Hollywood production company trying to cook up a film
about disaster in order to avert a financial disaster of its own, or is
humanity cultivating the art of disaster in a gratuitous effort to
gain control over the unavoidable drift towards the holocaust?
In the same way that individuality keeps shifting, strands in the
storyline keep splitting, as Shepard teases his situation into an
extraordinary tangle of vagueness and precision, generalisation
and particularity, combining inconsequential triviality with
apocalyptic prophecy, social satire and cultural parody with
surrealism and abstraction.

The stage is almost bare, with a scrim on the back wall, which
can be lit in different colours, and in front of it a neon rectangle
frames the actors when they are on the platform. Rabbit Brown
has bundles of various sizes attached to him by long leather thongs
and dragging on the floor behind him. He claims mystical medical
properties for them. What the film magnates expect from him is
not precisely definable. It involves a cure not only to Wheeler's
malady but to their troubles, artistic and financial.

> LANX: Right. So what we need in this case is a three-dimensional
> invention. Something altogether unheard of before. We have
> the story, the plot, the stars, the situation, but what's missing
> is this uh – this development. Something awesome and totally
> new.
> RABBIT: I see.
> LANX: It has to somehow transcend the very idea of 'character'
> as we know it today.

This is one of the aims Shepard is setting himself in the play.
In a note to the actors, he invites them to think not in terms of a
'whole character' but of collage construction or jazz improvisa-

tion. Each actor should be 'mixing many different underlying elements and connecting them through his intuition and senses to make a kind of music or painting in space without having to feel the need to completely answer intellectually for the character's behaviour. If there needs to be a "motivation" for some of the abrupt changes which occur in the play, they can be taken as full-blown manifestations of a passing thought or fantasy, having as much significance or "meaning" as they do in our ordinary lives.'

Shepard excels at these abrupt changes. Lanx, Wheeler's partner, switches from cordiality to rudeness, and in a sequence comparable to the opening of Handke's *Die Unvernünftigen sterben aus* he is suddenly dressed like a boxer, shadow-punching all over the stage. Wheeler swings between shy subservience and domineering aggression, Miss Scoons between secretarial meekness and rebellious self-assertion. When she reads from a script she claims to have written or goes into a trance (as characters do very often in Shepard's plays) her personality changes again. These abrupt shifts of character are reminiscent of Ionesco's plays,[12] but an amoeba-like splitting of character has occurred in Shepard's work from the beginning. In many of the early plays, a boy puts on the voice of an old man or an old woman, sustaining the identity he has assumed, half playfully, half seriously, only to drop it abruptly and perhaps pick it up again later. In *The Tooth of Crime*, alternating between an old man's voice and his own, Hoss has an imaginary dialogue with his father. In *La Turista* (produced New York 1967, London 1969) the characters change costume, nationality, attitude and identity with disconcerting casualness. After putting on a Mexican poncho, the American girl addresses the audience in a mixture of Spanish and English, declaiming as if she were selling slaves in a crowded marketplace; in *The Holy Ghostly* Shepard splits the character of Pop into two bodies. After an Indian ghost has told him that he is already dead, a witch brings on a corpse dressed in clothes identical with the old man's. When *rigor mortis* has set in, she says, the ghost will come back to collect him. She leaves the corpse in a sitting position: gradually it stiffens into the horizontal. Which does not mean that it cannot answer when he asks a question. Like his son, who refuses the name Stanley, insisting on being called Ice, the old man oscillates between ordinary American and old-time Western speech patterns. For neither of them is identity stable.

Directing *Red Cross* in 1968, Jacques Levy found that he could achieve a crisp style by encouraging the actors to move very sharply in and out of character, abandoning consistency of behaviour to comment implicitly on what particular pieces of behaviour signified. A monologue about skiing was delivered in the manner of an excited radio sports commentator, while the actress posed on a bed like a photograph of a skier. Mannerism in performance could parody mannerism in the text, which would itself be parodying mannerism in behaviour. While giving a mock swimming lesson to the maid, who was lying across a bed to go through the motions, the actor spoke as if he were a drill-sergeant reading from a military manual.[13] Shepard is a writer who has learnt a great deal from his directors, not merely incorporating business into stage directions, but integrating into the action ideas developed out of directorial devices for achieving stylistic discontinuity. This is why stylistic self-consciousness, which is so often a handicap to Albee, is an advantage to Shepard.

There is nothing new about the reaction against the idea that a character must be a self-consistent whole. The 'Note to the Actors' at the beginning of *Angel City* is oddly reminiscent of Strindberg's preface to his play *Frøken Julie* (written 1888; produced 1889):

> I have drawn my people as split and vacillating, a mixture of the old and the new . . . My souls (or characters) are agglomerations of past and present cultures, scraps from books and newspapers, fragments of humanity, torn shreds of once-fine clothing that has become rags in just the way that a human soul is patched together.[14]

Shepard writes:

> Instead of the idea of a 'whole character' with logical motives behind his behaviour which the actor submerges himself into, he should consider instead a fractured whole with bits and pieces of character flying off the central theme.

But why should it still be necessary to argue against wholeness and logicality ninety years after Strindberg's play?

Though his characters are more volatile than Ibsen's, Strindberg did not manage to break with the moral tradition in which character was seen as residing in a consistent pattern of behaviour governed by strongly internalised rules. In Ben Jonson's comedy of humours, the intention was didactic and character was little more than a personification of a particular propensity or foible. Strindberg's characters are incomparably more complex, but behaviour always corresponds to the functioning of will-power, and moral judgment is always implicit in the presentation. In Beckett's plays the functioning of will-power is suspended: whether they want to hang themselves, or merely to go somewhere else, Vladimir and Estragon lack the power to fulfil their intentions. Like Proust, they veer between being unable to want anything and being able to want nothing.[15] Shepard goes a long way towards completing the dissociation of will-power, behaviour and personality. Theatrical identity in his plays depends almost entirely on style, while strength depends partly on ability to change style. In *The Tooth of Crime* Crow, left alone on stage, imitates Hoss's walk, showing his power by the speed at which he perfects it. He can put on a style or take it off as effortlessly as changing his clothes. Towards the end of the play Hoss tries to learn Crow's style. His ineptitude as a mimic is the cause of his defeat in this final round of what is continuing to be a duel of styles. Crow, therefore, must seem to be the better actor.

Strindberg's attempts at dissolving the consistency of the ego had been quite different, partly because the underlying motive was autobiographical. He made one of his narrators say: 'I burn with desire to accuse myself and defend myself at the same time.'[16] It was his own soul Strindberg was thinking of when he wrote that his characters were 'fragments of humanity, torn shreds of once-fine clothing' all patched together like the human soul.[17] In *To Damascus* (1898), the Unknown Man is partly an Everyman figure, partly an autobiographical projection, while the Beggar, Caesar and the inmates of the asylum are partly dream figures, partly exteriorisations of inner impulses and personality traits. Fantasy and external reality interpenetrate. *A Dream Play* (1901) presents the world as an illusion which exists only because of a sin. The divisions of space and time are abolished as the structure

imitates both a dream and a symphony, patterning the relationships between sequences without providing narrative links or
logical explanations. Though Strindberg's Expressionism is
intensely autobiographical, the German playwrights who learnt
from him tended to depersonalise their material in the interest of
universality. Ionesco and Genet, in some of their plays, move
back towards autobiography, but neither Beckett nor Shepard
ever does this.

Generally, in Shepard's work, the distinction between actor
and character is disappearing.* The character is often a performer
of one sort or another, or at least someone who uses mimicry.
The actor is forced not only to use his own personality but to
cultivate self-consciousness about style. Unless he knows exactly
what he is doing, he cannot drop it to do something different.
Sometimes the effect is as if a drug were being used to move a
consciousness out of its customary groove. Everything is either
fluid or deliquescent, and the play itself may be thrown into the
melting pot. At the end of *Cowboys No 2* (produced Los Angeles
1967, London 1972) two young men come on with scripts in their
hands, reading in a monotone, starting from the beginning of the
play. At the end of *The Holy Ghostly*, after the corpse has spoken,
Pop throws it into the fire. Flames flicker all over the audience
as if the whole theatre were burning. The script of *Angel City*
contains several extracts from scripts allegedly written by the
characters, but disparaging criticism from other characters impli-
cates the whole play:

> MISS SCOONS *travels around the space and speaks with a different
> voice.* TYMPANI *watches her closely.*
> MISS SCOONS: The ambition to transform valleys into cities.
> To transform the unknown into the known without really
> knowing. To make things safe. To beat death. To be victori-
> ous in the face of absolute desolation.
> LANX: Whose script is that? Where did she memorize that?

* In an article published since this chapter was written he says: 'The
similarity between the actor's art and the playwright's is a lot closer
than most people suspect. In fact the playwright is the only actor who
gets to play all the parts.' *The Drama Review*, Vol. 21, No 4, December
1977.

TYMPANI: It's coming from her!

LANX: Don't give me that! I recognize the style. Sounds like
Fritz Lang or early Howard Hawks.

She may be in a trance, but in Shepard's plays trance is merely
one way of shunting a consciousness on to a different track, and
the discontinuities, like Brechtian alienation effects, work anti-
illusionistically. We may occasionally forget that what we are
watching is only a play, but we will receive frequent reminders.

Though he may never have felt so hostile towards the theatre as
Ionesco or Handke, Shepard has said 'I much prefer playing
music really to theatre'.[18] It would be simplistic to call his playwriting addictive or to argue that he is a prisoner of his own talent,
but it cannot be accidental that so many of his plays centre on
artists or dreamers who are forced at gunpoint to be creative. In
Melodrama Play (produced New York 1967) two men shut up in a
room with a gunman are ordered to compose a hit tune. In
Cowboy Mouth (produced Edinburgh and New York 1971, London
1972) a girl has kidnapped a boy with an old ·45 and she is keeping
him prisoner, determined to make him into a rock-and-roll star. In
Geography of a Horse Dreamer (produced London 1974) a man who
can pick winning horses in his dreams (like the small boy in D. H.
Lawrence's story 'The Rocking-Horse Winner') is chained to a
bed in the hotel room, guarded by two gangsters. In *Angel City*
Rabbit is told that he is not allowed to go away, but later he
realises that the compulsion to stay is internal. 'Nobody's holding
a gun to my head.'

It is possible that the anti-theatre elements in Shepard's work are
necessary to him as reminders of his freedom. For Genet, theatre
was intolerable unless it took as its point of departure the story
about the boy who was told to be Night, only to be demoted back
into playing a soldier when he made Night approach too fast. For
Shepard, who is much more prolific than Genet, the pressure
under the output is tolerable if he can remind himself often
enough that drama is a game, that he is under no obligation to
play it, that when he does play he can change the rules, that with
different rules a game is not the same.

8 *Antonin Artaud and the Devaluation of the Word*

The art of the director is comparatively young. Until the middle of the nineteenth century, timing, interaction and relative positions on stage were left more to chance than they are today. The detail of what happened in performance was controlled – in so far as it was controlled at all – by the playwright and the leading actors. Rehearsal periods were brief, and they were not used to develop characterisations or mould the *mise-en-scène*, but mainly to arrange where the entrances and exits would be made and to teach the supporting actors what the stars required of them. In England William Charles Macready, who was active as an actor-manager from 1827 to 1843, helped to refine and discipline the rehearsal process and, after 1850, Charles Kean, Squire Bancroft, W. S. Gilbert and Dion Boucicault continued the progress towards disciplining the production. But in 1881, when the Duke of Saxe-Meiningen brought his company to London, it became obvious that *mise-en-scène* could be brought to a much finer art if a director combined the talents of artist, planner and choreographer. In 1890 Stanislavski watched the Duke's stage manager, Ludwig Chronegk, directing the company in a Moscow rehearsal. 'I started to imitate Chronegk,' he wrote, 'and with time I became a producer-autocrat myself, and many Russian directors began imitating me as I had imitated Chronegk.'

This was the beginning of an autocratic tradition in which the director planned not only the shape but the detail of his production before he had his first rehearsal with the actors. Stanislavski has described how he prepared *The Seagull*:

> I shut myself up in my study and wrote a detailed mise-en-scène as I felt it and as I saw and heard it with my inner eye and ear. At those moments I did not care for the feelings of the actor! I sincerely believed it was possible to tell people to live and feel as I liked them to; I wrote down directions for everybody and those directions had to be carried out. I put down everything in those production notes; how and where, in what way a part had to be interpreted and the playwright's stage directions carried out, what kind of inflections the actor had to use, how he had to move about and act, and when and how he had to cross the stage. I added all sorts of sketches for every mise-en-scène – exits, entries, crossings from one place to another, and so on and so forth. I described the scenery, costumes, make-up, deportment, gaits, and habits of the characters, etc.

The text was completed by the writer before he handed it to the director; the moves and stage business were fully planned before the first rehearsal. It is only recently that procedures have become less rigid, functions less separate. Today it is commonplace for the director to work with the writer on the script and to arrive at the first rehearsal without having decided on any of the moves. But it still often seems to the outsider that the writer is solely responsible for the words that are spoken, but not for how they are spoken, for the pauses between them or for the action. Beckett's two *Acts without Words* and Handke's *Das Mündel will Vormund sein* are examples of silent plays, choreographed by writers, while Peter Brook's *US* and *Les Ik* exemplify the way in which the author can be reduced to a subsidiary role in the creation of dialogue. Brook may have been influenced during his twenties by his friendship with Edward Gordon Craig, who believed that writers were super-fluous in the theatre, that the director should be dominant, that theatre was an art in its own right, born out of gesture, move-ment and dance.[1] The designer Adolphe Appia, ten years Craig's senior, gave acting primacy over text and all the other elements.[2] The Russian director Vsevolod Meyerhold, who was strongly anti-literary, hoped to achieve a Dionysian concentration on the inner life. He anticipated Brook in borrowing heavily from circus, gymnastics and Noh Theatre, as well as from opera and *commedia dell'arte*. Script became less and less important for him. During the thirties (the last decade of his life) he was trying for a Wagnerian synthesis of words, music, lighting and rhythmic movement with 'all the magic of the plastic arts'.[3]

The two most brilliant, dynamic and influential directors alive today, Brook and Jerzy Grotowski, may have gone still further in devaluing the text, continuing a tendency that was likely, anyway, to become more dominant. If Meyerhold's prose had been less boring, it might have exerted more influence, but it was left for Artaud to write by far the liveliest and most persuasive words arguing that words should be relegated to a subordinate role. Though he had very little influence before his death in 1948, his ideas began to infiltrate theatrical practice after *Le Théâtre et son double* was reprinted in 1964. By then the cultural climate had changed considerably. Generally there has been a withdrawal of confidence from literature and language, together with a surge of interest in Oriental culture, which depends less than ours does on a verbal tradition. At the same time, a work of art has come to be regarded more as an object in its own right and less as a represen-tation of something else. As George Steiner has shown, realism in painting and sculpture 'corresponds to that period in which lang-uage is at the centre of intellectual and emotive life. A landscape, a still life, a portrait, an allegory, a depiction of some event out of history or legend are renditions in colour, volume and texture of realities which can be expressed in words . . . We say: this is a portrait of a man with a golden helmet; or, this is the Grand Canal at sunrise.'[4] But it was not only painting that was to become less representational: it was also words. In 1968, when Handke said that a sentence did not mean anything other than itself, he was repeating a point which had been made in 1799 by Novalis: 'The ridiculous and amazing mistake people make is to believe they use words in relation to things. They are unaware of the nature of language – which is to be its own and only concern.' But literature took a long time to catch up with this view, and drama took even longer. Writing in 1931, William Carlos Williams said that 'the principal movement in imaginative writing today' was 'that away from the word as a symbol towards the word as reality'.[5] The growth of art into anti-art and literature into anti-literature has ensued on the abandonment of representation, the cult of the aleatory, the refusal to continue the dialogue with the audience. The artist turns silently inwards.

As Susan Sontag has said,

> Explicitly in revolt against what is deemed the desiccated, cate-gorized life of the ordinary mind, the artist issues his own call for a revision of language. A good deal of contemporary art is moved by this quest for a consciousness purified of contamin-ated language and, in some version, of the distortions produced by conceiving the world exclusively in conventional verbal (in their debased sense, 'rational' or 'logical') terms. Art itself becomes a kind of counterviolence, seeking to loosen the grip upon consciousness of the habits of lifeless, static verbalization, presenting models of 'sensual speech'.[6]

Artaud, who was central to this development, was predisposed towards it by a stammer, which heightened his sense of the need for more immediate expression than words could give him. Believing that all thought was physical, he had the feeling that articulation was lagging badly behind it. As he put it in a letter to Jacques Rivière, 'I am constantly in pursuit of my intellectual being. So when I can catch hold of a form, however imperfect, I fix it, out of fear of losing all thought.'[7] It seemed to him that he would be fully alive only if he could feel that he was fully in touch with every element in his mental and physical being. Unlike Brook, he was less successful in directing actors than in mani-pulating words. Born in Marseilles, the son of a shipowner, he started writing poetry while he was still in his teens. The first onsets of melancholy came in the same period. Barrault compares him with de Quincey: 'he took drugs because he was ill, did not become ill because he took drugs.'

His career as an actor began when he went to Paris, where the director Lugné-Poë, who saw him in the street, was sufficiently struck by the expressiveness of his face to offer him a part in a play. He went on to play leading parts for Charles Dullin, in Abel Gance's *Napoléon* (1925) as Marat, and in Carl Dreyer's 1927 film *La Passion* de Jeanne d'Arc as Frère Massieu. Artaud joined the Surrealist group in 1924 and in 1925 he took over direction of the Bureau des Recherches Surréalistes and wrote several tracts, but he left the group in 1927, when Breton attacked him for wanting to found a theatre.

By now he had come to hate the sexual and excretory functions. He suffered agonies of revulsion against his own flesh. He believed that the world could never be saved so long as men and women went on making love. His passionate faith in the reality of evil, his insane diatribes pleading for chastity, and his hatred for the bourgeois theatre of words and titillation all have the same neurotic roots. Later on, unable to bear the idea that he had grown inside a womb, he claimed to be self-created. His activities as a theatrical revolutionary were fired partly by the need to use theatre as an escape from the human condition which he so hated – theatre was to become 'de la métaphysique en activité' – but, far from invalidating his ideas, the hysteria charged them with intensity.

> We must believe in a sense of life renewed by the theatre . . . Furthermore, when we speak of life, it must be understood that we are not referring to life as we know it from its surface of fact, but to that fragile, fluctuating centre which forms never reach.
>
> The theatre exists primarily to teach us that we are not free and that the heavens can at any moment fall about our ears.

Artaud's strongest drive was anti-dualistic. He refused to differentiate between mental and physical consciousness: having only himself to consult, he read his own body as if it were a map of the universe. As he put it in 'Position de la chair' (December 1925): 'I must examine this sense of flesh which ought to give me a metaphysics of Being and definitive knowledge of Life ... There is an intelligence, quick as lightning, in the flesh, and the agitation of the flesh shares in the highest activity of the mind.' At the same time he could not help thinking of his personal problem in terms of duplication, displacement, deviation from the self. In 'Le Poème de St François d'Assise' (1922) he wrote:

I am this eternal absence from myself
Always going near my own path.

One of his clearest statements of his predicament comes in a letter written to Rivière on 6 June 1924:

To have in oneself the inseparable reality and the material clarity of a feeling, to have it at the point where it cannot but express itself, to have a wealth of words and syntactic devices which could join in the dance, be brought into play; and just when the soul is getting ready to organize its wealth, its discoveries and this revelation – at this unconscious moment when the thing is on the point of emerging – a superior and malicious will attacks the soul like acid ... I ask nothing more than to feel my brain.

Here, as so often, Artaud seems to be measuring himself against Rimbaud, who had claimed that he could be present at the hatching of his thought.[8] In the same paradoxical letter Rimbaud made the classic statement of alienation from the self. 'I is another.' '*Je est un autre.*' Artaud echoed this when he said it was always other people that he heard in his unconsciousness, and it is in his ability to dramatise this fracturing of the self that Artaud anticipates Beckett. In the prose poem 'Paul les Oiseaux' (1924–5) Artaud identified with Paolo Uccello, who is represented as having lost his way in a huge mental tissue. Artaud makes him talk as if he were simultaneously inside and outside himself:

Leave your tongue, Paolo Uccello, leave your tongue, my tongue, my tongue, shit, who's talking, where are you? Proceed, proceed, brain, brain, fire, tongues of fire, fire, eat your tongue, old dog, eats its tongue, eats, etc. I tear my tongue out. YES.

In Beckett's play *Not I* (1972) the speaker is constantly trying to fend off her own identity. Whose voice is it that is talking inside her head? Partly Rimbaudesque, partly Artaudian, the idea was developed in Beckett's novel *L'Innommable* (written 1949–50), where the prose was being made to explore the conditions of its own creation, curling back on itself in long sentences like a tongue trying to find its own roots:

> . . . where are you, what are you seeking, who is seeking, seeking who you are, supreme aberration, where you are, what you're doing, what you've done to them, what they've done to you, prattling along, where are the others, who is talking, not I, where am I, where is the place where I've always been, where are the others, it's they are talking, talking to me, talking of me, I hear them, I'm mute . . . you don't feel a mouth on you, you don't feel your mouth any more, no need of a mouth, the words are everywhere, inside me, outside me, well well, a minute ago I had no thickness, I hear them, no need to hear them, no need of a head, impossible to stop them, impossible to stop, I'm in words, made of words, others' words . . .

From the beginning, Artaud had been ambivalent towards words, but his genius was, above all, literary, and when he first attempted to create a theatre of his own, his premisses were not altogether anti-literary. He did not like mindless subservience to the words, but did not want to undercut the importance of the playwright.

Together with Robert Aron and the playwright Roger Vitrac, he founded the Théâtre Alfred Jarry in 1926. The articles he wrote in newspapers and the brochure for the first season (1926–7) were ambivalent towards the script: the intention was to show a minimum of respect to the spirit of it. There should be no docile subservience to the script: what should be achieved as the production evolved was 'a kind of magnetic intercommunication between the spirits of playwright and director . . . Applying ourselves to a text, forgetting ourselves, forgetting theatre, we should lie in wait for the images that are born in us, naked, natural, excessive, and we should go to the end of these images.'[9] At the same time, the script was the only thing that seemed either 'invulnerable' or 'true', and it was important to cut down on the 'hateful and cumbersome apparatus' which 'turns a written play into a show, instead of letting it stay within the limits of words, images and abstractions'.

Artaud's Surrealism had left its mark on his theatrical ideas. We should free ourselves not only from all reality and all probability, he said, but from all logic. 'We must learn to be mystical again.' His Catholic upbringing had also left its mark. The choice of words with religious overtones tallies with the assumption that there should be some kind of communion with the audience. 'They would no longer come merely to see but to participate.' 'We suffer from a huge inability to *believe*.' The theatre should be able to proffer 'a world ephemeral but true, a world in contact with reality'. 'We are not addressing ourselves to the mind or the senses of the spectators, but to their whole existence. Theirs and ours. We stake our lives on the show performed on the stage.' It would be presented with a profound sense that 'a part of our deepest life is involved in it'.

He committed himself to a more consistently anti-literary position in July 1931, when he got the central idea for his 'Theatre of Cruelty' from seeing a troupe of Balinese dancers at the Colonial Exhibition in the Bois de Vincennes. Watching the performance, Artaud thought he could see theatre being used as a means of overcoming the dualism between inner and outer realities, bridging the gap between impulse and articulation.

> The thoughts it aims to evoke, the spiritual states it tries to generate, the mystical solutions it proposes are moved, sustained, achieved without delay or circumlocution. It all seems to be an exorcism for making our demons FLOW.

The story was told, he wrote, through 'inner states' (*états d' esprit*) themselves ossified and reduced to gestures, schemes . . . Like realisation, conception has no existence except in so far as it is objectified on the stage. They triumphantly demonstrate the absolute domination of the director, whose creativity *eliminates words*. The 'idea of a metaphysic' appeared to emerge out of 'a new utilization of gesture and voice'.[10] What he did not understand was that the reason words were virtually superfluous was that Balinese audiences were so familiar with the Ramayana story, on which the plays were based. He overestimated the contribution of the director, and he was wrong in saying that the dances were not religious. But his misunderstandings had results which have contributed powerfully and usefully to the development of theatre.

He developed his ideas in letters to critics and friends. Writing to Benjamin Crémieux on 15 September 1931, he argued that 'theatre should become a sort of experimental demonstration of the profound identity of the concrete and the abstract'. He attacked Western languages for desiccating ideas, while he praised Oriental languages for 'setting in motion a system of natural analogies'. Theatre should be where 'ideas are stopped in flight at a point where they have not yet become abstract'. The ideal theatre 'reconciles us philosophically with Becoming'. Just over a year later, in a letter to Jean Paulhan, editor of the *Nouvelle Revue Française*, he spoke of 'an alternative natural language':

> Words do not wish to say everything. By their nature and because they are fixed once and for all, they stop and paralyse thought instead of allowing it free play and encouraging it to develop . . . To spoken language I am adding another language and trying to restore its old magical efficacity, its power of enchantment, which is integral to words, whose mysterious potential has been forgotten.[11]

The phrase 'Theatre of Cruelty' was coined in March 1932, and, as he explained in a letter to Paulhan, cruelty, in his sense, was not exclusively a matter of sadism or bloodshed or horror.[12] In using the word he wanted 'to return to the etymological origins of language, which always evoked a concrete notion through abstract concepts . . . Essentially, cruelty means strictness, diligence, and implacable resolution, irreversible and absolute determination.'[13]

The theories Artaud evolved for his Theatre of Cruelty were intended to inaugurate a new phase of theatrical practice in which 'the director becomes author – that is to say creator'.[14] Though the dualism is not altogether destructible, and though Artaud's

influence cannot be isolated from that of the designers Appia and
Craig or the directors Meyerhold, Max Reinhardt, and Erwin
Piscator, his formulations have had an impact which is described
by Susan Sontag as 'so profound that the course of all recent
serious theatre in Western Europe and the Americas can be said to
divide into two periods – before Artaud and after Artaud'.[15]

The first manifesto for the Theatre of Cruelty[16] promised that
'without taking account of text', his productions would include
an excerpt from the Zohar, and a story by the Marquis de Sade,
with its eroticism transposed, pruned, and allegorically represented
– the cruelty would be violently externalised and everything else
covered up. A play from the Shakespearian period would be
adapted to the current spiritual confusion, while other Elizabethan
plays would be stripped of their dialogue to retain only costume,
situations and characters. The influence of the Surrealist attitude
to dreams is visible at several points in the manifesto, and Jan Kott
has compared this attitude to the Elizabethan text with Picabia's
trick of dismantling an alarm clock to make an *objet-dada* out of the
parts.

Artaud's violence was itself nourished by the violence of the
Elizabethan theatre, just as Jarry's *Ubu Roi* drew on *Macbeth*.
Many of the anti-literary elements in the modern movement had
literary sources, and Artaud's extremist reaction against conventional theatre and rationalistic language was inseparable from
the fascination with evil that was characteristic of the *poète maudit*.
Theatre must be used to bring the public into contact with the true
nature of experience, which is cruel.

> Cruelty, is, above all, lucid, a kind of rigid directedness, a sub-
> mission to necessity. There is no Cruelty without conscious-
> ness, without a kind of applied consciousness. It is this which
> gives to each act of life its bloodcolour, its cruel nuance,
> because it is understood that Life is always the Death of some-
> one . . . The erotic Desire is Cruelty, because it burns of
> necessity; Death is Cruelty, the Resurrection is Cruelty,
> Transfiguration is Cruelty.

One of the most influential passages in his Manifesto deals with the architectural relationship between acting area and auditorium:

> We are abolishing stage and auditorium, replacing them with a
> sort of common space without any kind of division or barrier
> . . . Direct communication will be re-established between
> spectator and performance, actor and spectator, by the placing
> of the audience in the centre of the action . . . Abandoning
> existing theatres, we will take some hangar or barn, recon-
> structing it according to the architectural principles expressed
> in certain churches, certain holy places, certain Tibetan temples
> . . . The four walls will be bare of any ornament, while the
> public will be seated in the middle of the floor on swivel chairs
> which allow it to watch the performance going on all round it.
> . . . Special positions in the four corners of the hall will be
> reserved for the actors and the action. Sequences will be played
> in front of whitewashed walls designed to absorb light. Over-
> head, as in certain primitive paintings, galleries will run all
> round the hall. These will allow the actors to pursue each other
> from one position to another whenever the action demands it,
> whilst the action can spread to different levels and differing
> perspectives. A shout uttered at one end of the hall can be
> transferred from mouth to mouth with successive modulations
> and amplifications till it reaches the other end. The action will
> unfurl, will extend its trajectory from level to level, point to
> point, paroxysms erupting suddenly in different places, as in a
> great fire.

It was not until after the war that this began to have its effect on
theatre design and production. The effort to break down the
dividing line between stage and auditorium has been central to
the development of theatre. In some productions (such as Ariane
Mnouchkine's 1970 staging of *1789*) the audience has been in the
centre of the action, and Buzz Goodbody's *Hamlet*, which trans-
ferred from The Other Place at Stratford-on-Avon to the Round
House Downstairs, used so many ideas from the paragraph
I have quoted that it could almost be read as a preview of the
production.

The directors most profoundly influenced by Artaud are Brook,
Grotowski and Joseph Chaikin, but in the Paris theatre, his ideas,

somewhat vulgarized, filtered into the mainstream through the work of Jean-Louis Barrault. Admiring his powers as a mime, Artaud befriended him and taught him much of what he knew. In December 1935 he may have been thinking partly of Barrault when he wrote 'Un Athlétisme affectif', which advances the idea that the actor should think of a human being as a double or an 'eternal ghost radiating affective powers'. The ideas about breathing and screams put forward in this essay and in 'Le Théâtre de Séraphin' are remarkably similar to the ideas Barrault himself was later to advance in 'An attempt at a Little Treatise on the Alchemy of the Theatre' and 'Alchemy of the Human Body'.[17]

They met almost every day. Artaud introduced Barrault to Tantrist Yoga, Hatha Yoga, the Tibetan *Book of the Dead*, the works of Fabre d'Olivet, the Upanishads, the *Bhagavad-Gita, Milarepa*, and Pythagoras's *Golden Verses*. He called the actor 'an athlete of the emotions'. Artaud was now trying to fulfil vicariously his personal ideal of being fully alive through being closely in touch with every element in his physical and mental make-up. He taught Barrault about the Cabbala, which divides human breathing into six main 'arcana', each involving a different combination of masculine, feminine and neuter. As in acupuncture, said Artaud, there are pressure points in the body which support physical exertion and come into play when affective thought is emerging. The solar plexus, for instance, is the centre for anger, aggressive and gnawing emotions. The secret is to agitate these pressure points as if whipping muscles into action.

Barrault made extensive use of Artaud's ideas. What he learned may be inferred from Paule Thévenin's accounts of what Artaud taught her: 'He gave me exercises to do . . . I learned to scream, to sustain the cry to the point of annihilation, to move from falsetto to a lower pitch, to prolong a syllable till breath was totally spent'.[18] Barrault was even able to physicalise Artaud's idea of merging the human with the non-human. Writing about the Balinese dancers and describing the movements and sounds that constituted the 'new physical language based on signs', nearly all Artaud's images were non-human: 'angular postures', 'brutal jerks', 'syncopated modulations at the back of the throat', 'musical phrases cut short', 'insect flights', 'rustling branches', 'the musical

angle formed by arm and forearm', 'a rarefied aviary where the
actors themselves are the fluttering', 'hollow drum sounds',
'machines creaking', 'animated puppet dances'. He praised the
asymmetrical robes that made the actors look 'like moving hiero-
glyphs'. In 1935, rehearsing for *Les Cenci*, his only production
under the Theatre of Cruelty banner, he advised the actors that it
would be easier to think of themselves as rapacious men of the
Renaissance if they chose an animal and modelled their performance on it. He believed that in the play, as in Lucas Van Leyden's
painting of *Lot and His Daughters*, the theme of incest precipitated
a revelation of 'cosmic cruelty'. 'I have imposed on my tragedy
the movement of nature, this kind of gravitation which works
alike on plants and creatures, and which is also to be seen in the
volcanic upheavals of the sun.' The text – Artaud's adaptation of
Shelley's play and Stendhal's 1837 translation of extracts from
archives in the Cenci palace – is replete with images of cosmic
viciousness, but, from the reviews, it would seem that very little of
this came across to the audience. In any case, the production was a
failure, running for only seventeen performances. Rejecting an
opportunity to work with Barrault, Artaud left for Mexico. 'There
the theatre which I imagine, which perhaps I contain within myself, expresses itself directly, without the intervention of actors
who can betray me.'[19]

After leaving for Mexico in January 1936, he spent only nine
months in Paris (November 1936 – August 1937) before his eight
and a half years in lunatic asylums. In his letters from the asylum
at Rodez, and in the verse and letters he wrote during the two
years of freedom between his release in 1946 and his death in
March 1948, he interpolated nonsense words which he did not
believe to be meaningless.

voctrovi
cano dirima
cratirima
enectimi

vonomi
cano victrima

> calitrima
> endo pitri
>
> calipi
> ke loc tispera
> kalispera
> enoctimi
>
> vanazim
> enamzimi

Some of the sounds are not dissimilar from those of Orghast, the language created by Ted Hughes for Peter Brook's production in Persepolis (1971)*:

> Khervackya doma Pramanath figgadagleg
> vuckluongleggada . . .
> gra gra glasta sheer
> glasta curblot
> gra blogauss sjoum blot
> gra bashotta hoan blot
> gra nullvuggun strutta hoan.

Artaud felt a similar need for a language which would not depend on other people's words. Before he left Rodez he wrote, in 'Révolte contre la poésie':

> In the forms of the human word there is I don't know what rapacious operation, what rapacious self-devouring, in which the poet, limiting himself to the object, watches himself being eaten by this object. There is a crime weighing on the word made flesh, but the crime was to admit it. Libido is animal thinking and these are all animals who one day sloughed off their non-humanity.

He believed he had already created a language which could become comprehensible to everybody. In his letter of 5 October 1945 to Henri Parisot he referred to the book he imagined he had written in 1934, under the title *Letura d'Eprahi Falli Tetar Fendi Photia o Fotre Indi*, 'in a language which was not French but which everyone would be able to read'.

Rimbaud, who had believed in the possibility of creating 'a

* See below, pp. 212–16.

poetic speech accessible, sooner or later, to all languages', could hardly have made a more determined series of efforts to transcend the existing structures of language and literature; he could hardly have admitted defeat more abjectly than he did in 'Adieu', the final section of *Une Saison en Enfer*:

> I have tried to invent new flowers, new stars, new flesh, new languages. I believed I could gain supernatural powers. Well, I must bury my imagination and my memories. What artistic glory – a story-teller who got carried away!

Shortly afterwards Rimbaud gave up writing. He had always detested 'literature', and he called himself a literaturicide. His equation of art with consciousness and consciousness with suffering had a profound influence on Artaud, who said: 'Rimbaud taught us how to live.' Lecturing in Mexico on 'Le Théâtre d'après-guerre à Paris', Artaud reported that the attempt had been made 'to rediscover the secret life of theatre just as Rimbaud managed to rediscover the secret life of poetry'. Undeterred by Rimbaud's self-confessed defeat, Artaud had struggled both towards a universal language and towards a theatre language that could wordlessly express this secret life. Under the influence of the Cabbala, which teaches that words, being an emanation from God, form the basis of all creation, he had accepted the primitive belief that words possess intrinsic physical strength. Incantation could therefore be a powerful weapon.

In his *Nouvelles révelations de l'Être*, which was published in 1937 after his return from Mexico, he wrote explicitly about the void:

> It is a long time now that I have been aware of the void but refused to throw myself into it.
> I have been a coward like everyone I see.
> I now know that when I thought I was rejecting this world,
> I was rejecting the void.
>
> For I know that this world does not exist and I know *how* it does not exist.
> What I have been suffering from till now is having rejected the void.
> The void that was already inside me.

> I know the desire was there to enlighten me through the void, and I have refused to be enlightened.
>
> If I have been made into a bonfire, it was to cure me of being in the world.

And in one of his last works, *Van Gogh le suicidé de la société*, describing the 'Self-Portrait with a Straw Hat', he went still further:

> Van Gogh has seized the moment when the pupil of the eye is going to spill into the void . . . and, what is more, nothingness has never harmed anybody, but what pushes me back inside myself is this desolating absence which passes and momentarily submerges me, but I see there clearly, very clearly. I even know what nothingness is, and I will be able to say what there is inside it.

The loss of faith in language is partly a loss of faith in rationality. Nothing is to be learned from the words that explain the solid crust of the world's surface. Artaud's influence has helped to precipitate a new interest in the discourse of madness. Hölderlin, Nietzsche, Poe, Nerval, Baudelaire, Lautréamont, Rimbaud, van Gogh – it is the artists in delirium who may be able to teach us about the void, and one consequence of this revaluation is the recurrence of delirium and madness, whether as a theme or as an ingredient of method, in the work of Beckett, Ionesco, Genet, Handke, Brook, Grotowski and Chaikin.

9 The Anti-Director – Peter Brook

During the first twenty years of his professional life, Peter Brook worked his way dialectically between opposites. After directing a Shakespeare play, he would go on to a West End comedy or a musical; after an opera, to a television play or a film. Far from adopting an anti-theatre attitude, he seemed to feel at home in every corner of showbiz, always producing interesting results in spite of or because of his ability to accommodate his creativity to varying physical and financial circumstances. One of his best productions, the 1970 *Midsummer Night's Dream*, was evolved for the amateurishly designed theatre at Stratford-on-Avon, 'where, if you don't face front and speak at a certain pitch . . . you can't be heard'.[1] It also has bad sight-lines. The production came to life in a different way when it was performed, once, in the Round House. Had it been evolved for a theatre-in-the-round or an open stage theatre with good acoustics, he might have been able to contrive an even closer relationship between performers and public.

His decision to work mainly outside the existing theatrical set-up was a refusal to go on compromising. He had long been aware that actors do most of their best work in the rehearsal room, that repetition is a deadly enemy of creativity, that a long run – the result of success – produces a steady deterioration. Since 1963 he has been experimenting with different means of exposing work to audiences before it has hardened into a finished product. In 1962, when he was invited to become a director of the Royal Shakespeare Company, he agreed on condition that the company should subsidise experimental work which would be carried on separately from its seasons at Stratford and London. The first twelve weeks of experimental work, directed by Brook and Charles Marowitz, culminated in five weeks of performances at the LAMDA Theatre in January 1964 under the Artaudian title *Theatre of Cruelty*. The programme carried a note comparing the experiment to a scientific research project, and warning the audience that it was watching 'a public session of work-in-progress: improvisation, exploration, and a re-examination of accepted theatre forms'. In 1968 the phrase 'work in progress' and the comparison with laboratory work again figured on the duplicated programme issued to the audience that came to the Round House to see acting exercises based on brief extracts from *The Tempest*. But like the critics, the public tends to ignore such warnings and to react as if it is being offered a finished work. Since the foundation of Brook's International Centre of Theatre Research in Paris (earlier in 1968) he has tended to spend most of his time working with actors, experimenting, doing exercises, working on lines taken from plays, ideas taken from myths, developing expressive sounds and movements as alternatives to dialogue, approximating as closely as possible to perfecting the voice and body as performing instruments, but rarely exposing the work in public performance and then only when the work needs exposure, never for the sake of publicity or money. If all theatrical work takes place in a quadrilateral with writer, director, actor, and audience at the four points, Brook has thickened the line between director and actor at the expense of the other three lines.

If there was any doubt about whether he had moved into an anti-theatre position, it was dispelled in October 1976 when he stated his belief in

> the need for the destruction – not of the present Theatre, because why should we want to destroy it? – but for the destruction of the belief that there is any validity in the present Theatre . . . The Theatre that we know, over a long period of time has been the Theatre of the Lie rather than the Theatre of the Illusion – simply because its points of contact with the life around it are almost entirely cut. Cut on a social level, cut on a political level, cut on an emotional level, and cut on an intellectual level . . . The fact that, in the whole range of emotions, nine-tenths of them are squeezed out of the Theatre means that the Theatre is operating in a closed building with a very, very thin strand of experience. These are the deadly factors which mean that any belief in this form as it stands has to be taken and destroyed.[2]

As with most anti-artists, there is a long-term optimism underlying the short-term pessimism. If it is true, as he went on to say, that only a tiny part of the audience's consciousness is being touched by current theatrical activity, the negative gesture of withdrawing (incompletely) from the rehearsal–performance treadmill is inseparable from an affirmation of belief in the possibility of finding ways to touch on a larger part of the audience's consciousness. At the same time, Brook's withdrawal cannot be understood fully unless it is seen in the context of contemporary anti-art. Like Duchamp, he is rejecting the conventions and channels by which the average practitioner sells his wares to the consumer. The ideal of communication is still there, but it seems better to stay in harbour than to risk being wrecked on the rocks of commercialisation and corruption. Research takes priority over contact with the public, the exploration of inner space over the compulsion to fill an empty canvas or an empty theatre. In so far as art or acting can still be seen as a spiritual project, material considerations seem inimical. The performer's responsibility is to his own sense of truth, and the public is seen partly as an embodiment of materialist values. Instead of flattering it by giving it what it wants or insulting it with theatrical provocation, Brook has opted for a period of ignoring it, staging very occasional productions in Paris or London or Stratford-on-Avon, but working mainly in the privacy of a research centre, forming audiences by private invitation (sometimes to children), and making major expeditions to Persepolis or Africa, implicitly rejecting the Western European audience, and the limitations normally imposed by language and culture.

Is Brook's attitude anti-literary? He has involved the poet Ted Hughes not only in creating an alternative language, Orghast, for a performance in Persepolis (1971) but in producing sounds, ideas and scenarios to be developed in improvisation. In *Les Ik* (1975) the playwright Denis Cannan was involved in adapting Colin Turnbull's book *Mountain People*, but the last time Brook concerned himself with material originated by a living playwright was in 1970, when he worked in Paris on Handke's *Kaspar*. First of all he stuck to the script:

> But we found we could communicate the play in that way only to a tiny cross-section of humanity, because it can only be played to an equally small number of people who can mentally make themselves ready to take on a Handke set of rules; for those able to listen to language exactly on Handke's wavelength it was fine, but for those who are not, for a million legitimate human reasons, if only because it was written for a particular social class in the language of the intelligentsia, then those people are not going to make the first step to come into tune with it. The barrier couldn't be in any way breached. So we found we had to change the form until in the end Handke's austere and verbal play became a musical with very little dialogue (half the words went entirely), movement, dancing, songs, and eventually we came to a fine version that could scoop in any audience – and then what the play was about came to life. Handke saw both versions and liked the free one much better.[3]

Brook's predilection for working through the creative collectivity of a group was announced in his 1968 book *The Empty Space*: 'Group creation can be infinitely richer, if the group is rich, than the product of weak individualism.' In England the great pioneer of group creativity had been Joan Littlewood, who maintained

> I do not believe in the supremacy of the director, designer, actor or even the writer. It is through collaboration that this knockabout art of theatre survives and kicks . . . No one mind or imagination can foresee what a play will become until all the physical and intellectual stimuli which are crystallized in the poetry of the author, have been understood by a company, and then tried out in terms of mime, discussion and the precise music of grammar; words and movement allied and integrated.[4]

She carried her principles triumphantly into practice in her apparently authorless 1963 production of *Oh What a Lovely War*. Charles Marowitz, who reviewed the production for *Encore*, was quick to recognise its importance as an essay in discontinuity: 'No sooner has the production adopted one stance than it flips into another, but despite these endless modulations, there is no sense of contradiction. This is not merely the simplex two-dimensionalism of black comedy where laughter freezes up into menace, but the multi-dimensionalism of true Epic Theatre where styles appear in order to serve the nature of what is being said, and what is being said is constantly being varied.' For Marowitz the experience was crucial, and nothing he has done in the theatre is more important than carrying the germ of discontinuity from Joan Littlewood to Peter Brook when the two men collaborated at the end of 1963 on preparations for their *Theatre of Cruelty* season.

This Artaudian experience seems to have made Brook more aware of his dissatisfaction with the limitations of playing to a minority united by linguistic, cultural and educational qualifications. Later it was the same dissatisfaction that led him into the Orghast project and into the African expedition. The human body is almost exactly the same everywhere, so there must be a way of communicating simple information about physical states (elation, dejection and so on) without using anything more than postures and sounds. Artaud had spoken of 'an alternative natural language'. Music, singing, dancing, acrobatics and conjuring tricks can almost infallibly bridge any cultural or linguistic barrier, so is it possible to build up an international theatrical vocabulary, using sounds and movements, for communicating with any audience anywhere?

Brook could be accused of failing to make up his mind about what part words should play in this theatre language; he could retort that this is what he is trying to find out. Never one to baulk at impossibility, he set himself the task of evolving 'a theatre language as agile and penetrating as the Elizabethans created . . . intensity, immediacy, and density of expression'.[5] Like Artaud, he believes that all thought is physical, that an actor should be able to short-circuit the gap between impulse and expression, like a cat. 'A cat actually thinks visibly. If you watch him jump on a shelf, the wish to jump and the action of jumping are one and the same thing.'[6] Undeniably, working with Brook in Paris has helped actors to increase their range of vocal and physical expressiveness, and it is arguable that in the long term, the contributions he is making to the theatre from outside will prove more valuable than any he could have made from inside. It may have been no part of his intentions to put himself beyond the range of the critics, but it is virtually impossible to assess any of the work he has done since 1968 except the outcrops in four public productions seen in Europe – *A Midsummer Night's Dream, Timon of Athens* in French (Paris 1974), *Les Ik* and *Ubu*.[7] The Persepolis production of *Orghast* was exposed to the international press, but the most sympathetic and understanding review came from an opera critic who was likelier than his non-musical colleagues to respond to the choric subtleties. In one passage, a solo voice rose above bass chanting; several times words were chanted in set rhythms scored by Richard Peaslee.[8]

Writing about Artaud in 1961, Brook tried to explain 'our current obsession with improvisation':

Anti-author, anti-director and anti-audience, the anti-actor improvises – in search of what? The anti-movie director improvises his movie – in search of what? . . . First of all the forms of order have let us down. In fact all the structure of nine hundred years is now open to question . . . If I had a drama school, the work would begin very far from character, situation, thought or behaviour. We would not try to conjure up past *anecdotes* of our lives . . . We would search deeper: not for the incident but for the quality, the essence of this emotion, beyond words, beyond incident . . . to me, what matters is the difference between the man who stands motionless on the stage and rivets our attention and the man who fails to do this . . . Star quality, personality. No. That's too easy and it's not the answer . . . But I know it's just here, in the answer to this question, that we can find the starting point of our whole art.[9]

The article goes on to launch an Artaudian attack on our Occidental way of separating principles from 'the massive and energetic spiritual state that belongs to them'. As it says, rehearsal conditions provide a common ground on which there is no need for director or actors to discuss the scale of values by which something is better or worse than something else. What matters is what 'works' theatrically, and the idea of communicating to an audience is strongly present, even when the only audience is the director. The constant aim is to make contact in a way that transcends the limitations of ordinary social intercourse and heightens awareness. 'A real experience in the theatre is qualitatively better than one from a drug because it demands an activeness from the audience as well as the stage.' But, like Artaud, who also used the Elizabethan theatre as a point of reference, Brook argues that words could no longer perform such a central function:

I believe in the word in classical drama, because the word was their tool. I do not believe in the word much today, because it has outlived its purpose. Words do not communicate, they do not express much, and most of the time they fail abysmally to define. There have been great theatres in the history of the world with a concrete language of their own that is not the language of the streets nor the language of books – all great theatre is religious . . . I want to see outer realism as something in endless flux with barriers and boundaries that come and go – people and situations forming and unforming before my eyes. I want to see identities changing not as clothes are changed . . .

but as scenes dissolve in a film, as paint drips off a brush. Then I
want to see inner realism as another state of movement and
flux – I want to sense the energies which, the deeper one goes,
become stronger and clearer and more defined . . . I want to feel
the true forces that impel our false identities: I want to sense
what truly binds us, what truly separates us.

The idea of having a drama school was fanciful, but the underlying urge to train or re-train actors was gratified when he and
Marowitz recruited ten young actors – their average age was
twenty-four – to work experimentally together for twelve weeks
before giving five weeks of performances at the LAMDA Theatre.
The preliminary work was designed partly to break down
Stanislavskian habits of continuity with Artaudian disruptions.
Instead of encouraging the actors to think in terms of 'through-
lines' and 'super-objectives', beading sequences together on a
single string of intention, phasing development along a consistent
line of 'character', Brook and Marowitz worked 'to create a discontinuous style of acting'.[10] Improvisation exercises were devised
in which transition and adjustment to interruption were more
crucial than what was being interrupted. Two actors in mid-scene
would be cut short by the entrance of a third performing an
unrelated series of actions. They would have to adapt theirs to his,
until all three were interrupted by a fourth. 'Little by little,' wrote
Marowitz,

we insinuated the idea that the voice could produce sounds
other than grammatical combinations of the alphabet, and that
the body, set free, could begin to enunciate a language which
went beyond text, beyond sub-text, beyond psychological
implication and beyond monkey-see-monkey-do facsimiles of
social behaviorism . . . Sounds were created which had the
resonance of wounded animals; of pre-historic creatures being
slain by atomic weapons. Movements became stark and unpredictable. Actors began to use the chairs and tables as sculptural
objects instead of functional furniture. Facial expressions, under
the pressure of extended sounds, began to resemble Javanese
masks and Zen sculpture.[11]

In one improvisation, a writer was confronted with his landlady, his girlfriend, his father, his drinking companion, an old school-friend and an insurance salesman, each making a different kind of demand on him. After the six sequences had been played separately, they were made progressively to overlap until all six were running simultaneously. Before the pressure had become intolerable the exercise would have built to a Ionesco-like farrago of contradictory statements and gestures. Another experiment in simultaneous contradiction centred on casting several actors as conflicting components of a single personality and making them speak at the same time in answer to an interviewer's questions. Being unable to take in so many words all spoken at the same time, they had to concentrate on tone, inflection, innuendo, vibration.

As Marowitz suggests, 'The potential superiority of an Artaudian theatre – compared even to an overhauled and much-improved realistic theatre – lies in the fact that its language is not yet discovered, therefore not yet tarnished and empty.'[12] The five weeks of performances, with a programme that varied from night to night both in content and in casting, represented the results of Brook's first sustained attempts to evolve an Artaudian language. Sometimes the programme included three minutes from Genet's *Les Paravents*. One of the exercises had already been based on the idea of speaking with paint: after a strongly emotional encounter, the actor had to express his attitude in a painting. In performance, the process was incorporated not only in the excerpt from *Les Paravents* but also in the production of Artaud's brief play *Le Jet de sang*, which was first performed wordlessly, through inarticulate sounds, and afterwards as Artaud wrote it. Another text (by Paul Ableman) was performed without direction or rehearsal.

The next phase of work began with the enlargement of the group from ten to seventeen for a private production in the Donmar Rehearsal Rooms of Genet's *Les Paravents* (omitting the last five scenes). Using some of the same exercises, the group worked towards evolving a style for the play. One of the best moments was the sequence of chalking red flames on the screens to denote the burning of the orchard, and Brook achieved the kind of effect Artaud had intended to produce in his *Theatre of Cruelty* when a gigantic dummy, bedecked with medals and ribbons, dominated the scene, and when Sir Harold left his huge glove in the fields to keep order in his absence. Something frightening was in each case being stylised into something that seemed absurd without ceasing to be disturbing.

Brook had long been interested in Genet's work. In 1960 he had directed the French première of *Le Balcon*, and in 1962, working on *King Lear*, he had treated the Goneril–Regan relationship in terms of *Les Bonnes*, with Goneril as dominant, hardened by disaster, and Regan as softer, though fired by the masculinity of her sister.[13] The production was also influenced by Beckett, and especially by *Endgame*. Brook aimed for the same timelessness, the same truthfulness and the same self-denial. No luxuriating in despair. In an article titled '*Endgame* as *King Lear*'[14] Brook wrote: 'He does not say "no" with relish: he forges his merciless "no" out of a longing to be able to say "yes".' The production of *Lear* did the same.

Many of the same actors and the same techniques of discontinuity were used later on in the year for Peter Weiss's *the persecution and assassination of Marat as performed by the inmates of the asylum of Charenton under the direction of the marquis de Sade*. On the first day of work for the *Theatre of Cruelty* season the actors had each been given something to bang with and something to bang on – sticks, ladles, spoons, boxes, tins, crates. They then elaborated rhythms, sometimes using fingers, knuckles, elbows instead of or in combination with their instruments. In the Weiss play, while Sade was lecherously coaching Charlotte Corday in how to stab Marat, orchestrated lunatics were using wooden spoons to beat out Dionysiac rhythms on legs, knees, ankles. Brook's production went a long way towards translating the principles behind Theatre of Cruelty into theatrical practice, combining Brechtian alienation effects with semi-ritualised delirium and the Artaudian compulsion to express the inexpressible. The production at once made audience provocation into a refined art, and came as close as Brook has ever come in a modern play to finding 'a theatre language as agile and penetrating as the Elizabethans created'. In his Preface to the printed edition he wrote:

A good play sends many such messages, often several at a time, often crowding, jostling, overlapping one another. The intelligence, the feelings, the memory, the imagination are all stirred ... Starting with its title, everything about this play is designed to crack the spectator on the jaw, then douse him with ice-cold water, then force him to assess intelligently what has happened to him, then give him a kick in the balls, then bring him back to his senses again. It's not exactly Brecht and it's not Shakespeare either but it's very Elizabethan and very much of our time. Weiss not only uses total theatre, that time-honoured notion of getting all the elements of the stage to serve the play. His force is not only in the quantity of instruments he uses; it is above all in the jangle produced by the clash of styles.

The production style shifted unsettlingly between realism and stylisation. Straightforward dialogue was interspersed with songs and passages of rhymed verse, abrasive and apocalyptic, sung or chanted from between the painted lips of doll-like prostitutes and string-wigged lunatics. Threatening outbursts of manic behaviour kept interrupting the play-within-the-play. The imitation of schizoid and erotomaniac behaviour was realistic, unlike the chalky make-up with blood-red lipstick and exaggerated lines around the mouth. The guillotine was frightening; the buckets of red, white and aristocratically blue blood were comically reassuring. Charlotte Corday's knocking on Marat's non-existent door was portentous; and she used her hair to flagellate de Sade, accompanied by whistling from the lunatics. The action ended in pandemonium as the patients overpowered the nuns and nurses who, egged on by Coulmier, the director of the asylum, were belabouring them with batons. Music was playing, the frantic movement took up the rhythm of a 'mad marchlike dance', while there was rhythm in the shouting and screaming. In the script, the play ends with a signal from Coulmier for the curtain to be lowered; in Brook's production the lunatics, who were fighting and smashing up the set, abruptly desisted at his signal. When the audience applauded, the cast, faces expressionless, replied with a slow hand-clap.

The experimental work done during rehearsals of the *Marat/Sade* had been designed to culminate in a marriage between *mise-en-scène* and a text that already existed in its entirety. For his next production, *US* (1966), Brook and the actors rehearsed for fifteen weeks without any such restriction. Some scripted material was provided by Dennis Cannan, but much of the text was invented during rehearsal by the actors. The ambiguity of the title posed the question of how far the British should feel involved in American responsibility for the Vietnam war, which was still going on. The preparatory work forced the actors to think in theatrical terms as they searched for the answer to such questions as: 'If I say I care about Vietnam, how does that influence the way I spend my time?'[15]

As in *Les Paravents*, a gigantic dummy was used, this time representing a US marine commando, who crashed on to the stage. As in the *Marat/Sade*, there were well-directed scenes in which the actors were apparently running berserk, and again powerful effects were generated from clashes of style and abrupt transitions. A solemn discussion of American interrogation methods dissolved into a stage picture of a Vietcong prisoner writhing in the grip of two American soldiers. Suddenly he was transformed into a rock-singer writhing through a number. With an unpredictable transition into a Chinese theatre-style, a symbolic history of Vietnam was enacted in mime. Often the action would shift into comedy. As Brook said, 'We were continually moving into burlesque and farce as being perhaps the only way that one can deal with extreme horror.'[16] (Since about the beginning of the sixties, he had been under the influence of Jan Kott, author of *Shakespeare Our Contemporary*, who believes that the old tragic themes – fate, the meaning of life, freedom and inevitability, the discrepancy between humanity and the absolute – can today be handled only in grotesque comedy.)[17] The comic sequences in *US* also added to the opportunities for stylistic gear-changes, from light-hearted satirical ballads, for instance, into horrific air-raid sound effects. The first half of the show ended with a group of whimpering war victims, paper bags over their heads, blindly groping their way through the auditorium towards the exits.[18]

No attempt was made to offer facile solutions or to prescribe attitudes for the audience to adopt. The sequence that relied most on dialogue was about a man who had decided on a protest suicide, parallel with those of the Vietnamese Buddhist monks who were pouring petrol over themselves to die in the flames. He was seen in argument with a girl of liberal convictions who had no faith in the effectiveness of self-immolation. The scene culminated in hysteria as she screamed out her demand that the war should spread to this country. Kenneth Tynan, who accuses Brook of 'shallow and factitious pessimism', and of being a 'pure master of the theatrical gesture', has complained that he was merely using the Vietnamese war to 'get at' the Hampstead intellectuals,[19] but Ronald Bryden, writing in *The Observer*, argued that the production contained 'moments of brilliance which advance the theatre's frontiers historically', while, in *The Times*, Irving Wardle wrote that he had never experienced such a successful theatrical assault on the audience's detachment.

The collaboration with Ted Hughes began when Brook commissioned him to adapt Seneca's *Oedipus* for the National Theatre production, which opened at the Old Vic in March 1968. Hughes was probably quite wrong to believe that in Seneca's version the Oedipus story 'becomes something close to the scenario of a mystery play in the religious sense',[20] but though his translation was very free, it was vivid, vicious and highly speakable, piling images of barbarity and animality into lines of variable stress.

For the first three of the ten rehearsal weeks, Brook did not allow any of the actors to see a script. They worked at physical and psychological gymnastics, and he played records of Tibetan monks resonating, encouraging the actors to try, like singers, to produce resonation from the chest. As the audience came into the theatre, it saw some of the cast assembling on stage in uniformly black clothes, while others were positioned about the auditorium at picked vantage points, sitting or standing on specially constructed platforms or leaning against metal pillars. A rap from on stage cued the first sound, a low hum proceeding from all over the theatre and growing louder. The chorus was among the audience. In the centre of the stage a huge gold-clad cube was rotating, painfully reflecting the spotlight beams that fell on it. The on-stage actors had gold-clad wooden boxes, which they now beat with their hands, while the others beat against their pillars. More than in any of his previous productions, Brook fragmented words into component sounds, using choric echoes of syllables and sounds as rhythmic backing to speeches by the principal characters. Oedipus's first speech, which was transposed from much further on in Seneca's text, encapsulated the whole story, so that less depended on narrative suspense, and he was not ignorant of what was going to happen to him.

Terror runs through the action, and the effect of Brook's production style was to de-individualise it, making it into a social reality. After listening in silence when Oedipus began to address the gods, the chorus came in with a heavy, loud, rhythmic breathing, which was used again to back Jocasta's first speech. The next chorus was divided between voices on stage and voices in the auditorium, so the audience felt surrounded by the events that were being narrated. The lamentations were punctuated with a loud sound half way between a swallow and a groan; then dry clicking sounds started as concerted accompaniment to individual speaking voices. Each line denying the existence of the gods was followed by a hollow, rhythmic, choric laugh. Some notes were sung, and some were stretched into sounds reminiscent of Noh Theatre. The chorus then began fragmenting its lines more than ever, repeating and overlapping phrases. The atmosphere was by now so doom-laden that Creon's line, 'I didn't know what terror was; I feel it now as I speak', could be rendered quite matter-of-factly. Quoting the oracle's words at the shrine, he was speaking against a background of humming, and he used a high-pitched monotone. Tiresias made his entrance to a background of 'Kssh' and 'Psst' noises; a sound like a whip whistling through the air continued as he spoke, and as he interrogated his daughter, Manto. Her delivery was solemn, flat, the alarm held down. When Tiresias acted out the embarrassment of the silent gods, the chorus produced a stylised equivalent of the helpless sounds a dumb man makes. The noises grew louder, quicker – a groaning, grunting, humming, which took on a sexual overtone as it mounted to a climax of excitement. On the line, 'the Queen and her womb', with Oedipus cowering in an almost foetal position, with Jocasta thudding across the whole width of the stage in a strange straddling gait, knees bent but rigid, legs stiffly spread, doing a half-turn at each awkward stride, and with Creon crawling on his belly inside the opened golden cube, thumping the floor like an angry baby, we had the feeling that these three figures represented phases of human development between birth and death.

Oedipus's blinding of himself was described by the Messenger in short phrases all ending on the same note, but gradually the note was pushed higher. Though the declamation was flat, pain and bitterness seemed to be tearing into the restrained sound from underneath, while the breaks in the flow of words became impressive. Any display of emotion would have made less impact than the unimpassioned statement of facts like 'Blood came spouting out over his face and head. In a moment he was drenched'. The speech ended with a hiatus: the Messenger's exit was a carefully prepared anti-climax, an expressive silence which had the effect of a shrug. 'What can we do?'

In the on-stage action, the blindness was denoted by black eye-patches which the blind Tiresias fixed over the King's eyes. His head held stiffly, Oedipus stood motionless as Jocasta moved towards the erect golden spike, which had been fixed into the floor of the golden cube. Standing about a foot away from it, she impaled herself symbolically, groaning with pain and satisfaction in her excited struggle towards the climax of death. The production ended with a modern Bacchanalian revel. Led by a six-piece band raucously playing 'Yes We Have No Bananas', the cast – all sporting gold carnival cloaks over their black clothes, some wearing animal masks – danced through the auditorium and around the golden phallus which had replaced the spike. The audience's laughter was boosted by the need to release tension that had accumulated during two hours of Senecan horror.

Hughes's text allowed Brook and the actors more freedom than a Shakespeare text to arrive at stresses, rhythms and syllabic values that had been evolved out of exercises and rehearsal work. Brook has written:

A word does not start as a word – it is an end product which begins as an impulse, stimulated by attitude and behaviour which dictate the need for expression. This process occurs inside the dramatist; it is repeated inside the actor. Both may only be conscious of the words, but both for the author and then for the actor the word is a small visible portion of a gigantic unseen formation . . . The only way to find the true path to the speaking of a word is through a process that parallels the original creative one. This can neither be by-passed nor simplified.

In a Shakespeare play the pressure of the blank verse line constantly influences the actor's decisions about the weight, the shape and the value to give each syllable. In the rehearsals of *Oedipus* Brook asked actors to feel free about warping words. As Ronald Pickup (the Messenger) has testified, 'The word *stand* didn't have to sound like *stand*. One could do anything with any of the series of words, but one was really concentrating on sound from back beyond the time words were invented. Just having the words vaguely sitting on top of it. I remember that exercise most vividly because I think that was the time when I felt it really broke through. And the most ugly, awful – but for that speech real and right – sounds were coming out. And then, as time went on, it was possible to integrate them.'[21] At one stage Brook helped him by telling him to imagine that he was a gargoyle on a Gothic cathedral or a monster in a voodoo ceremony. He found himself producing grotesque noises which could not be used in the performance, but the fact of having made them helped him towards it.

It was in the spring of 1968, immediately after this production, that Brook began to work in Paris with an international group of actors. Just before *Oedipus* opened in March, he had been invited by Jean-Louis Barrault to run a theatre workshop during the two-month *Théâtre des Nations* season, so that actors from visiting companies could join in. Wanting more continuity, Brook offered to form an international group and work with it through the two months. He recruited nine English actors, five Americans, seven French and one Japanese. He involved three other directors – Geoffrey Reeves, an Englishman; Victor Garcia, an Argentinian; and Joseph Chaikin, director of the Open Theatre in New York. They began work on 6 May, concentrating on medieval mystery plays and sequences from *The Tempest* and from Calderón's plays, but in face of the student rebellion, the French government cancelled the *Théâtre des Nations*, and the group would have been homeless but for an invitation to London from the RSC.

For a week at the end of July some of the work based on *The Tempest* was exposed to public view in the Round House. This time, instead of planting actors among the audience, Brook seated some of the audience on scaffolding structures which could be wheeled into the centre of the acting area. Without attempting to present more than disconnected fragments of Shakespeare's play, the actors would condense lines into keywords, and keywords into isolated syllables or sounds, translating words into physical movements and moods into rhythmic chants. In this early phase of his work towards achieving a new balance between verbal and non-verbal elements, Brook was continuing the experiments he had started for the *Theatre of Cruelty* season, testing how much could be expressed through the body movements of actors working in pairs or small groups and through sounds that had nothing to do with words – humming, resonating, groaning. Some of Shakespeare's lines were chanted, some repeated so many times that they became almost like a litany. The Japanese actor beautifully suggested the wind with a sound derived from Noh theatre, while the others responded fearfully to the imaginary tempest, huddling together and whimpering – a collective response to an act of theatre projected out of one man's imaginative reaction to an imaginary storm.

Some parts of the play could be physicalised more effectively than others. The conflict between Prospero and Caliban could not survive on such a meagre ration of words, and it was odd to see Prospero swinging athletically by one arm from the top of some scaffolding throughout a narrative speech. The dangling actor's shouts became almost meaningless because he could not concentrate on what he was saying. But, Brook has said:

We had no sense of obligation to deliver *The Tempest*. Consequently we were free, we could do a *Tempest* in which nine-tenths of the text was inaudible, incomprehensible . . . It would have meant many months of work before we could have recovered that same freedom and yet made every word and every line live completely. To do neither thing would have been a horrid half-way house where we would have had to become much stiffer and conventional to deliver the text, or we would have had to say 'To hell with the text. This is ruining our newly found freedom.' . . . The only good solution would have been to have gone on working month after month to the point where in presenting the text, we could have found all the freedom there was in the exercises.[22]

The duplicated programme warned the audience that it was being asked to participate in 'exploring questions that are concerning the theatre everywhere . . . What is a theatre? What is a play? What is an actor? What is a spectator? What is the relation between them all? What conditions serve this relationship best?'

This formulation may seem naïve, but its explicitness indicated a reductionist concern to go back to the beginning of theatre art, and, if necessary, start all over again. The very fact of posing such fundamental questions implied that Brook was prepared to find himself in total disagreement with the solutions provided by the theatrical *status quo*.

But for his next production, he went back to a Shakespearian text, which would be presented *in toto, A Midsummer Night's Dream*. Again he began rehearsals with exercises and discussions aimed at exploring the play's theme, not intellectually but through the bodies and the personal experiences of the company. Visually the most striking feature of the production was the trapezes and the other elements imported from Chinese circus. According to the designer, the starting point was the need 'to delimit a specific small-sized acting area, a neutral place to introduce other elements of the play. There are points for instance where people are "sleeping" while action is going on. At first we wanted the actors stuck on the walls . . . Then I suddenly realised that we already had a marvellous mechanism – the flies – for lifting people up and down, and so the trapezes came in. They also accentuated the floating and dreaming aspect of the play. We could use the stage vertically as well as horizontally.'[23]

There was no condescension in the way Brook treated the

amateur actors in the play-within-the-play. The emphasis was not on what differentiated them from the courtiers but on what the two groups had in common. Nor were the fairies made to seem generically different from the humans. Incorporating elements of circus, music hall, conjuring tricks, ballet, songs and ritual at the same time as democratising the poetry, the production tallied with what Brook was later to say about Shakespearian theatre. 'The Shakespearian theatre speaks simultaneously in perform-ance to everyone, it is "all things to all men", not in general, but at the moment when it's being played, in actual performance. It does so by reconciling a mystery, because it is simultaneously the most esoteric theatre that we know in a living language and the most popular theatre.'[24] This version of *A Midsummer Night's Dream* aimed to offer something to every conceivable kind of audience, and so it tended towards removing the barrier that usually divides actors from spectators. The sensation was of belonging to a circle of people celebrating all the contradictions and compensations of the human condition. At the end, when the actors walked through the auditorium, shaking hands with the nearest spectators, the sense of solidarity was confirmed.

The reaching towards communion and the tendency to mini-mise differentiation of class within the play were characteristic of Brook's concern to make contact with a broader social spectrum. In a 1970 interview he had fantasised about giving performances of a play in eighty different milieux – 'On Broadway, in Harlem, to farmers in Iowa, in a prison, and so on.' One performance 'might be at midnight unconfined by space and time – a perfor-mance playing maybe to two thousand people with actors and spectators staying and talking until dawn'. It should be possible for theatre to transcend not only social but national frontiers; when he returned to work with the multi-national group, which was reinstated in Paris, and when he commissioned Ted Hughes to invent a new language, he was not only showing his dissatis-faction with the degenerated English we now speak and write, he was wanting to test how far human beings could ignore differences of race, language and cultural tradition, communicat-ing through movements and sounds, using the lowest common multiples of human expressiveness and raising them to a higher power. As Brook asked in *The Empty Space*, 'Is there another language, just as exacting for the author, as a language of words? Is there a language of actions, a language of sounds – a language of word-as-part-of-movement, of word-as-lie, word-as-parody, of word-as-rubbish, of word-as-contradiction, of word-shock or word-cry?' And can new words be minted out of sounds that will have a comprehensible meaning dependent on their sound and regardless of the different semantic connotations they might have in different countries? After an interview with Ted Hughes, Tom Stoppard wrote: 'It is Mr Hughes's conviction, indeed the point of Orghast, that hypothetically there are some meanings, basic mental states, for which there are optimum sounds irrespective of the audience, Arab or Eskimo . . . It was Mr Hughes's task to offer the actor the sound which he felt was best suited to convey a given meaning . . . When Mr Hughes decides that "help me" is *moama ya*, he is working a deeper vein where physiology, philology, psychology and a touch of mysticism are combining to form an ore which in a certain light is not self-evidently fool's gold'.[25] Hughes's intention was to create an 'organic language' in which abstractions were always referred back to a physical root.

Before launching into either the language or rehearsals for the production which were both called 'Orghast', Brook made the actors work for a long time on a dozen or so syllables which had no specific meaning, loading them with connotation and association. The idea was to find areas of the actors' expressive powers which were not brought into play through normal language.

Watching the actors working in Paris, Hughes felt that the effects of *Orghast* were liberating:

> When they have a new sound which has no precise intellectual content they have to search their resources for an actuality which will give it content – unless they're just going to make an empty noise. They reach for the most living feeling in them at that moment – a feeling that might have been evoked by imagination, by their precise situation in a dramatic action, or just by their life.[26]

If the implication is anti-literary, Brook's premiss was anti-art:

None of us believe that the so-called frontiers and the so-called definitions of art, or of what a particular art today is for, or what they're doing, are in themselves particularly valid or particularly worthy of respect. We're trying to go beyond the outline formed by certain cultural patterns. We say 'Look beneath'.[27]

The production of *Orghast*, which was the culmination both of Brook's first year's work with his group and of the whole Artaudian phase in his work that had begun with *Theatre of Cruelty*, implied a total rejection of English literature, the English theatre and the English language. No director in the history of theatre had ever made a more dismissive gesture to his mother-tongue, and the cultural traditions built up in it. This is the negative aspect of what Brook was doing; the inseparable positive is that he was trying to create a form of drama immediately comprehensible to any human being.

Before the performance of *Orghast* at the royal arts festival of Persepolis, the company put on a show in a much simpler style in one of the Persian villages, an experience which prefigured the African expedition of 1972–3. The two styles of playing corresponded to the two levels on which the company had been working to develop 'on the one hand a very simple, naïve popular theatre work, and on the other a very intense, cool, hieratic theatre work'.[28] He had taken ten Persian actors into the company, which now also included actors from England, the United States, France, Spain, Portugal, Mali and the Cameroons, but, on both simple and hieratic levels, he was trying to turn the language difficulty into an advantage, working towards a performable *lingua franca*.

One of the central problems was how sounds, words, actions and other visual elements should be blended in making up this new theatrical language. This is not a question Brook would have attempted to answer theoretically: the idea was to evolve an answer through studio work and performance, using different audiences in different places as sounding-boards. The words spoken during *Orghast* were not all invented by Ted Hughes. The text also included sequences in Ancient Greek, Latin and Avesta, a dead language used during the fourth century by Zoroastrian magi. In the same way that a transition from French to Russian would be noticeable to an audience that understood neither, movements between the four languages made their effect, but few people realised that the Greek and Latin sequences were excerpts from Aeschylus's *Prometheus* and Seneca's *Hercules Furens*. For the unprepared spectator, it was impossible to follow the story that was being enacted. The first part of *Orghast* drew both on Western and Asian myths, and on a mixture of literary sources – including Calderón and Shakespeare. Inevitably some members of the audience would be more alert than others to the borrowing and the allusions. Some of the visual effects were spectacular. No one could have failed to be affected by the moving ball of fire, the flaming torches, the groupings and movements, well devised by Brook and the three other directors in relation to the tomb of Artaterxes, a two-tiered platform cut into the rock. Some of the vocal sounds were moving, many were striking. But the reactions of most spectators must have been tarnished by a resentful awareness of missing out on the meaning. Many would have guessed that it was Prometheus who was chained or roped to a ledge high on the rockface; not everyone understood that the shrieking girl was a vulture, or why, later on, she dragged a scared boy out of the tomb to be taught language. (This was possibly an outcropping remnant of the work done the previous year on Handke's *Kaspar*.) Similarly, it is questionable whether *Orghast* would have had references to *La vida es sueno* (*Life is a Dream*) built into it if they had not been working on Calderón. His play is about a prince imprisoned by his father; in *Orghast* the tyrant imprisons his own children. Finally, in a spectacularly ritualised duel, fighting with a flaming torch in one hand and a knife in the other, the tyrant, who is mesmerised by the torch of a freed African slave, blinds himself, like Oedipus.

Individual moments could hardly have failed to make their impact on virtually the whole audience – the opening chorus, staccato and disunited, of the squatting, earthbound creatures; the lament from inside the mouth of the tomb; the blues-like lullaby sung by a boy climbing down a ladder; the knife duel; the sequence of stamping the baby to death; the moans of Prometheus tormented by the vulture; the appearance of the blind tyrant, tapping his way with a stick and ringing a small bell. But the audience could understand neither the relationship between the characters, nor the interrelationship between the moments. Brook had allowed for partial incomprehension. Possibly he had not allowed sufficiently for resentment at being deprived of essential-seeming information.

The second part of *Orghast* was more operatic. It was staged separately, six kilometres outside Persepolis, in a vast open arena, edged by towering cliffs. As in the Round House *Tempest* exercises, the audience was forcibly involved in the action: it had to move about with the actors, who performed alternately on the cliff-face and on the plain. While a procession moved slowly through the middle of the site, the chorus zig-zagged freely across it, enacting the defeat in Aeschylus's *The Persians*. The vulture shrieked from the tomb of Xerxes. After the tyrant and other characters from Part One had reappeared, another action started on the low mounds across the valley. A recital of the names of Xerxes's commanders at Salamis provoked a frightened choric chant, heard over amplifiers. The two actions merged when the Persians invoked the ghost of the emperor Darius. When he appeared, they swarmed up a ladder to the tomb. There was a great deal of processional movement in the action that followed, ending with a procession up the mountain slope timed to synchronise with sunrise.

Between the Persepolis performances and the expedition to Africa the group did almost fifteen months of studio work in Paris, but from the book *Conference of the Birds* by John Heilpern, the journalist whom Brook had chosen to be his chronicler, it seems doubtful whether much of what the actors had learned could filter into the mainly improvised performances they gave in the African towns and villages. Not that what they had learned was valueless: Africa was not necessarily the right place to test it out. With songs and with slapstick comedy they seldom failed to arouse a favourable response from the villagers, but on a more serious level, the effort to communicate elicited a constant simplification of means, an erosion of formalisation. Eleven years earlier, in the article for *Encore*, Brook had expressed his interest in 'the man who stands motionless on the stage and rivets our attention'. In Africa there was an inclination to spiritualise the attempts at penetrating the mystery of what it is that commands attention. Certain moments of stillness or very simple action did transcend the cultural barriers in a way that had nothing to do with music or comedy or spectacle. Buskers, acrobats or circus performers could have played successfully to an audience of African villagers. Occasionally Brook's actors had moments of success that were generically different, and these moments may have had something to do with the self-mastery acquired from months of working at T'ai Chi. For at least some of the actors, the only explanation was religious. The Japanese actor, Katsuhiro Oida, said: 'Acting has become a way to find God. It's normal'. And Heilpern quotes Ted Hughes's reaction to comparable moments he had seen in the actors' work: 'that riveting near-holy or unholy experience where, as the Bible says, "a spirit passed before my face, the hair of my flesh stood up."'[29]

Three days after they entered the desert, Brook gave the actors an idea based on a loaf of bread. The object itself acquired a meaning it could not have in places where bread is not scarce. Placed in the centre of the carpet which served to mark out the acting area, the loaf became a powerful symbol. A confrontation between possessor and would-be dispossessor almost led to blows. Through improvising around the strong, simple drives that the loaf generated, the actors tried to build up a dramatic framework, struggling against the impulse to fall back on clichés, conventions, habits, mannerisms. Brook is good at detecting and rejecting commonplaces, but the process of stripping them away is arduous, and, if it went on long enough, what would be discovered at the centre? An essence or merely an attention-riveting moment?

One exercise Brook developed almost daily during the second half of the journey was related to the *Theatre of Cruelty* interruption exercises. With the group standing in a circle, one actor was asked to make a simple movement. In silence the others followed him. Eventually the actor next to him introduced a variation on it, which the others followed. Each new movement spread around the circle until everybody had introduced one. For actors addicted to making an impression the difficulty was to be simple.

As in Paris, one of the most valuable exercises was done with sticks. Led by the Noh-trained Katsuhiro Oida, the group developed collective awareness by working in unison with long bamboo poles, almost as if they were an extension of the body, and using them for exercises in rhythm and timing, balance and agility. The actors have developed admirable expertise with this communal stickwork, but the expertise is not an end in itself. Like the Zen master-archer, who can 'aim without aiming' and hit the target when blindfold, the actors, throwing and catching sticks, can come to feel that it is the sticks that are manipulating them. Skill is developed to such a degree that no skill and no will-power seem to be involved. In one of the stick exercises, which is based on Samurai swordsmanship, they try to perfect an exchange in which there is no time-lag between thrust and counter-thrust. The defender must anticipate the attacker's intention with enough precision to parry it almost before it is executed. The idea would be to arrive at a pitch of physical expressiveness where, as in Artaud's ideal, there would be no separation between idea and exteriorisation, impulse and articulation. The actor would be like a medium, directly relaying what went on inside him. It would then be possible to extirpate the habit of putting on an act and playing for effect. All thought and feeling would be apprehended in physical terms which would be directly communicated.

There can be no doubt about the usefulness of the stick exercises, but when the sticks were incorporated into performances in the African towns, educated members of the audience were confused because they tried to interpret what was happening. 'Some have suggested the crossing of the bamboo sticks as the Enactment of the Divine Comedy; others the *danse macabre* and others *Exodus*.'[30] As in Persepolis, the audience was stratified according to its familiarity with the mythical and literary sources of the material, but there was confusion on all levels.

It is possible that the African experience contributed more to the next eighteen months of studio work in Paris than the previous fifteen months of studio work had contributed to the African performances, but there is no means of quantifying or judging. Certainly both the expedition and the studio work contributed to Brook's November 1974 production of Shakespeare's

Timon of Athens in French at the Bouffes du Nord, an almost derelict theatre which had not been used for twenty years. The stage and the seats had been removed. Brook's main acting area was where the front stalls used to be; the characters made their entrances from a gaping hole where the stage was. Brook had come to the opposite extreme from the brightness and glitter of *A Midsummer Night's Dream,* though he made something of the same attempt to merge actors and audience. During the first half of the action, within the semi-circle formed by the audience, actors sat on cushions listening.

The French translation was by one of Buñuel's script-writers, Jean-Claude Carrière, and as Brook said in his preface to the published version, Shakespeare's Athens is as symbolic as Ubu's Poland. Accordingly, he made it as timeless and placeless as Beckett's *Waiting for Godot.* Timon (cast much younger than usual) wore a trendy white suit. His sycophantic friends made their first appearance in rich brocade gowns; later, when they visited him in his cave, frock coats and top hats. One of them carried an umbrella. During the first party, Timon's guests crouched down like praying Arabs, and Cupid's masque was like a parody of Kabuki. There was African chanting as the banquet assembled in a bright panoply of sparkling gowns and golden rugs. Apemantus was played by a black actor; Katsuhiro Oida was in the cast, and only twelve of the nineteen actors were French. French members of the audience complained about the bad accents of the other seven; English members complained that our best director was choosing to do Shakespeare in a foreign language. But this was part of the point – to place most of the emphasis on telling a story and relatively little on the words it was told in.

Les Ik, Brook's second production at the Bouffes du Nord, had in common with *Timon* a great stylistic simplicity and economy of means. The Ik, a hunting tribe, was forced into farming when the Ugandan government made its territory into a tourist game reserve, and now the tribe is living on the verge of starvation in consequence of its inability to adapt. Critics wondered whether Brook was allegorising about our own inclination to live beyond our evolutionary means, but it seems more likely that Colin Turnbull's book *The Mountain People* (which was dramatised by

Colin Higgins and Denis Cannan) appealed to him as a story which could be told on stage mainly through actions. Relatively few words are necessary. It was a singularly unspectacular production, but it quietly succeeded in knitting its international cast into a convincing tribe, and in making it look as though the well-nourished, well-exercised actors were dying of starvation.

Scenes which could have been sensational were presented matter-of-factly. A woman lured her child to her by holding food temptingly over a fire, only to withdraw it, letting the child burn its fingers. As in *Oedipus*, economic statement would have let the horror speak for itself, but it was the absence of horror that was horrifying. For the Ik, nothing is too embarrassing to be made into a joke. If they are dying out because they are too debilitated for procreation, if they leave the old to die, if they push out children to care for themselves from the age of three, if stealing and lying have become commonplace, if the only pleasures that remain, scantily, are eating and excreting, they can only laugh hollowly when they explain. The main virtues of Brook's production were negative: he neither sentimentalised nor complicated the situation. Because he never demanded pity for the Ik, we went on respecting them; because he never condemned them, we saw them as fellow-human beings, and because he never condemned the government, we were not distracted from the rudimentary issues by political indignation. Had he toured the production through Africa – or Asia or South America – much of it would have been comprehensible.

In London, critics and audiences were predominantly disappointed. The Round House was too large for the production, so the production appeared to be too small. It was not a show comparable with *A Midsummer Night's Dream*. It hardly seemed any more like a finished production than the 'work in progress' productions of 1964–8, and it hardly seemed like a work of art. In fact there was no category in which it could be placed, but that was because there had been no previous productions that were comparable.

10 The Director and the Group: Grotowski and Chaikin

Jerzy Grotowski has been called 'Artaud's natural son',[1] and Peter Brook has written: 'Grotowski's theatre is as close as anyone has got to Artaud's ideal.' According to Brook, 'No one since Stanislavski has investigated the nature of acting, its phenomenon, its meaning, the nature and science of its mental-physical-emotional processes as deeply and completely as Grotowski.'[2]

As in Brook's more recent work, research takes priority over performance. The company that Grotowski and his collaborator, Ludwick Flaszen, founded in 1959 was called Teatr Laboratorium. After more than five years in Opole, a small town in south-west Poland, it moved to the university town of Wroclaw, where it became an Institute for Research into Acting. With extraordinary persistence, dedication and self-discipline, Grotowski and his actors have gone on experimenting with the human organism, both in exercises and in performance, to find new combinations of spontaneity and artificiality. Like Artaud, he understands that they are not mutually exclusive:

> It is the true lesson of the sacred theatre; whether we speak of the medieval European drama, the Balinese, or the Indian Kathakali . . . that what is elementary feeds what is constructed and vice versa, to become the real source of a kind of acting that glows. This lesson was neither understood by Stanislavski, who let natural impulses dominate, nor by Brecht, who gave too much emphasis to the construction of a role.[3]

Sometimes it has seemed to Grotowski as though forms already exist inside the organism, that the actor must uncover them, like a sculptor working on a block of stone. But while Grotowski believes, as Brook does, that research is indispensable to creativity, he maintains that exercises and creative work should never be mingled.

He is as violently hostile as Genet or Ionesco to the norms of current theatrical practice. The average actor has only two choices, says Grotowski. He must play either for the audience, flirting with it narcissistically in order to be accepted, loved, affirmed, or work for himself, observing his own emotions, studying the richness of his own psychic states. Acting is not far removed from prostitution. 'A man who gives his bodily presence in return for material gain – in one sense or another – by this very fact puts himself in a false position; today even more so than in the past.'[4]

Grotowski professes himself to have been more influenced by Stanislavski than by any other man of the theatre, but he rejects both Stanislavski and theatre:

> For the theatre he was a great man, but I am not interested in theatre any more, only in what I can do leaving theatre behind . . . Many of us present here face the problem: to pursue the profession, or to do something else? As far as I am concerned, it's better to do something else . . . For us the question is: what do you want to do with your life; and then – do you want to hide or reveal yourself, do you want to discover yourself in both senses of the word . . . If one learns *how to do*, one does not reveal oneself; one only reveals a skill for doing. And if any-

one looks for means, resulting from our alleged method, or any
other method, he does it not to disarm himself but to find
asylum . . . For years one worked and wanted to know more,
to acquire more skill, but in the end one had to reject it all and
not learn but unlearn, not to know how to do but how not to
do, and always face doing – to risk total defeat, not a defeat in
the eyes of others – which is less important – but the defeat of
. . . a failure to meet with oneself.[5]

Rejection and reductionism had always been integral to Grotowski's approach. Instead of regarding theatre as a combination
of artistic activities, he wanted to define the minima, to isolate
what was essential to theatre. Could theatre exist without costumes or sets? Without music? Without lighting effects? Without
a text? None of these are indispensable, but there can be no
theatre without actors and spectators. Treating everything
inessential as superfluous, Grotowski evolved the idea of a 'poor'
theatre. Moving along a route parallel to Beckett's, Grotowski
has revealed the richness of the medium by repudiating most of
the resources available to it. All acoustic and musical effects were
to be produced vocally, all visual elements to be produced
through the actors' bodies, appropriately costumed, and scenic
design in which acting area and auditorium were not separate.
Each production has been conceived as a new way of deploying
bodies in space and involving the audience, sometimes making it
interpenetrate with the action, as in *Kordian*, which is set in a
mental hospital, spectators being treated as patients. According to
Grotowski, the producer has two ensembles to direct – actors and
audience. The performance should integrate them.

Grotowski's debt to Artaud is easily exaggerated. He was
ignorant of Artaud's work until 1960, when he read the essay
'Le Théâtre alchimique', and he did not read *Le Théâtre et son
double* until it was reprinted in 1964. (The incantation in Grotowski's 1961 production of Mickiewicz's *Forefathers' Eve* derived
not from Artaud but from the playwright's introduction.)
Nevertheless, the affinity between Grotowski and Artaud is
extremely strong, centring on the emphasis they both lay on
qualities which they describe as 'spiritual', and on the religious

element in theatrical performance. 'We suffer from a huge inability to *believe*,' wrote Artaud in his 1926 manifesto for the Théâtre Alfred Jarry. The performance should be imbued with the sense that 'a part of our deepest life is involved in it'. The audience should leave the theatre in a state of 'human anguish', having been 'shaken and turned back against itself by the inner dynamism of the production'. Grotowski has said: 'I don't see the possibility of being religious today.' But we still need to find a meaning. 'If one does not possess that meaning, one lives in constant fear.' Talking of Nazareth 2000 years ago he said: 'in the air there was a need to abandon force, to abandon the prevailing values and search for other values on which one could build life without a lie.'[6]

Like Artaud, he believes that we are being maimed by 'the tradition that man is divided into the inner and the external'. In theory the demands Grotowski makes on the actor are very similar to the demands Artaud made: that he should free himself 'from the time-lapse between inner impulse and outer reaction in such a way that the impulse is already an outer reaction. Impulse and action are concurrent: the body vanishes, burns, and the spectator sees only a series of visible impulses'.[7] This almost echoes a phrase of Artaud's which Grotowski has quoted: 'Actors should be like martyrs burnt alive, still signalling to us from their stakes.'[8] 'In the final result,' said Grotowski, 'we are speaking of the impossibility of separating spiritual and physical. The actor should not use his organism to illustrate a "movement of the soul", he should accomplish this movement with his organism.'

Many of the images Artaud used suggest that he would have liked the actor to be in a state of trance, surrendering his body to cosmic forces that would act through him, but Artaud had no system, no technique and little skill in making actors do what he wanted them to do. Grotowski has great ability to inspire devotion and loyalty from his actors, and he spent ten years on evolving a system of training. From 1959 to 1962, the object was positive – to extend their technical range. They did exercises to loosen up the muscles and the vertebrae, exercises based on setting different parts of the body into apparent conflict with each other (a fight between the two hands, for example), exercises based on the imitation of animals or of a plant's growth, exercises based on making the face resemble a mask, exercises to open the larynx and to change the voice and its carrying power by finding points all over the body where the pressure of the indrawn air can seem to cause vibration. After 1962, the vocal exercises were changed and although the components of the physical exercises were mostly retained, the method became more negative. Grotowski called it a *via negativa*, a process of elimination:

> The process itself, though to some extent dependent upon concentration, confidence, exposure, and almost disappearance into the acting craft, is not voluntary. The requisite state of mind is a passive readiness to realize an active role, a state in which one does not *'want to do that'* but rather *'resigns from not doing it.'* . . . In terms of formal technique, we do not work by proliferation of signs, or by accumulation of signs (as in the formal repetitions of oriental theatre). Rather, we subtract, seeking *distillation* of signs by eliminating those elements of 'natural' behaviour which obscure pure impulse. Another technique which illuminates the hidden structure of signs is *contradiction* (between gesture and voice, voice and word, word and thought, will and action, etc.) – here, too, we take the *via negativa*.[9]

The interest in contradiction is comparable to Brook's; the interest in the disparity between impulse and 'natural behaviour' is comparable to Handke's. The insistence on passivity in the actor – resigning from not doing it – is comparable to what Meyerhold called 'reflex excitability'; the system of practical exercises he developed in 1922 under the title 'Bio-mechanics' was designed partly to increase the actor's 'physical competence' by helping him to locate his centre of gravity at any moment, and partly to increase his quickness and expressiveness in responding to external stimuli. Grotowski's objective was to remove everything that obstructed the actor's progress towards total involvement. All his psycho-physical resources should be involved in the performance. The director can help only negatively, destroying the obstacles that stand in the way of self-surrender to creativity.

For neither Meyerhold nor Grotowski has it primarily been a

matter of volition, of willpower being asserted. Grotowski
demands that 'The actor makes a total gift of himself. This is a
technique of the "trance" and of the integration of all the actor's
psychic and bodily powers which emerge from the most intimate
layers of his being and his instinct, springing forth in a sort of
"translumination".' Grotowski's language is often reminiscent of
medieval theology, or of Artaud, whose concept of theatre
derived partly from ancient ritual, partly from alchemy. The concern is with a communal act conducive to metamorphosis in the
individual soul. Artaud implies an analogy with the Eleusinian
mysteries, which must, he says, have worked towards resolving
'all the conflicts produced by the antagonism between matter and
spirit, idea and form, concrete and abstract'. According to
Grotowski, Artaud needed anarchy and chaos 'as a spur for his
own character', and he reminds us that they 'should be linked
to a sense of order, which he conceived in the mind, and not as a
physical technique'.[10] But if Artaud had a personal need for anarchy
and chaos, Grotowski has a parallel compulsion towards outrage
and transgression:

> Why are we concerned with art? To cross our frontiers, exceed
> our limitations, fill our emptiness – fulfil ourselves. This is not
> a condition but a process in which what is dark in us slowly
> becomes transparent. In this struggle with one's own truth,
> this effort to peel off the life-mask, the theatre, with
> its full-fleshed perceptivity, has always seemed to me a place of
> provocation. It is capable of challenging itself and its audience
> by violating accepted stereotypes of vision, feeling, and judg-
> ment – more jarring because it is imaged in the human organ-
> isms's breath, body, and inner impulses. This defiance of
> taboo, this transgression, provides the shock which rips off the
> mask, enabling us to give ourselves nakedly to something
> which is impossible to define but which contains Eros and
> Caritas.[11]

He is aware that in his choice of play he has deliberately and
repeatedly involved himself with taboo. He has made use of
'archaic situations sanctified by tradition', wanting 'to attack
them, go beyond them, or rather confront them with my own

experience which is itself determined by the collective experience of our time'. If his treatment of them verges on the blasphemous, his blasphemy is like that of Dostoevsky, who called himself 'a child of unbelief and scepticism', though his 'longing for faith' was 'all the stronger for the proofs I have against it'.[12] In *The Possessed*, after Stavrogin has smashed a crucifix, the Bishop tells him: 'You honour the holy spirit without knowing it.'

The impulse is always towards a quasi-mythical transcendence of the personal and the circumstantial. Unlike Artaud, Grotowski has proved his ability to translate his metaphysics into compelling theatrical reality. His production of *The Constant Prince* plunges a Messianic hero into suffering that must culminate in martyrdom, surrounding the action with a fence reminiscent of a bullring, and implicating the audience by making it uncomfortable at its own passivity. There was no faking about the pain Ryszard Cieslak had to suffer: we saw his body bouncing and his back going red under flagellation from a folded cloak, and he was genuinely hurting himself when he slapped his own chest. He submitted with the same stoical passivity to the torture and humiliation as to the kiss that Rena Mirecka implanted on his groin, but the alternation between supinity and violent animation made his performance seem all the more dangerous.

Calderón's *The Constant Prince* is a rather wordy play about a Christian hero who accepts martyrdom in preference to paying the ransom demanded by his Moorish captors – a whole Christian town. In eliminating most of the words, most of the plot, and most of the characters, Grotowski was doing very much the same sort of stripping down that, in his first manifesto for a Theatre of Cruelty, Artaud had promised to perform on Elizabethan texts. Grotowski's basic attitude – like Artaud's and like Meyerhold's – is anti-literary. He rejects the idea that theatre's function is to 'illustrate' something which already exists, as the text does. He praises Artaud for discovering that theatrical reality is instantaneous, that it does not depend on illustrating life any more than it should illustrate literature. What matters is 'an act carried out *here and now* in the actors' organisms'. The actor who merely plays the text is taking the easy way out. 'The text has been written,

he says it with feeling and he frees himself from the obligation of
doing anything himself.' The encounter with the audience is therefore more important than the text. 'The entire value of the text is
already present once it has been written; this is literature, and we
may read plays as part of "literature".'

Grotowski's text for *The Constant Prince* is much shorter than
Calderón's, and quite different. There is a residue from the
seventeenth century, but Grotowski has treated the script as a
message from the past that 'contains certain concentrations of
human experiences, representations, illusions, myths and truths
which are still actual for us today'. His concern is to contrive a
new text 'as a sort of prism which reflects our experiences'. But
while it is easy for the audience to connect the behaviour of the
torturers with what it knows about concentration camps, ter-
rorists and sadistic policemen, the behaviour of the prince is
explicable only in terms of the spiritual, a mode which most of us
would say we have not experienced. Refusing to renounce his
faith, the prince neither resists nor argues. He submits to torture
and castration, and he suffers physically, but at the same time his
physical reactions make it apparent that there is another level on
which his feelings are closer to ecstasy than to agony. There is
something in him which his persecutors cannot touch. The impression Cieslak irradiated could be described only in religious
terminology: he appeared to be in a state of grace.

Wanting to save the theatre from 'human psychologising',
Artaud created a new metaphysics out of words, gestures and
expression, a new theatre language that would 'use human
nervous magnetism to transcend the ordinary limits of art and
language to realize actively – that is to say magically, *in real terms* –
a sort of total creation, where man has only to resume his position
between dreams and reality'. He was assuming the possibility of a
non-verbal, non-rational contact with the inner life of the
audience. Grotowski understood that if this could be achieved in
the theatre, it would be through myth. 'Only myth – incarnate in
the fact of the actor, in his living organism – can function as a
taboo. The violation of the living organism, the exposure carried
to outrageous excess, returns us to a concrete mythical situation,
an experience of common human truth.'[13]

Looking at the history of theatre in terms of psychology and cultural anthropology, he had seen that

> myth was both a primeval situation, and a complex model with an independent existence in the psychology of social groups, inspiring group behavior and tendencies. The theatre, when it was still part of religion, was already theatre: it liberated the spiritual energy of the congregation or tribe by incorporating myth and profaning or rather transcending it. The spectator thus had a renewed awareness of his personal truth in the truth of the myth, and through fright and a sense of the sacred he came to catharsis. It was not by chance that the Middle Ages produced the idea of 'sacral parody'.[14]

Nor is it by chance that so much of Grotowski's terminology, like Artaud's, derives from this period of cultural history. Writing in *Le Figaro*[15] about his adaptation of *Les Cenci*, Artaud said that he was calling the play a tragedy because it was a myth: 'the men, though less than gods, are more than men. Neither innocent nor guilty, they are subject to the same essential amorality as the gods of the Antique Mysteries, the source of all tragedy.' But he miscalculated the effect his characters would have on the audience. Grotowski does not attempt to theatricalise myth in such a way as to make it acceptable as a model of group behaviour. But 'we can attempt to incarnate myth, putting on its ill-fitting skin to perceive the relativity of our problems, their connection to the "roots", and the relativity of the "roots" in the light of today's experience. If the situation is brutal, if we strip ourselves and touch an extraordinarily intimate layer, exposing it, the life-mask cracks and falls away.'

In *Apocalypsis cum Figuris*, the production he launched in 1968, Grotowski made his bravest attempt at exploring the relativity of our problems by putting on the ill-fitting skin of myth. The performance assessed the relevance of the Christ story by subjecting it to various tests. The conflict between the quotations from the Bible, from the Grand Inquisitor sequence in Dostoevsky's *The Brothers Karamazov*, from Simone Weil and from T. S. Eliot carried the implication that modern consciousness is an echo chamber full of irreconcilable information. Whiling away the time with games, the effete figures in modern dress seemed to be incarnations of contemporary aimlessness.

The central game is sadistic and sacrilegious. The ring leader, who will become Simon Peter, distributes roles – Judas, Mary Magdalene, Lazarus, John. A simpleton is goaded into identifying with Christ. 'You died for us on the Cross.' At the climax of the teasing and manhandling, Peter leaps on his back, as if riding him. This provokes him into a demented dance. (Grotowski told a Polish critic that according to one of the New Testament Apocrypha, Jesus danced.)[16]

Parodic enactment of incidents from the Crucifixion story alternate with erotic episodes. Though much of the dialogue consists of quotation, the structure is not literary. The interconnection between the parts depends on *mise-en-scène* and acting. Though the Simpleton may sometimes remind us of Myshkin, it makes a big difference that he is not articulate or intelligent, that he expresses himself physically. Extraordinarily complex statements are made through the actors' bodies. An expression on a face may be contradicted by a posture, just as words may be contradicted by tone or an action countered by someone else's. Almost each moment of the production makes a complex pictorial statement, while the other moments add to the complexity, which is multiplied by the movement from moment to moment. One almost negates another, as in *Endgame*, where one piece of information about the basic situation is contradicted by another. Despite the density and complexity of the action in *Apocalypsis*, we get an evocation of the void, a suggestion that all this gameplaying is camouflage for the hollowness at the centre. The characters need diversion not because they are waiting for someone, but because there is no one to wait for, and nothing to do, though there is energy to be used up. There is a sequence of inertia at the beginning, and they often lapse back into lethargy between bouts of game-playing and sexual activity.

One of the main strands of imagery is about eating Christ's flesh and drinking his blood. While the Simpleton is in most ways less Christ-like than the Constant Prince, physical assaults on his body are simultaneously reminiscent of the earlier production and of the Crucifixion story. In one sequence the tormentors suck

from the side of his naked chest as if they were drinking wine or
blood. As he is drawn more deeply into the identification, he
begins, like the Prince, to rise above those who have him at their
mercy, submitting with so much meekness and dignity to every
torture and humiliation they can inflict. Again we feel challenged
to define the power he is visibly gaining. Is it 'spiritual'?

The quotations from Dostoevsky's Grand Inquisitor are especially telling.

> Twenty years have passed since he promised to come and found
> his kingdom. Twenty years have passed since his prophet wrote
> that he would come soon but that not even he knew the hour
> and day of his coming, only his father in heaven. But mankind
> has been expecting him with unchanging faith and with the old
> emotion. No, with greater perhaps, because the communion of
> man with heaven has ended . . .
> Instead of the old stern law, man was himself to decide in the
> freedom of his heart what is good and what is evil, with your
> image and your likeness before him. But did it never occur to
> you that he would eventually reject your image and your
> truth if you laid on him so terrible a burden as freedom of
> choice?

We feel under pressure to take sides. Are we rejecting his image?
Are we right to reject his image?

In a sequence which recalls both Golgotha and the Agony in
the Garden, quotation from T. S. Eliot is combined with ritual-
istic singing. In the flagellation sequence, a rolled up towel is used
instead of a cloak, and this time it is the Christ figure who is
inflicting the punishment, driving the money-lenders from the
temple. But the action has become a conflict which Christ cannot
win. The world does not want him. The last scene ends in darkness. Simon Peter's voice is audible: 'Go and come no more.'
When the lights are brought up, the acting area is empty.

After Grotowski and Brook, the director with the best claim to
the title 'Artaud's natural son' is Joseph Chaikin, whose life oddly
parallels Artaud's. Since childhood he has suffered from a cardiac

weakness. His career as an actor, which had begun in the commercial theatre, ended when he was warned not even to risk the strain of playing with his own company; his ideas, like Artaud's, have been conditioned by his own disability. The letters to Rivière are echoed, consciously or unconsciously, in Chaikin's insistence that the actor needs direct access to the life that is moving inside him. States of being should be externalised in performance.

Chaikin's hostility to the theatrical *status quo* grew rapidly out of his experiences as an actor. He played in a production of the comedy *No Time for Sergeants*: 'We counted laughs and adjusted nightly performances to the laughs. We tried to meet the audience on the dumbest common level.'[17] He realised that he had been trained to present character according to stereotype, and that implicitly members of the audience were being offered hints about how they ought to identify themselves and classify themselves. 'Such theatre sells the audience a moral order of social and internal life based on type and function.'[18]

In 1959 he joined the Living Theatre, and, playing in Jack Gelber's *The Connection* and in two Brecht plays, *Mann ist Mann* and *Im Dickicht der Städte* (*Jungle of the Cities*), he came up against a different treatment of character. Brecht required the actor to think, to respond critically to the predicament of the individual he was portraying, inviting the audience to share his response. So his attention must be partly on the audience's attitude. Gelber's play is like *Waiting for Godot* in immobilising characters in a waiting situation, but, waiting for a fix, the junkies are waiting to be taken out of themselves, and the actors have to realise not only the boredom, the frustration and the reluctant passivity, but the contrast between the two modes of being, drugged and undrugged.

Chaikin found that, as an actor, he was using himself in a way for which he had not been prepared either by his training or by his experience in the commercial theatre. But he felt that the directors of the Living Theatre, Julian Beck and Judith Malina, were not sufficiently concerned to explore either the potential of the actor or the ensemble experience, and in September 1963 the Open Theatre was founded in New York after Chaikin had called a meeting of seventeen actors and four writers. The name 'implied susceptibility to change'. It 'would serve to remind us of that early commitment to stay in process'.[19] During the first eight months of work there were two public performances, but the prime concern was to renounce 'the theatre of critics, box offices, real estate and the conditioned public . . . It is not possible to make discoveries under the pressure to please, to gain audiences and money. Only in a climate where people are listening to their own drumbeats can it be possible. It is then necessary to close off this impulse to "make it" in order to open oneself to other voices.'[18] Or as he said in an interview, 'What of us is for sale, someone can buy, but we're certainly not going to trim ourselves for a market we despise.'[20]

Working in freedom from any schedule of public performances, the group concentrated on improvisations and exercises, exploring ways of using the voice and body not to tell a story naturalistically but to exteriorise inner impulses.

> When we do use words we try to understand the unexpressed in the situation – not in a logical way, but rather through behaviour's irrational and more fragile qualities . . . When we locate the inside of a situation in its abstract and elusive texture, we then try to make this thing visible . . . We do characters who have the qualities of life or death, who are suspended or grounded; we play 'states' and 'things' as well as people. We want to know how to play Beckett, Ionesco, Genet, and the others who write about the man *not* in the street.[21]

Unlike Grotowski, Chaikin involved playwrights in the process of working out a new theatrical language that was not to depend primarily on words.

> I'd like to see each play have its own code in the use of words. Each play is only involved in its special poetry. It would become a kind of language, with the syntax carrying a special kind of meaning. The words have special meaning to the audience and the actor. That's what the playwright, finally, has to do. I despair of conversation and conventional language. It doesn't carry meaning any more. It's facile.[22]

The distrust of words is similar to Brook's and Grotowski's. In the Open Theatre, movements, silences and semi-articulate sounds would be no less important than dialogue, while words or disconnected phrases might be used in a non-logical sequence. Apart from actors and playwrights, the group included directors, musicians, a choreographer, a visual artist and two critics. Rhythms, ideas and theatrical images were developed out of improvisations. Sometimes lines would be written to fit a rhythm and a mode of physical expression which had already been fixed. (This happened with a speech about a New Orleans sorceress in the 1969 production *Terminal*.) Sometimes the playwrights would refine or elaborate themes introduced by the actors, and speeches would seldom be written without knowing who was going to deliver them, so the actor's personality would be one of the determining factors, with 'character' constructed either like a mask to fit a particular face or like a semi-transparent veil. (This does not mean that one actor would not be able to take over another's role.) From frequent attendance at rehearsal the writers would also learn how words could often be replaced by a sound or a gesture or a glance. After working with the group on *Terminal*, Susan Yankowitz said: 'It is clearer to me now that writing is not only about what is said but what is unsaid.'[23]

The first writers to attend regularly at the studio were Jean-Claude van Itallie, Megan Terry and Michael Smith. Van Itallie worked directly with the actors, interweaving his work with theirs; all three observed sessions before delivering scripts.

> After the writer has suggested a form – I don't like 'plot' because these things are often much simpler than a plot – we begin to improvise with them. We select what language to use. Very often this is a 'language' of our own, sounds which communicate . . . Sometimes we move in silence or use words or phrases rather than connected sentences in a logical sequence.[24]

In the trilogy of short plays by van Itallie which the company presented in 1966 under the title *America Hurrah*, sentences were sometimes split between several speakers, and in the scene with the psychiatrist in the first play, *Interview*, the whole cast formed a handshaking grand chain, chanting:

> Blah, blah, blah, blah, blah, blah, hostile.
> Blah, blah, blah, blah, blah, blah, penis.
> Blah, blah, blah, blah, blah, blah, mother.
> Blah, blah, blah, blah, blah, blah, money.

As in the Brook–Marowitz *Theatre of Cruelty*, the actors had to switch abruptly and unnaturalistically from one level to another, sometimes from one character to another, and at moments in the interview sequences the audience was included as if it were expected to answer the questions. The third play, *Motel*, was the most Artaudian of all. The motel-keeper and the couple who smashed up the room were represented by grotesque, outsize dolls with disproportionately big heads.

In 1967 van Itallie started working with Chaikin and the actors on the production which toured Europe during 1968 and was shown to the New York public in 1969 under the title *The Serpent*. Like Artaud, who explored his own origins in some of his poetry, Chaikin felt a compulsion to go back to the roots of the situation we are all in. The object in evolving a new version of Genesis was to evoke impressions of the primordial state, together with contrasting impressions of the current situation. As Chaikin said, 'Everyone has some sense of the Utopia we're not living in.'[25] Like Grotowski, he saw that myth could be a means of carrying performance beyond personal relationships, and liberating the 'spiritual energy' of the audience; like Grotowski, he understood the importance of pushing contemporary experience up against 'archaic situations sanctified by tradition'. When the actors reproduced moments from the Zapruder film of President Kennedy's assassination, the juxtaposition with Cain's murder of Abel added to the mythical resonance of the modern event by comparing an anonymous long-range shooting with a killing in which the murderer was feeling his way, doing something that had never been done before. (Brook had also been mythifying modern events in his equation of Mrs Kennedy with Christine Keeler.) Like Grotowski, Chaikin saw that he must violate taboo. 'In *The Serpent*,' he said, 'the point of crossing a boundary is a point of transformation, and the whole company crosses a boundary.

Because, when one person crosses a forbidden line, nothing is the same after that.'

The serpent itself was brilliantly suggested by a tangle of actors who divided sentences between them, producing quantities of apples to tempt the audience. For the opening procession around the theatre, van Itallie's stage direction is:

The players don't use their voices, but they explore every sound that can be made by the human body – slapping oneself, pounding one's chest, etc. The procession appears to be one of medieval mummers, and sounds like skeletons on the move. All at once all stop in a freeze. This happens three times during the procession. During a freeze each actor portrays one of the various motifs from the play such as: the sheep, the serpent, the president's wife's reaching gesture, Adam's movement, Cain's waiting movement, Eve's movement, the heron, and the old people.

Physical movement verged on the acrobatic, while the text, combining liturgical repetition with prosaic flatness, went beyond 'Prufrock' in ironically celebrating the private man's detachment from public events.

> I was not involved.
> I am a small person.
> I hold no opinions.
> I stay alive.
> I mind my own affairs.
> I am a little man.
> I lead a private life.
> I stay alive.
>
> I'm no assassin.
> I'm no president.
> I don't know who did the killing.
> I stay alive . . .

The staging distracted from the flatness of the language.

Like the Balinese actors Artaud saw, and like Brook's actors, the company was deriving some of its effects from observation of non-human movement. The Garden of Eden seemed to be pulsing with animal life. Through jerky, abrupt, mindless-seeming movements, through posture, through choreographed groupings, rhythmic breathing and subtle chanting, primordial life was tellingly evoked. *The Serpent* was the product of a profound collaborative effort. As Chaikin wrote in his Introduction,

> The collaboration requires that each person address to himself the major questions posited in the material: what are my own early pictures of Adam and Eve and the serpent, of the Garden of Eden, of Cain and Abel? These questions deal with a personal remembered 'first time'. They are questions we stopped asking after childhood. We stopped asking them because they were unanswerable (even though we gave or guessed at answers), and later we substituted 'adult' answerable questions for them. The group must also go into those deeply dramatic questions of the 'first man' and 'first woman', 'first discovery of sex', and also into the character of God in the Old Testament. I would state that the premise of the piece is that Man made God in his own image, and held up this God to determine his own, Man's, limits.

This concern with the frontiers of human experience led naturally on to the work that culminated in the production of *Terminal*.

Exploring the meeting points between life and death, the actors brought material taken from their dreams; ideas and attitudes were discussed; body and voice were used improvisationally to probe at the experience of dying. What would it feel like? An embalmer came in to describe his professional technique; Joseph Campbell came in to discuss the treatment of death in myth and in different primitive societies. Three writers, including Sam Shepard, worked with the actors before Susan Yankowitz was asked to take over responsibility for the text. Together with Chaikin and the company she arrived at the notion of guides who could move freely between the living and the dead, or act as mediums through which spirits of the dead can take possession of living bodies.

Reading the text of *Terminal* is quite unlike reading a script which was completed before rehearsals started. It looks like a score for a ceremony. Incantation is interwoven with music, voices overlap each other. Bodies move between trance and dance. Pregnancy is juxtaposed with dying, and, as in *The Serpent*, the audience is pushed into awareness of fundamental existential questions, partly through the isolation of the act of breathing, and of the other fundamental actions, including eating and defecating. The process of dying is brought keenly into focus by a sequence in which an actor is told: 'This is your last chance to use your eyes.' He makes a final effort to take advantage of them and when his vision fails, he is handed a piece of black tape, which he sticks across his eyes. Given his last chance to use his voice, he makes a sound before his mouth is sealed off. Taking his last chance to use his legs, he stumbles weakly forward before being put on a small cart. For years Chaikin had been living privately with the possibility that death could interrupt his work at any moment, but he seems to have been quite unsentimental about placing his fears at the disposal of the actors, who were able to touch chillingly on each other's nerve centres, working with neither reverence nor irreverence, but with a sensitivity that helped them towards a series of effective theatrical statements about death. As in Brook's *US*, the results showed that theatre can be a medium for collective thinking, provided that the group has received instruction and direction in the technique of thinking in theatrical terms.

After this exploration of the borderline between life and death, the group went on to a less verbal, more physical exploration of human mutation. There was a 'writer-in-residence', W. E. R. La Farge, from October 1970 to June 1971 when most of the preliminary work was done for *The Mutation Show*, but no writer was credited for the text. The concentration on basic activities like breathing and walking was correlated with stories about wolf-children and satire on social rituals, such as marriage. Like Handke's *Kaspar*, the show focuses on the losses and limitations involved in initiation into adult human society, and the recurring sentence which parallels Kaspar's 'I want to be someone like somebody else once was' is 'I don't know if it happened to me or to somebody else, but I know that it happened'.[26]

Both *The Serpent* and *Terminal* started with processions;

The Mutation Show started with a parade, as in a circus. The Barker presented the freaks – the Thinker ('She thinks she thinks but she doesn't know what it is that she thinks'), the Man Who Smiles ('If he didn't smile, he would have no face'), the Man Who Hits Himself, the Bird Lady, the Petrified Man. These freak characters were not consistently retained in what followed. The birth trauma enacted in *Kaspar* by a tentative, blundering entrance, was represented by the forcible removal of an actor from a box. He was lifted on to the shoulders of another actor, who carried him forwards, resisting his efforts to shift position in order to see for himself.

In one sequence five actors had to tame a sixth, making her less like a bird, forcing her to conform with human society. Her resistance was oddly touching. Like Brook, Chaikin has achieved interesting results by shifting abruptly from one style to another, and there was an unexpected monologue about the unwillingness of the bourgeoisie to confront the pain of separation, followed by a second physicalisation of birth as another actor emerged from the box, his body covered with a sticky mixture representing amniotic fluids. The action then modulated into farcical satire on marriage, starting with a parade of unhappy couples. A blankly unaware bride was parcelled from father to groom; another undignified groom signalled his sexual appetite by honking incessantly at the bicycle horn between his legs. The denunciation of marital ceremonies and marital norms mounted to a climax reminiscent of Ionesco, with frenetic, nonsensical action fleshing out a logical-seeming progression of nonsensical lines. 'The father of the groom is now dancing with the mother of the bride.' 'The butcher is now dancing with the cow.' 'The people are now dancing with the laws.'

When I saw the company's final production, *Nightwalk*, in June 1973, it was still being presented as a 'work-in-progress', though preparations for it had begun in December 1972. The long incubation is characteristic of anti-art, while Chaikin, like Brook, felt that it was essential to have audience reactions before putting the finishing touches to a work.

The central concern was to investigate the function of consciousness during sleep. Two bird-like creatures presided over

sequences that seemed to represent a nocturnal stream of consciousness in the minds of the others. The swift movement between comedy and high seriousness itself suggested modulations
and states of mind that occur in fantasy and dream. Actors were
pushed on stage, sometimes alone, sometimes in small groups, on
trolleys, as if they were images occurring to the sleepers. The
surrealistic social satire of *The Mutation Show* was developed in a
very funny meal-table scene. The dialogue was in gibberish, but
speech patterns emerged clearly and meaningfully. Once again
anti-art was launching an ironic attack on the inadequacy of our
stratagems to disguise the disparity between animal appetites and
civilised behaviour patterns: carrying a rose and wearing an
elegant evening dress, an actress went on singing a sentimental
lyric and preserving the air of being unperturbed while she was
obscenely assaulted by an actor who wore a top hat and trousers
with a large hole that displayed his bottom.

A comparison with performances at the Cabaret Voltaire might
seem to carry the implication that Chaikin had learnt nothing
significant from Artaud, Brook or Grotowski, or from his years of
experimenting with his company in studio work and in protracted
rehearsal periods, which continued long after the 'work in progress' was being exposed to the public. Presumably acting and
production at the Cabaret Voltaire were fairly unpolished, while
the scripts of the Open Theatre plays are better integrated than
most Dada texts, standing up to comparison with the best
Expressionist plays and the best plays that Artaud directed at the
Théâtre Alfred Jarry, such as Roger Vitrac's *Victor*. The advantage of the Open Theatre writers was that they could benefit from
collaboration with a group of creative actors. Writing and rehearsing became almost indistinguishable parts of a single process, with the result that in text, as in performance, each element
could enrich every other element.

This is one of the great paradoxes of anti-art and anti-theatre –
that the parts need the optimum relationship with each other,
while needing, at the same time, if not to cancel each other out, at
least to undercut each other, so that the resultant gesture is predominantly negative, the total statement veering towards silence.

The negative force directed against previous art needs to be strong enough for some of it to seep into the new work, which therefore seems partly aimed against itself. Pure anti-theatre is not only anti-realistic, it is also hostile to reality, though the anti-world it creates can never provide a viable alternative to reality. And though anti-theatre, like all anti-art, can provide a valid alternative to realism, this validity depends on the survival of realism. At least the audience must go on expecting realism, or new means will have to be found of frustrating it.

Notes

Where full publication details of books are not given in the Notes, these can be found in the Select Bibliography on p. 263.

1 Godot and After

1 See Ronald Hayman, *Tom Stoppard*, 1977.
2 Quoted by Martin Esslin in *Theatre of the Absurd*, 1962.
3 'La Peinture des van Veldes, ou le monde et le pantalon', *Cahiers d'art*, Nos 20 and 21, Paris, 1945–6.
4 *Samuel Beckett*, London, 1976.
5 *The Writer in Extremis*, Stanford, 1959.
6 Nicholas Hern, 'Expressionism' in Ronald Hayman (Ed.), *The German Theatre*, 1975.
7 'Peintres de l'empêchement' in *Derrière le miroir*, Nos 11–12, June 1948.

2 Beckett and Before

1 Octavio Paz, *Marcel Duchamp or the Castle of Purity*, tr. Donald Gardner, London, 1970.

2 Beckett, *Proust*, 1951.
3 See Renato Poggioli, *The Theory of the Avant-garde*, Cambridge, Mass., 1968.
4 'The Aesthetics of Silence' in *Styles of Radical Will*, New York and London, 1969.
5 Pierre Cabanne, *Dialogues with Marcel Duchamp*, London, 1971.
6 Richter, op. cit.
7 *Three Dialogues with George Duthuit*.
8 Letter of July 1866 to Théodore Aubanel.
9 *Proust*, 1931.
10 In *Scrutiny* (Vol. V, No 4, March 1937) Martin Turnell objects 'one thing is certain – a poem which can equally well be a description of the sexual act or of the act of writing poetry must have something badly wrong with it'. This is to miss the point.
11 *La Musique et les Lettres*.
12 Edmund Wilson, *Axel's Castle*, New York and London, 1931.
13 'Dante, Bruno. Vico . . . Joyce' in *Our Exagmination Round the Factification for Incamination of Work in Progress*. *Work in Progress* was the only title given to the section of *Finnegan's Wake* that had been published.
14 *The Novel in France*, London, 1950.
15 André Gide, *Journal 1889–1939*, Paris, 1948.
16 *Monsieur Proust*, tr. Barbara Bray, London, 1974.
17 Gilles Deleuze, *Proust and Signs*, tr. Richard Howard, London, 1973.
18 Journal of Beckett Studies, Vol. I, No I, Winter 1976.
19 *Proust*.
20 *Three Dialogues with Georges Duthuit*.
21 By Lawrence E. Harvey in *Samuel Beckett: Poet and Critic*, Princeton, 1970.
22 Richard L. Admussen, 'Samuel Beckett's Unpublished Writing' in *Journal of Beckett Studies*, No 1.
23 A number of photostats has been made available, and there are discussions of it in John Fletcher and John Spurling, *Beckett: a Study of His Plays*, 1972, and in John Pilling's *Samuel Beckett*, 1976.

3 Ionesco and the Anti-Play

1 *Notes and Counter-Notes*, tr. Donald Watson, London, 1964.
2 Simone Benmussa, *Ionesco*, Paris, 1971.
3 Cf p. 18.
4 Claude Bonnefoy, *Conversations with Eugène Ionesco*, tr. Jan Dawson, London, 1970.
5 '*The Bald Soprano* and *The Lesson*: an Inquiry into Play Structure' in *Ionesco*, Ed. Rosette Lamont, New Jersey, 1973.
6 Ionesco in *Cahier des Saisons*, No 15, Winter 1959.
7 'Richard Wagner, rêverie d'un poète français.'
8 Walter Sokel, *The Writer in Extremis. Expressionism in 20th Century German Literature*, Stanford, 1959.

9 *Notes and Counter-Notes.*
10 *Notes and Counter-Notes.*
11 *Conversations with Eugène Ionesco.*
12 *Notes and Counter-Notes.*
13 *Plays*, Vol 2, tr. Donald Watson.
14 *Notes and Counter-Notes.*
15 See Richard N. Coe, *Ionesco: a Study of his Plays*, 1961; and the interview with Ionesco in Ronald Hayman *Ionesco*, 1972.
16 'Spéculations' in *La Revue Blanche*, 1900–03.

4 Genet's Anti-Worlds

1 A letter to the publisher Jean-Jacques Pauvert printed to preface the 1954 edition of *Les Bonnes*.
2 Another extract from it had been published in *L'Express*, 4 September 1958.
3 *Lettres Nouvelles*, September 1957.
4 The letter to Pauvert.
5 Antonin Artaud 'Sur le théâtre Balinais,' reprinted in *Le Théâtre et son double*, Paris, 1938.
6 'Comment jouer *Les Bonnes*', *Oeuvres complètes*, Vol. IV.
7 'Motifs du crime paranoiaque' in the review *Minotaure*, 1933. Reprinted in *Obliques*, No 2, 1972.
8 Jean-Paul Sartre, *Saint Genet; comédien et martyr*, 1952.
9 An earlier version had been published in the review *La Nef*, No 28, March 1947.
10 *Tel Quel*, No 30, 1967, reprinted in Vol. IV of the *Oeuvres complètes*.
11 Interview with Hubert Fichte, tr. Patrick McCarthy, *The New Review*, No 37, April 1977.
12 *Advertisements for Myself*, New York, 1959; London, 1961.
13 *Lettres à Roger Blin*, Paris, 1966.

5 Peter Handke and the Sentence

1 *Offending the Audience*, the title of the published translation, is misleading.
2 Interview with Artur Joseph, tr. E. B. Ashton, *The Drama Review*, Vol. 15 No 1, Fall 1970.
3 *Preliminary Studies for the 'Philosophical Investigations'. Generally known as the Blue and Brown Books*, Oxford, 1958.
4 *Ich bin ein Bewohner des Elfenbeinturms (I Live in the Ivory Tower)*, 1972.
5 Nicholas Hern's *Peter Handke* draws attention to the relationship between the play and the essay.
6 Interview with Artur Joseph.
7 *Ich bin ein Bewohner des Elfenbeinturms.*
8 Karen Malpede Taylor, 'Two Kaspars – by Peter Handke and the Open Theatre', *Performance*, No 6, May–June 1973.

9 The title is the German version of Prospero's question: 'What, I say, My foot, my tutor?' in *The Tempest*. Literally it means 'The ward wants to be the guardian'.
10 *Ich bin ein Bewohner des Elfenbeinturms*.
11 *They Are Dying Out* is the title of the published translation.

6 *Pinter and Stoppard*

1 Martin Esslin, *The Peopled Wound: The Work of Harold Pinter*.
2 Clive James, 'Count Zero Splits the Infinite', *Encounter*, November 1975.
3 Ibid.
4 Interview in *Theatre Quarterly*, No 16, November 1974–January 1975.
5 See Ronald Hayman, *Harold Pinter*, 1968.
6 See p. 2.
7 'A Valediction: of Weeping.'
8 First Interview in Ronald Hayman: *Tom Stoppard*.
9 Ibid.

7 *Albee and Shepard*

1 Interview with Michael Nardacci and Walter Chura published in *Beverwyck*, Winter 1965, and reprinted in *The Playwrights Speak*, Ed. Walter Wager, 1969.
2 Edward Albee interview with Digby Diehl. *Transatlantic Review*, No 13, Summer 1963. Reprinted in *Behind the Scenes*, Ed. Joseph F. McCrindle, 1971.
3 *Biographia Literaria*, Chapter 13.
4 Ibid. Chapter 14.
5 See p. 85.
6 Peter Farb. Cited by Richard Schechner. 'The Writer and The Performance Group: Rehearsing *The Tooth of Crime*' in *Performance*, No 5, March–April 1973.
7 Cp Schechner.
8 Interview in *The Guardian*, 21 February 1974.
9 Ibid.
10 Cp p. 26.
11 *Theatre Quarterly* Interview.
12 Cp pp. 48–70.
13 See 'Notes on *Red Cross*' in Sam Shepard *Five Plays*, London, 1969.
14 Michael Meyer's translation.
15 See p. 5.
16 In the 'Wresting Jacob' section of *Legends*.
17 Preface to *Miss Julie*.
18 *Theatre Quarterly* Interview.

8 Antonin Artaud and the Devaluation of the Word

1 *The Art of the Theatre*, Berlin, 1905; London, 1911.
2 *L'Oeuvre d'Art vivant*, 1911.
3 See *Meyerhold on Theatre*, Ed. Eduard Braun, London, 1970.
4 'The Retreat from the Word' in *Language and Silence*, London, 1967.
5 'Excerpts from a Critical Sketch' reprinted in *Selected Essays of William Carlos Williams*, New York, 1954.
6 'The Aesthetics of Silence' in *Styles of Radical Will*, New York and London, 1969.
7 5 June 1923.
8 Letter to Georges Demeny, 15 May 1871: 'J'assiste à l'éclosion de ma pensée'.
9 'L'Évolution du décor' in *Comoedia*, 19 April 1924.
10 'Sur le théâtre balinais' published in the *NRF*, October 1931, and reprinted in *Le Théâtre et son double*, 1938.
11 28 September 1932.
12 Letter of 13 September.
13 Ibid.
14 Letter of 7 August 1932 to André Gide.
15 'Approaching Artaud', *The New Yorker*, 19 May 1973. Reprinted as the Introduction to Antonin Artaud, *Selected Writings*, New York, 1976.
16 *NRF*, October 1932. Reprinted in *Le Théâtre et son double*.
17 'An attempt at a Little Treatise . . .' is included in Barrault's *Reflections on the Theatre*, and 'Alchemy of the Human Body' in his *Memories for Tomorrow*.
18 *Tel Quel*, Nos 20 and 39.
19 Letter of 19 July 1935 to Paulhan.

9 The Anti-Director – Peter Brook

1 Peter Brook. Interview with Ronald Hayman in *Playback*, London, 1973; New York, 1974.
2 Interview in *Transatlantic Review*, No 57.
3 Interview summarised in *The Guardian*, 20 March 1974 and printed in Judith Cook, *Directors' Theatre*, London, 1974.
4 Statement quoted by Charles Marowitz in his *Encore* review and reprinted in *Confessions of a Counterfeit Critic*, London, 1973.
5 Quoted in A. C. H. Smith, *Orghast at Persepolis*, London, 1972.
6 Brook, quoted in John Heilpern, *Conference of the Birds: The Story of Peter Brook in Africa*, London 1977.
7 In October 1978 he directed *Antony and Cleopatra* at Stratford-on-Avon.
8 Andrew Porter of *The Financial Times*, who had seen the production five times. What it *immediately* communicated was no longer fresh in his mind.

 9 Cp Ossia Trilling, 'Playing with Words in Persepolis', *Theatre Quarterly*, Vol. II, No 5, January–March 1972.
10 Charles Marowitz, 'Notes on the Theatre of Cruelty', Tulane Drama Review, No 34, Winter 1966.
11 Ibid.
12 Ibid.
13 Cp. Interview in *Plays and Players*, December 1962.
14 *Encore*, No 53, Vol. 12, No 1, January–February 1965.
15 J. C. Trewin, *Peter Brook*, 1971.
16 See Ronald Hayman, *Playback*.
17 Brook's 1962 *King Lear* owed some of its Beckettian elements to Kott's essay '*King Lear* or *Endgame*'.
18 Later this sequence was cut.
19 *Theatre Quarterly*, Vol. VII, No 25, Spring 1977.
20 Preface to printed text, London, 1969.
21 *Playback* interview.
22 Ibid.
23 Statement by Sally Jacobs, in *Stage Design throughout the World since 1960*, International Theatre Institute, 1973.
24 Statement at a press conference (quoted in Ossia Trilling 'Playing with Words in Persepolis'), *Theatre Quarterly*, Vol. II, No 5, January–March 1972.
25 *Times Literary Supplement*, 1 October 1971.
26 A. C. H. Smith, *Orghast at Persepolis*.
27 Statement at a press conference, *Theatre Quarterly*, Vol. II, No 5, January–March 1972.
28 Ibid.
29 *Conference of the Birds*.
30 'The Brook Experience'. Two articles in the newspaper *West Africa* by Ming Tsow, a member of the English department at the University of Ife, who had made a statistical survey of audience reactions to three performances by the group in West Nigeria.

10   The Director and the Group: Grotowski and Chaikin

 1 Raymonde Temkine, 'Fils naturel d'Artaud', *Les Lettres nouvelles*, May–June 1966, and *Grotowski*, Lausanne, 1970.
 2 Preface to Jerzy Grotowski, *Towards a Poor Theatre*, Ed. Eugenio Barba, Denmark, 1968; London, 1969.
 3 *Towards a Poor Theatre*.
 4 Statement to a conference at New York University, 1970, reprinted in *Theatre Quarterly*, Vol. III, No 9.
 5 Ibid.
 6 Ibid.
 7 *Towards a Poor Theatre*.
 8 In an article on him in *Les Temps modernes*, April 1967.
 9 *Towards a Poor Theatre*.
10 Ibid.
11 Ibid.

12 Letter of 1854.
13 *Towards a Poor Theatre.*
14 Ibid.
15 5 May 1933.
16 Konstanty Puzyna 'Grotowski's Apocalypse' in *Polish Perspectives*, Vol. XIII, No 2. Reprinted in *The New Theatre: Performance Documentation*, Ed. Michael Kirby, New York, 1974.
17 Interview in *Time Out*, 1–7 June 1973.
18 'Notes on Character . . . and the Setup' in *Performance*, No 1, December 1971.
19 *Time Out* interview.
20 Statement by Chaikin quoted in the programme for the Open Theatre's season at the Round House, June 1973.
21 *Tulane Drama Review*, No 26, Winter 1964.
22 Interview quoted by John Lahr in *Up Against the Fourth Wall* (New York, 1970; published in the UK under the title *Acting Out America*, London, 1972).
23 Interview in *Performance*, No 1, December 1971.
24 Joseph Chaikin, Interview in *Tulane Drama Review*, No 26, Winter 1964.
25 *Time Out* interview.
26 Cp Karen Malpede Taylor, 'Two Kaspars – by Peter Handke and the Open Theatre', in *Performance*, No 6, May–June 1973.

Chronology of
Performances

Samuel Beckett (b. 1906)
1953 *En attendant Godot* at the Babylone, Paris, directed by Roger Blin
1955 *Waiting for Godot* at the Arts Theatre, London, directed by Peter Hall.
1957 *All That Fall* broadcast on the BBC Third Programme, directed by Donald McWhinnie
       Fin de Partie at the Studio des Champs-Elysées, Paris, and at the Royal Court, London, directed by Roger Blin
1958 *Krapp's Last Tape* at the Royal Court, directed by Donald McWhinnie
1959 *Embers* broadcast on the BBC Third Programme, directed by Donald McWhinnie
1961 *Happy Days* at the Cherry Lane Theatre, New York, directed by Alan Schneider
1962 *Words and Music* broadcast by the BBC

1963   *Play* (translated into German) premièred at Ulm, directed by
        Derek Mendel
        Cascando broadcast by Radio France directed by Roger Blin
1964   *Film* made in New York directed by Alan Schneider
1965   *Come and Go* (translated into German) premièred in Berlin,
        directed by Derek Mendel
1966   *Eh Joe* televised by BBC, directed by Michael Bakewell
1969   *Breath* staged as opening sketch in *Oh Calcutta* at Eden Theatre,
        New York, directed by Jacques Levy
1973   *Not I* at the Royal Court directed by Anthony Page
1976   *That Time* and *Footfalls* at the Royal Court directed (respectively)
        by Donald McWhinnie and Samuel Beckett
        Radio II broadcast on Radio 3 directed by Martin Esslin
1977   *Ghost Trio* and *but the clouds* televised by the BBC, directed by
        Donald McWhinnie

Eugène Ionesco (b. 1912)
1950   *La Cantatrice chauve* (*The Bald Prima-Donna*) at the Noctambules
        directed by Nicholas Bataille
1951   *La Leçon* (*The Lesson*) at the Théâtre de Poche, directed by
        Marcel Cuvelier
1952   *Les Chaises* (*The Chairs*) at the Lancry, directed by Sylvain
        Dhomme. *Le Salon de l'automibile* produced as a radio play
1953   *Victimes du devoir* (*Victims of Duty*) at the Quartier Latin directed
        by Jacques Mauclair
        La Jeune fille à marier (*Maid to Marry*), *Le Maître* (*The Leader*) and
        Le Salon de l'automobile (*The Motor Show*) at the Huchette, directed
        by Jacques Poliéri
1954   *Amédée ou Comment s'en débarrasser* (*Amédée or How to Get Rid of
        It*) at the Babylone, directed by Jean-Marie Serreau
1955   *Le Nouveau locataire* (*The New Tenant*) premièred in Finland in a
        Swedish translation, directed by Vivica Bandler
        Jacques ou la Soumission (*Jacques or Obedience*) and *Le Tableau* (*The
        Picture*) at the Huchette, directed by Robert Postec
1956   *L'Impromptu d'Alma ou le Caméléon du berger* (*The Impromptu of
        Alma or the Shepherd's Chameleon*) at the Champs-Elysées,
        directed by Maurice Jacquemont
1957   *L'Avenir est dans les oeufs ou Il faut tout pour faire un monde* (*The
        Future Is in Eggs or It Takes All Sorts to Make a World*) at the
        Cité Universitaire, directed by Jean-Luc Magneron

1959   *Tueur sans gages (The Killer)* at the Récamier, directed by José Quaglio
        Scene à quatre (Foursome) premièred at the Spoleto Festival
1960   *Rhinocéros* (translated into German) at the Düsseldorfer Schauspielhaus, directed by Karl Heinz Stroux
1962   *Délire à deux . . . tant qu'on veut (Frenzy for two . . . and the Same to You)* at the Champs-Elysées, directed by Antoine Bourseiller
        Le Roi se meurt (Exit the King) at the Alliance Française directed by Jacques Mauclair
        Le Piéton de l'air (A Stroll in the Air) premièred in a German translation at the Düsseldorfer Schauspielhuas
1964   *La Soif et la faim (Hunger and Thirst)* premièred in a German translation at the Düsseldorfer Schauspielhaus
1965   *La Lacune (The Oversight)* at the Centre Dramatique du Sud-Est
1970   *Jeux de massacre (Here Comes a Chopper* or *Killing Game)* premièred in a German translation at the Düsseldorfer Schauspielhaus directed by Karl Heinz Stroux and Frantisek Miska
1972   *Macbett* at the Rive Gauche, directed by Jacques Mauclair
1973   *Ce formidable bordel (What a Bloody Circus* or *What a Hell of a Mess)* at the Moderne, directed by Jacques Mauclair

Jean Genet (b. 1910)
1947   *Les Bonnes (The Maids)* at the Athénée, directed by Louis Jouvet
1949   *Haute Surveillance (Deathwatch)* at the Michodière, directed by Pierre Fresnay
1957   *Le Balcon (The Balcony)* at the Arts Theatre, London, directed by Peter Zadek
1959   *Les Nègres (The Blacks)* at the Lutèce, directed by Roger Blin
1966   *Les Paravents (The Screens)* at the Théâtre de France, directed by Roger Blin
        (The first twelves scenes had been premièred in London at the Donmar Rehearsal Rooms directed by Peter Brook with Charles Marowitz in 1964)

Peter Handke (b. 1942)
1966   *Publikumsbeschimpfung (Offending the Audience)* at the Theater am Turm, Frankfurt, directed by Claus Peymann
        Weissagung (Prophecy) and *Selbstbezichtigung (Self-Accusation)* at the Städtische Bühnen, Oberhausen, directed by Günther Buch
1967   *Hilferufe (Cries for Help)* in Stockholm with actors from the Oberhausen company directed by Günther Buch

1968   *Kaspar* at the Theater am Turm, Frankfurt, directed by Claus
       Peymann and (simultaneously) at the Städtische Bühnen,
       Oberhausen, directed by Günther Buch
1969   *Das Mündel will Vormund sein* (*My Foot My Tutor*) at the Theater
       am Turm, Frankfurt, directed by Claus Peymann
1970   *Quodlibet* at the Basler Theater, Basle, directed by Hans Holl-
       mann
1971   *Der Ritt über dem Bodensee* (*The Ride across Lake Constance*) at the
       Schaubühne am Halleschen Ufer, Berlin, directed by Claus
       Peymann and Wolfgang Wiens
1974   *Die Unvernünftigen sterben aus* (*They are Dying Out*) at the Schau-
       bühne am Halleschen Ufer, directed by Peter Stein

Harold Pinter (b. 1930)
1958   *The Birthday Party* at the Lyric, Hammersmith, directed by Peter
       Wood
1959   *A Slight Ache* on BBC Third Programme
1960   *The Room* and *The Dumb Waiter* at the Hampstead Theatre Club
       directed by Anthony Page and James Roose Evans
       A Night Out on BBC Third Programme
       The Caretaker at the Arts Theatre, directed by Donald Mc-
       Whinnie
1961   *The Collection* on Associated Rediffusion
1963   *The Lover* on Associated Rediffusion
1965   *Tea Party* on BBC Television
       The Homecoming at the Aldwych (RSC), directed by Peter Hall
1967   *The Basement* on BBC Television
1968   *Landscape* on BBC Third Programme
1969   *Landscape* and *Silence* at the Aldwych (RSC), directed by Peter
       Hall
1971   *Old Times* at the Aldwych (RSC), directed by Peter Hall
1973   *Monologue* on BBC Television
1975   *No Man's Land* at the Aldwych (RSC), directed by Peter Hall
1978   *Betrayal* at the National Theatre, directed by Peter Hall

Tom Stoppard (b. 1937)
1963   *A Walk on the Water* (adaptation of stage play later re-titled
       Enter a Free Man) transmitted by ITV, directed by Peter Moffatt
1964   staged at Hamburg
       The Dissolution of Dominic Boot broadcast by the BBC, produced
       by Michael Bakewell

'*M*' *is for Moon among Other Things* broadcast by the BBC, produced by John Tydeman

1965   *The Gamblers* staged by the Drama Department of Bristol University

Rosencrantz and Guildenstern Are Dead on the fringe of the Edinburgh Festival, produced by the Oxford Theatre Group, directed by Brian Daubney

1966   *If You're Glad I'll Be Frank* broadcast by the BBC, produced by John Tydeman

A Separate Peace transmitted by BBC Television, directed by Alan Gibson

1967   *Teeth* transmitted by BBC Television, directed by Alan Gibson

Rosencrantz and Guildenstern Are Dead at the Old Vic (National Theatre), directed by Derek Goldby

Another Moon Called Earth transmitted by BBC Television, directed by Alan Gibson

Albert's Bridge broadcast by the BBC, produced by Charles Lefeaux

1968   *Enter a Free Man* at the St Martin's, directed by Frith Banbury

The Real Inspector Hound at the Criterion, directed by Robert Chetwyn

Neutral Ground transmitted by Thames Television, directed by Piers Haggard

1970   *The Engagement* (a new version of *The Dissolution of Dominic Boot*) transmitted by NBC Television, directed by Paul Joyce

After Magritte at the Green Banana Restaurant, directed by Geoffrey Reeves

Where Are They Now? broadcast by the BBC, produced by John Tydeman

1971   *Dogg's Our Pet* at the Almost Free Theatre, directed by Ed Berman

1972   *Jumpers* at the Old Vic (National Theatre), directed by Peter Wood

Artist Descending a Staircase broadcast by the BBC, produced by John Tydeman

1974   *Travesties* at the Aldwych (RSC), directed by Peter Wood

1976   *Dirty Linen* and *New-Found-Land* at the Almost Free Theatre, directed by Ed Berman

1977   *Every Good Boy Deserves Favour* at the Royal Festival Hall, directed by Trevor Nunn

Professional Foul transmitted by BBC Television, directed by Michael Lindsay-Hogg

Edward Albee (b. 1928)

1959   *The Zoo Story* at the Schiller Theater, Berlin (in German translation), directed by Walter Henn

1960   *The Death of Bessie Smith* at the Schlosspark Theater, Berlin (in German translation)

        The Sandbox at the Jazz Gallery, New York, directed by Laurence Arrick

1961   *The American Dream* (in a double bill with *The Death of Bessie Smith*) at York Playhouse, New York, directed by Alan Schneider

1962   *Who's Afraid of Virginia Woolf?* at the Billy Rose Theatre, New York, directed by Alan Schneider

1963   *The Ballad of the Sad Café* (adapted from Carson McCullers's novel) at the Martin Beck Theatre, New York, directed by Alan Schneider

1964   *Tiny Alice* at the Billy Rose Theatre, New York, directed by Alan Schneider

1966   *Malcolm* (adapted from James Purdy's novel) at the Shubert Theatre, New York, directed by Alan Schneider

1967   *Everything in the Garden* (adapted from Giles Cooper's play) at the Plymouth Theatre, New York, directed by Peter Glenville

1968   *Box* and *Quotations from Chairman Mao Tse-Tung* at the Studio Arena Theatre, Buffalo, directed by Nancy Kelly and (six months later) at the Billy Rose Theatre, New York, directed by Alan Schneider

1971   *All Over* at the Martin Beck Theatre, New York, directed by John Gielgud

1975   *Seascape* in New York directed by Edward Albee

1976   *Counting the Ways* at the National Theatre, directed by Bill Bryden. *Listening* broadcast by the BBC, produced by Edward Albee and John Tydeman

Sam Shepard (b. 1943)

1964   *Cowboys* at Theatre Genesis, New York

        The Rock Garden at Theatre Genesis, directed by Ralph Cook

1965   *Up to Thursday* at Theatre 65, Playwrights Theatre

        Dog and *Rocking Chair* at La Mama Experimental Theatre Club

        Chicago at Theatre Genesis, directed by Ralph Cook

        Icarus's Mother at Caffé Cino, directed by Michael Smith

        4-H Club at Theatre 65

1966   *Fourteen Hundred Thousand* at Firehouse Theatre, Minneapolis, directed by Sydney Schubert Walter

Red Cross at Judson Poets' Theatre directed by Jacques Levy

1967 *La Turista* at the American Place Theatre, New York

Melodrama Play at La Mama Experimental Theatre Club, directed by Tom O'Horgan

Cowboys No 2 at Mark Taper Forum, Los Angeles, directed by Edward Parone

Forensic and the Navigators at Theatre Genesis, directed by Ralph Cook

1969 *The Holy Ghostly* produced by the New Troupe branch of La Mama on tour, directed by Tom O'Horgan

The Unseen Hand at La Mama Experimental Theatre Club, directed by Jeff Bleckner

1970 *Operation Sidewinder* at Lincoln Center, directed by Michael A. Schultz

Shaved Splits at La Mama Experimental Theatre Club, directed by Bill Hare

1971 *Mad Dog Blues* at Theatre Genesis, directed by Robert Glaudini

Cowboy Mouth at the Traverse Theatre, Edinburgh, directed by Gordon Stewart

Back Bog Beast Bait at the American Place Theatre, directed by Tony Barsha

1972 *The Tooth of Crime* at the Open Space, London, directed by Walter Donohue and Charles Marowitz

1973 *Blue Bitch* on BBC Television

1974 *Geography of a Horse Dreamer* at the Theatre Upstairs, Royal Court, directed by Sam Shepard

Little Ocean at the Hampstead Theatre Club, directed by Stephen Rea

1975 *Killer's Head* and *Action* at the American Place Theatre directed by Nancy Meckler

1976 *Angel City* at the Magic Theatre, San Francisco, directed by Sam Shepard

1977 *Suicide in B Flat* at the Open Space, directed by Kenneth Chubb

Antonin Artaud (1896–1948)

May 1925 *Au pièd du mur* by Louis Aragon at the Vieux-Colombier

June 1927 *Le Ventre brulé* by Artaud; *Gigogne* by Max Robur (Robert Aron); *Les Mystères de l'amour* by Roger Vitrac: all with the Théâtre Alfred Jarry at the Théâtre de Grenelle

Jan. 1928   Act III of *Partage de midi* by Paul Claudel with the Théâtre Alfred Jarry at the Comédie des Champs-Elysées

June 1928   *Dream Play* by Strindberg, with the Théâtre Alfred Jarry at the Théâtre de l'Avenue

Dec. 1928 } *Victor* by Roger Vitrac, with the Théâtre Alfred Jarry
to Jan. 1929 } at the Comédie des Champs-Elysées

Feb-Mar.   Assistant director to Louis Jouvet on *La Patissière du*
1932   *village* by Alfred Savoir

May 1935 *Les Cenci*, at the Folies Wagram

Peter Brook (b. 1925)

1945   Cocteau's *The Infernal Machine* (*La Machine infernale*) at the Chanticleer
       Rudolf Besier's *The Barretts of Wimpole Street* at the Q
       Shaw's *Pygmalion* for an ENSA tour
       Shaw's *Man and Superman*, Shakespeare's *King John* and Ibsen's *The Lady from the Sea* at Birmingham Repertory Theatre

1946   Shakespeare's *Love's Labour's Lost* at Stratford-on-Avon
       Alec Guinness's adaptation of Dostoevsky's *The Brothers Karamazov* at the Lyric, Hammersmith
       Sartre's *Vicious Circle* (*Huis Clos*) at the Arts

1947   Shakespeare's *Romeo and Juliet* at Stratford-on-Avon
       Sartre's *Men without Shadows* (*Morts sans sépulture*) and *The Respectable Prostitute* (*La Putain respectueuse*) at the Lyric, Hammersmith

1949   Howard Richardson's and William Berney's *Dark of the Moon* at the Lyric, Hammersmith

1950   Anouilh's *Ring Round the Moon* (*L'Invitation au chateau* adapted by Christopher Fry) at the Globe
       Shakespeare's *Measure for Measure* at Stratford-on-Avon
       André Roussin's *The Little Hut* (*La Petite hutte* adapted by Nancy Mitford) at the Lyric, Shaftesbury Avenue

1951   Arthur Miller's *Death of a Salesman* at the Belgian National Theatre
       John Whiting's *A Penny for a Song* at the Haymarket
       Shakespeare's *A Winter's Tale* at the Phoenix
       Anouilh's *Colombe* at the New

1953   Otway's *Venice Preserv'd* at the Lyric, Hammersmith
       The Little Hut at the Coronet, New York

1954   Christopher Fry's *The Dark Is Light Enough* at the Aldwych
       Arthur Macrae's *Both Ends Meet* at the Apollo

1955 Anouilh's *The Lark* (*L'Alouette* adapted by Christopher Fry) at the Lyric, Hammersmith

Shakespeare's *Titus Andronicus* at Stratford-on-Avon

Shakespeare's *Hamlet* at the Phoenix

1956 *The Power and the Glory* adapted from Graham Greene's novel by Dennis Cannan and Pierre Bost at the Phoenix

Eliot's *The Family Reunion* at the Phoenix

Miller's *A View from the Bridge* at the Comedy

La Chatte sur un Toit Brûlant André Obey's translation of Tennessee Williams's *Cat on a Hot Tin Roof* at the Théâtre Antoine, Paris

1957 Shakespeare's *The Tempest* at Stratford-on-Avon

1958 *Vu du Pont* Marcel Aymé's translation of Miller's *View from the Bridge* at the Antoine

Dürrenmatt's *The Visit* (*Die Besuch der alten Dame* adapted by Maurice Valency) at the Lynne Fontanne Theatre, New York

Irma la Douce with book and lyrics by Alexander Breffort, Julian More, David Heneker and Monty Norman at the Lyric, Shaftesbury Avenue

1959 *The Fighting Cock*, Anouilh's *L'Hurluburlu* translated by Lucienne Hill at the ANTA Theatre, New York

1960 Genet's *Le Balcon* (*The Balcony*) at the Théâtre de Gymnase, Paris (French première)

The Visit at the Royalty, London

Irma la Douce at the Plymouth Theatre, New York

1962 Shakespeare's *King Lear* at Stratford-on-Avon (RSC)

1963 Dürrenmatt's *The Physicists* (*Die Physiker* translated by James Kirkup) at the Aldwych (RSC)

Shakespeare's *The Tempest* at Stratford-on-Avon (RSC)

The Perils of Scobie Prilt musical by Julian More and Monty Norman at the New Theatre, Oxford

La Danse de Sergent Musgrave translated from John Arden's *Serjeant Musgrave's Dance* at the Théâtre de l'Athénée, Paris

Rolf Hochhuth's *Le Vicaire* (*Der Stellvertreter, The Deputy*) co-directed with François Darbon at the Athénée, Paris

1964 *Theatre of Cruelty* co-directed with Charles Marowitz at the LAMDA Theatre, London (RSC)

Genet's *The Screens* (*Les Paravents* translated by Bernard Frechtman) at the Donmar Rehearsal Rooms (RSC)

Weiss's *Marat/Sade*, translated by Geoffrey Skelton and Adrian Mitchell, at the Aldwych (RSC)

1965   Weiss's *The Investigation* (*Die Ermittlung*) translated by Alexander
        Gross at the Aldwych (RSC)
1966   *US* at the Aldwych (RSC)
1968   Seneca's *Oedipus* translated by Ted Hughes at the Old Vic
        (National Theatre)
1970   Shakespeare's *Midsummer Night's Dream* at Stratford-on-Avon
        (RSC)
1971   Ted Hughes's *Orghast* at the Shiraz Festival, Persepolis
1972–3 Performances in Africa with actors from the International
        Centre for Theatre Research
1974   Shakespeare's *Timon of Athens* at the Bouffes du Nord, Paris
        Les Ik at the Bouffes du Nord
1977   Alfred Jarry's *Ubu* at the Bouffes du Nord
1978   Shakespeare's *Antony and Cleopatra* at Stratford-on-Avon (RSC)

Jerzy Grotowski (b. 1933)
1957   Ionesco's *Les Chaises* (*The Chairs*) at the Stary Theatre, Cracow
1959   appointed Artistic Director of the Theatre of Thirteen Rows,
        Opole. Cocteau's *Orphée* in Opole
1960   Byron's *Cain* in Opole; Goethe's *Faust* at Poznan
1961   Mickiewicz's *Forefathers' Eve*
1962   Theatre renamed Theatre Laboratory of Thirteen Rows
        Wyspianski's *Acropolis* adapted by Jerzy Szajna
        Acropolis (second version)
1963   Marlowe's *Doctor Faustus*
        Acropolis (third version)
1965   company moved to Wroclaw
        Acropolis (fourth version)
        Calderón's *The Constant Prince* (adapted by Slowacki)
        The Constant Prince (second version)
1967   *Acropolis* (fifth version)
1968   *The Constant Prince* (third version)
1968–73 *Apocalysis cum figuris*

Joseph Chaikin (b. 1935)
1963   Founded Open Theatre
        Performances of short plays by van Itallie, Megan Terry and
        Brecht at Sheridan Square Playhouse and the Martinique, New
        York

1964–5   Short plays by T. S. Eliot, John Arden and Maria Irene
         Fornes added to repertoire
1966–7   Megan Terry's *Viet Rock* at Yale and Off-Broadway
         co-directed van Itallie's *America Hurrah* with Jacques Levy at
         Yale
1968   van Itallie's *The Serpent* premièred in Rome
1969   co-directed *Terminal* with Roberta Sklar
1971   *Mutations* on tour
1972   *The Mutation Show* and *Nightwalk* in New York

Select Bibliography

Beckett

Coe, Richard N.   *Beckett*, Edinburgh and London, 1964.

Cohn, Ruby   *Samuel Beckett: the Comic Gamut*, New Brunswick, NJ, 1962.

Esslin, Martin (Ed.)   *Samuel Beckett: a Collection of Critical Essays*, Englewood Cliffs, NJ, 1965.

Fletcher, John   *The Novels of Samuel Beckett*, London, 1964.

Harvey, Lawrence E.   *Samuel Beckett: Poet and Critic*, Princeton 1970.

Hayman, Ronald   *Samuel Beckett*, London, 1968.

Kenner, Hugh   *Samuel Beckett: a Critical Study*, New York, 1961; London, 1962.

——, Hugh   *A Reader's Guide to Samuel Beckett*, London, 1973.

Pilling, John   *Samuel Beckett*, London, 1976.

Worth, Katherine (Ed.)   *Beckett the Shape Changer*, London, 1975.

Ionesco

Benmussa, Simone   *Ionesco*, Paris, 1966.

Coe, Richard N.   *Eugène Ionesco*, Edinburgh, 1961. Revised: *Ionesco: A Study of His Plays*, London, 1971.

Donnard, J. H.   *Ionesco, dramaturge*, Paris, 1966.

Hayman, Ronald   *Eugène Ionesco*, London, 1975; New York, 1976.

Lamont, Rosette C. (Ed.)   *Ionesco: a Collection of Critical Essays*, Englewood Cliffs, NJ, 1973.

Pronko, Leonard   *Eugène Ionesco*, New York, 1965.

Vernois, Paul   *Le Dynamique théâtre d'Eugène Ionesco*, Paris, 1972.

L'Avant-Scène   Special Ionesco Issue, Nos 373–4.

Tulane Drama Review, No 7   (Spring 1973).

Genet

Bonnefoy, Claude   *Jean Genet*, Paris, 1965.

Coe, Richard N.   *The Vision of Jean Genet*, London, 1968.

—— Richard N.   (Ed.) *The Theatre of Jean Genet: a Casebook*, New York, 1970.

McMahon, Joseph H.   *The Imagination of Jean Genet*, New Haven, 1963.

Sartre, Jean-Paul   *Saint Genet: comédien et martyr*, Paris, 1952.

Thody, Philip   *Jean Genet: a Critical Appraisal*, London, 1968.

Obliques, No 2   (Special Genet issue).

Handke

Hern, Nicholas   *Peter Handke: Theatre and Anti-Theatre*, London, 1971; New York, 1972.

Scharang, Michael (Ed.)   *Über Peter Handke*, Frankfurt, 1972.

Pinter

Baker, William, and Tabachnik, Stephen Ely   *Harold Pinter*, Edinburgh 1972.

Esslin, Martin   *The Peopled Wound: the Work of Harold Pinter*, London, 1970; New York, 1970.

Hayman, Ronald   *Harold Pinter*, London, 1967, 3rd ed. 1975; New York, 1973.

Kerr, Walter   *Harold Pinter*, New York, 1967.

Trussler, Simon   *The Plays of Harold Pinter*, London, 1973.

Stoppard

Hayman, Ronald   *Tom Stoppard*, London, 1977.

Albee

Bigsby, C. W. E.   *Albee*, Edinburgh, 1969.

——, C. W. E.   *Edward Albee: A Collection of Critical Essays*, Englewood Cliffs, NJ, 1975.

Cohn, Ruby   *Edward Albee*, Minneapolis, 1969.

Hayman, Ronald   *Edward Albee*, London, 1971; New York, 1973.

Paolucci, Anne   *From Tension to Tonic: the Plays of Edward Albee*, Carbondale, 1972.

Rutenberg, Michael E.   *Edward Albee: Playwright in Protest*, New York, 1969.

Shepard

Theatre Checklist, No 3, *Sam Shepard, Theatrefacts*, August–October 1974.

Artaud

Brau, Jean-Louis   *Antonin Artaud*, Paris, 1971.

Gouhier, Henri   *Antonin Artaud et l'essence du théâtre*, Paris, 1974.

Hayman, Ronald   *Artaud and After*, London, 1977.

Sollers, Philippe (Ed.)   *Artaud*, Paris, 1973.

Virmaux, Alain   *Antonin Artaud et le théâtre*, Paris, 1970.

Obliques, Nos 10–11 (1977)   (Special Artaud issue).

Brook

Heilpern, John   *Conference of the Birds: the Story of Peter Brook in Africa*, London, 1977.

Smith, A. C. H.   *Orghast at Persepolis*, London, 1972.

Trewin, J. C.   *Peter Brook: a Biography*, London, 1971.

Grotowski

Temkine, Raymonde   *Grotowski*, Lausanne, 1970.

Index